D0723427

ANTICIPATING
MADAM
PRESIDENT

NO LONGER PROPERTY OF
SEATTLE PUBLIC LIBRARY

ANTICIPATING MADAM PRESIDENT

EDITED BY
ROBERT P. WATSON
ANN GORDON

LYNNE
RIENNER
PUBLISHERS

BOULDER
LONDON

Published in the United States of America in 2003 by
Lynne Rienner Publishers, Inc.
1800 30th Street, Boulder, Colorado 80301
www.rienner.com

and in the United Kingdom by
Lynne Rienner Publishers, Inc.
3 Henrietta Street, Covent Garden, London WC2E 8LU

© 2003 by Lynne Rienner Publishers, Inc. All rights reserved

Library of Congress Cataloging-in-Publication Data
Anticipating madam president / edited by Robert P. Watson, Ann Gordon.
    p. cm.
  Includes bibliographical references and index.
  ISBN 1-58826-137-9 (alk. paper) — ISBN 1-58826-113-1 (alk. paper)
  1. Presidents—United States—Election. 2. Presidential candidates—
United States. 3. Women political candidates—United States. I. Watson,
Robert P., 1962– . II. Gordon, Ann, 1971–
JK524 .A77   2003
324'.0973—dc21   2002073942

British Cataloguing in Publication Data
A Cataloguing in Publication record for this book
is available from the British Library.

Printed and bound in the United States of America

      The paper used in this publication meets the requirements
 ∞   of the American National Standard for Permanence of
      Paper for Printed Library Materials Z39.48-1984.

  5 4 3 2 1

To Shirley Chisholm, Geraldine Ferraro,
Pat Schroeder, and Elizabeth Dole
for their courage

Contents

Part 3 The Media, Voters, and Public Opinion

Part 4 Governing

Foreword

Pat Schroeder, former U.S. Representative

I have never had the slightest problem anticipating Madam President and have been eagerly waiting for the rest of you to join me! Since the phrases "Commander in Chief" and "Leader of the Free World" are always automatically used to describe the president of the United States, it seems an important stepping-stone for achieving this goal is first to have a woman as secretary of defense. Madeleine Albright as secretary of state did a lot to show that a woman could be a world leader. The concern that a woman could lead the armed services is one that must be dealt with. We have had presidents and secretaries of defense who have not served in the military, and it was never an issue. Nevertheless, it will be an issue for a woman to have a real shot at becoming Madam President.

Did all of this change in America on September 11, 2001? My friend, Congresswoman Nancy Pelosi, was running for Democratic Whip. It would be the highest elected position ever held by a woman in Congress. The election was October 10, 2001, and I was very worried about the potential fallout from the tragic terrorist events. When you look at reports of which political leaders get the most air time in the media, elected women almost drop off the charts during periods of hostilities. The media turns almost entirely to men to analyze what is going on. Remembering those charts increased my anxiety about the outcome of the election. The good news is Nancy Pelosi won this historic election in a landslide, and I exhaled.

When we look at the region of the world breeding this current terrorism, we find many countries have already had Madam Presidents. Benazir Bhutto was elected twice in Pakistan to its highest office. The Philippines, Bangladesh, India, and Malaysia have all had women leaders. How could countries with strong Islamic populations break down the gender barrier to national leadership before the United States did?

What keeps holding us back? We have an incredibly strong farm club full of qualified women.

This book should make all of us ponder the remaining barriers. Polls are taken every year or so on how many people would vote for a woman. The good news is the number gets higher every year. The bad news is there are still many who say they would not. Presidential elections in this country are usually very close, and it is hard to win when there is a group that won't even consider your qualifications because of your gender. Those polls usually include another question asking if a person thinks his or her friends would vote for a woman presidential candidate. Interestingly, many who say they have no trouble voting for a woman don't think their friends are as progressive. Makes one wonder! We need to dig deeper and find out what motivates people to feel a woman should not even be considered for president, rather than just measure how many feel that way.

The White House has been America's ultimate tree house, with a "No Girls Allowed" sign posted on it. *Anticipating Madam President* should help all of us reflect and figure out how to rip that sign down. Ready, get set, read!

Preface

In September 1995, after customers complained that a product was "too political," the Wal-Mart store manager pulled the item. What was the offensive product in question? Amazingly, it was a T-shirt featuring "Margaret," the bespectacled, fluffy-haired girl from the *Dennis the Menace* cartoon strip, saying: "Someday a woman will be PRESIDENT." That a corporate giant believed this T-shirt "went against their philosophy of family values" and that customers would find offense in the message is a wake-up call for all women and men interested in the principles of democracy. What kind of family values, after all, would find such a message disturbing? The answer is the kind that would not vote for a qualified, capable candidate simply because of the candidate's sex.

That was one of those memorable events that calls one to arms and seems to take on meaning larger than the initial sequence of actions that occasioned the controversy in the first place. We still remember first reading this story in disbelief. It is also one of those events that would seem to justify producing a book such as the one you are reading. Indeed, the fact that readers would pick up a book, or scholars would feel compelled to publish a book, on presidential campaigns, the nature of the presidency, and the challenge of governing the White House—all from the perspective of the president being a woman—would seem to suggest that gender matters. Although we might find the controversy of the Margaret T-shirt unthinkable, others might find the concept of women as leaders unthinkable.

The happy ending to this story is that Wal-Mart's actions sparked a nationwide protest. To Wal-Mart's credit, company officials admitted an "overreaction" and agreed to stock the shirts. The creator of the T-shirts—Ann Moliver Ruben, a family psychologist in Miami—went on to create "Margaret for President" clubs for children and a series of programs to promote women as leaders (and sell a lot of T-shirts). But, the other happy ending to this story—the eventual fulfillment of Margaret's message on the T-shirt—remains to be written.

As of the date of this book's publication, we have yet to elect a woman to the U.S. presidency. So, one might ask: why read a book about the first woman president, if we have not yet had one? We hope the book helps to explain *why* she has not yet been elected, what challenges are in store for the first woman to successfully campaign for the nation's highest office, how Madam President will change the nature of the presidency, and the significance for women's equality, the nation, and democracy of finally having a woman serve in that capacity. Indeed, we believe the topic is important and fascinating. *Will* a woman ever become president? *When* will it happen? *Who* will it be? We hope that *Anticipating Madam President* will help you anticipate her election.

The genesis of this project began simultaneously in the desert of Las Vegas and the lush rainforests of Hawaii. Ann Gordon brought presidency scholars together with women and politics scholars for the Western Political Science Association meeting in Las Vegas in the spring of 2001. The panel she convened on a woman president generated interest among the participants to find a journal in which the work could be published. Ann contacted Robert Watson, the editor of the journal *White House Studies,* who was at the time teaching at the University of Hawaii at Hilo and, by happy coincidence, also researching the question of when a woman would become president. Robert and Ann ended up collaborating on a special issue of *White House Studies* devoted to the first female presidency. During the process, the two realized that little had been written on the topic and that there was much more to say. Thus, *Anticipating Madam President* was born. We hope events are such that we will soon be collaborating once again to produce a book titled *Madam President: The First Four Years!*

This book offers chapters on a wide array of topics pertaining to the prospects for, challenges facing, and significance of electing the first woman president. Our intention in producing this book was to assemble leading scholars from such diverse fields as political science, presidential studies, women and politics, women's studies, communication, and media studies to produce one of the first comprehensive examinations of the first female presidency. Every effort was made to include essays that are highly readable and accessible to scholars, students, and general readers alike from varying backgrounds and degrees of familiarity with the subject.

A special thanks to Pat Schroeder and Geraldine Ferraro, two leaders who blazed trails and truly helped the nation anticipate Madam President, for so generously giving their time to answer our questions. It has been a rewarding experience to work with women who so exemplify the spirit of public service and who, although they did not know it, personally influenced the editors to undertake this book. Thank you also to Eleanor Clift, contributing editor at *Newsweek;* Marie Wilson, president of the White House Project; Michael Devine, Scott Roley, and Kathy Knotts of the Truman Presidential Museum and Library; Carol Davis, Colleen Kelly, Joan Wurth, Deborah Kemp, and many others at the University of Missouri at Kansas City; and Mary Kay McPhee of the Starr Symposium for taking time out of their full schedules to support our interest in this topic. This project would not have been possible without our talented colleagues who contributed so enthusiastically to the book. We believe they represent the very best academia has to offer, and it was a pleasure to work with them. We would also like to acknowledge Ohio University, which provided Ann Gordon with support for this project; Beth Partin; and Lynne Rienner, Leanne Anderson, Shena Redmond, Penny Monroe, Liz Miles, and the rest of the staff at Lynne Rienner Publishers for publishing this book. Lastly, to Claudia Pavone Watson and David Shafie, thank you for your continued support and interest in our idea.

We hope you, the reader, find the book intellectually stimulating and enjoyable.

—*Robert P. Watson*
—*Ann Gordon*

1

Introduction:
The White House as Ultimate Prize

Robert P. Watson

When It Happens

It is not a matter of *if*, but rather, *when* a woman will be elected as president of the United States. Of course, the occasion of the election of the first woman to the nation's highest office will not pass unnoticed. Surely it will be *the* political story of the year, reported in exhausting detail by the press, followed closely by the public, and analyzed for generations to come by scholars and presidential historians.

And rightfully so! The fulfillment of the ultimate prize in U.S. politics will mark the shattering of the final glass ceiling that has blocked half the U.S. populace for well over 200 years. It will be cause for much celebration (and possibly some gnashing of teeth), as the first female presidency brings with it the promise of a new era in the women's movement. Women will have finally attained every possible elected office in the United States, from mayor to governor to senator to president. The message sent to countless young girls that a woman is in the Oval Office will be one of immeasurable encouragement and confidence.

But it is doubtful that the event will signal the end of inequality faced by women in political life and other facets of society. This great feat should not and will not be reason for advocates of women's equality to abandon their work. Sadly, the existence of Madam President will be less an end than simply a means to an end to a long history of disenfranchisement and inequality experienced by women. When will that be? Not until women are successfully *elected* in roughly the same proportion to the number of those *pursuing* public office. Not until women are elected in the same proportion one finds for men pursuing elected office. Not until women are elected in a proportion that reflects the female population as a whole. Not until elected officials support and promote issues

1

of importance to women in a way that is proportional to the impact those issues and decisions have on women's lives. And, ultimately, not until an individual's sex is unimportant as a factor in the voting booth or a story by the media or is no longer reason to treat one poorly or indifferently. Not until then will women's advocates be able to put down their signs or marching shoes.

Likewise, the election of a female president will not mark the end of the inaccessibility of high political office to women but will mark the beginning of the challenge of governing for the new president. Indeed, with each act (and inaction), she will be setting precedents and proceeding into uncharted territory.

Her election will raise a number of questions: How will she govern? Will her sex or gender influence the way she is viewed by the public, press, and other political leaders? Will her sex be an asset or liability in meeting the day-to-day challenges of the office? The very nature of the presidency as it has been known could change. Or, nothing fundamental about the office could change. About all that is certain is that the election of the first woman president will go a long way toward promoting and achieving the objectives of the women's movement and the event will be both interesting and worth studying. In the meantime, questions remain: When will it happen? How will she be elected? Who will it be? Why has it not yet occurred?

When Will She Be Elected?

When contemplating the question of *when* a woman will be elected, the words of Charles Dickens might be appropriately paraphrased. When it comes to women in politics, these are, in a way, both the best and worst of times. The progress made by women and the status of women are vastly improved over those which existed just a generation ago. The number of women elected to the U.S. Senate, for instance, has increased almost sevenfold in just one decade, from two to thirteen from 1991 to 2001.[1] In the year 2001, for the first time in U.S. history, women found themselves enjoying double-digit percentages of representation in state legislatures (22 percent), statewide elected executive offices (27 percent), governorships (10 percent), and both houses of Congress (13 percent). New perspectives on feminist thought and scholarship and a growing recognition of women's rights have refocused debate on women's issues. More women than ever before have entered medical schools, law schools, and veterinary schools; in veterinary schools, for instance, women comprise the majority of enrolled students. Women in the United States are narrowing the pay gap, living longer, and achieving success in heretofore inaccessible leadership positions in medicine, industry, science, diplomacy, entertainment, and other sectors of society. With each accomplishment, more and more positive role models are offered to impressionable young minds.

Yet, the United States ranks only forty-ninth in the world in terms of the percentage of women serving in public office. The 2004 presidential election will mark the twentieth anniversary of Geraldine Ferraro's historic vice presidential nomination on the Democratic ticket. But no woman has followed in her footsteps. During this period, spouses, mothers, and even daughters of presidents have generally occupied more prominent roles in presidential campaigns and as presidential advisers.[2] But during that same period—as before—women have not even come close to gaining the presidency. Only Elizabeth Dole's brief candidacy in 1999 mounted what could have been considered a viable campaign. But Dole was forced to abandon her bid because of difficulties raising money, an interesting fact given her considerable political connections and work as head of the Red Cross, an organization noted for fund-raising. Well-known congresswoman Pat Schroeder contemplated pursuing the office in 1987 but also had trouble raising money, one of many important factors pertaining to the election of a woman president that will be discussed in this book.

Women at the dawn of the twenty-first century are facing some of the same issues and challenges as their mothers and grandmothers. Pay equality, abortion rights, access to quality, affordable child care and health care, sexual harassment, and the threat of domestic violence remain in the headlines. Women must still contend with the burden of the "second shift syndrome," years after it was brought to the public's attention that most married men did little to no housework, whereas working women had to perform both their paying job and the lion's share of domestic responsibilities, including child rearing. First ladies and female candidates for public office at all levels are still asked by the press about their hairstyle and clothing. And the status of women in much of the world remains precarious and distinctly second class.

Although the U.S. presidency remains elusive for women, an ever-increasing number of nations have elected or selected female leaders of government, many of whom served with great distinction and commanded great respect. As prime minister, Indira Gandhi led India for many years before she was assassinated by Sikh religious extremists in 1984. Golda Meir served as Israel's prime minister in the late 1960s and early 1970s, and Margaret Thatcher was Britain's prime minister for over a decade. Benazir Bhutto succeeded in twice gaining the prime ministership in Pakistan, a Muslim nation.

Most studies of women leaders overwhelmingly suggest that it is much more difficult for women to attain the office of presidency than the prime ministership because of the need to win a nationwide election.[3] Yet, women have served in that capacity. Ireland's Mary McAleese, Nicaragua's Violeta Chamorro, and other women succeeded in winning nationwide presidential elections. Indeed, Ireland has had female presidents since 1990. Iceland's Vigdis Finnbogadottir holds the distinction of being the first woman *popularly* elected to lead her nation. Table 1.1 lists women who have led their nations.

Why Hasn't She Been Elected?

It would seem that Madam President should have been elected by now. As was mentioned above, the United States has elected women to other high-level offices. With the passage of the Nineteenth Amendment to the Constitution, women gained the right to vote in 1920. Since 1980, women have been turning out to vote at rates higher than men.[4] Moreover, the United States has often been a leader in promoting human rights and the rights of women. So, if women have shown that they can be elected to head governments worldwide, then why has no woman been elected to do so in the 200-plus year history of the United States?

Initially, it should be noted that surprisingly little research has been done on this topic.[5] Not only does this dearth of information point to the need for further scholarly attention on the subject, but it reflects the larger obstacles facing women. Ample research has been done on female candidates, most of it focusing on the challenges women face pursuing legislative office.[6] Scholars study women in legislative office because women pursue legislative office. Women pursue legislative office because it has become an attainable goal. However, it is difficult to study women in executive office because so few women have served as governors or mayors of major cities. Of the 100 largest cities in the United States, for instance, only sixteen have female mayors.[7] No woman has yet served as president, and until only recently, very few women served in this capacity internationally. Comparatively few women have pursued high executive office in the United States because it is not easily attainable. To the voters, political reporters, financiers of campaigns, party leaders, and others playing a role in determining who gets elected president, women have not been widely viewed as viable presidential material. It is necessary for scholars to "put the cart ahead of the horse" and anticipate Madam President.

One area of research on women that is useful to any effort to anticipate a female president is scholarship on women governors. This research

Table 1.1   Women World Leaders

Name	Country	Position	Years
Sirimavo Bandaranaike	Ceylon (Sri Lanka)	PM	1960–1965, 1970–1977, 1994–2000
Indira Gandhi	India	PM	1966–1977, 1980–1984
Golda Meir	Israel	PM	1969–1974
Isabel Perón	Argentina	President	1974–1976
Elizabeth Domitien	Central African Republic	PM	1975–1976
Maria de Lourdes Pintasilgo	Portugal	PM	1979–1980
Lidia Gueiler	Bolivia	President	1979–1980
Margaret Thatcher	Britain	PM	1979–1990
Mary Eugenia Charles	Dominica	PM	1980–1995
Vigdis Finnbogadottir	Iceland	President	1980–1996
Gro Brundtland	Norway	PM	1981, 1986–1989, 1990–1996
Agatha Barbara	Malta	President	1982–1986
Milka Planinc	Yugoslavia	President	1982–1986
Maria Liberia Peres	Nicaragua	President	1984–1985
Marie Liberia-Peters	Netherlands Antilles	PM	1984–1986, 1988–1994
Corazon Aquino	Philippines	President	1986–1992
Benazir Bhutto	Pakistan	PM	1988–1990, 1993–1997
Violeta Chamorro	Nicaragua	President	1990–1996
Ertha Pascal-Trouillot	Haiti	President	1990–1991
Kazimiera Prunskiene	Lithuania	PM	1990–1991
Mary Robinson	Ireland	President	1990–1997
Edith Cresson	France	PM	1991–1992
Begum Khaleda Zia	Bangladesh	PM	1991–1996, 2001–present
Hanna Suchocka	Poland	PM	1992–1993
Susanne Camelia-Romer	Netherlands Antilles	PM	1993, 1998–1999
Kim Campbell	Canada	PM	1993
Sylvie Kinigi	Burundi	PM	1993–1994
Marita Peterson	Faroe Islands	PM	1993–1994
Agathe Uwilingiyimana	Rwanda	PM	1993–1994
Tansu Ciller	Turkey	PM	1993–1996
Chandrika Kumaratunga	Sri Lanka	President	1994–present
Claudette Werleigh	Haiti	PM	1995–1996
Sheikh Hasina Wazed	Bangladesh	PM	1996–2001
Ruth Perry	Liberia	President	1996–present
Pamela Gordon	Bermuda	Premier	1997–1998
Janet Jagan	Guyana	President	1997–1999
Jenny Shipley	New Zealand	PM	1997–1999
Mary McAleese	Ireland	President	1997–present
Ruth Dreifuss	Switzerland	President	1998–1999
Jennifer Smith	Bermuda	Premier	1998–present
Helen Clark	New Zealand	PM	1999–present
Mireya Moscoso	Panama	President	1999–present
Vaira Vike-Freiberga	Latvia	President	1999–present
Tarja Halonen	Finland	President	2000–present
Gloria Macapagal-Arroyo	Philippines	President	2001–present
Megawati Sukarnoputri	Indonesia	President	2001–present

is important because we have not yet had a female president. However, there is a challenge in drawing inferences based on such a small sample of cases (only a few women have ever served as governor), just as it will one day be difficult to draw conclusions from the experience of the first female president. Sara J. Weir, for instance, provides a model for understanding women and executive governance based on the study of female governors.[8] She points out that the women she studied—those elected governor since 1974—have had to contend with a host of rigid gender stereotypes. For instance, female candidates for high executive office face perceptual problems from a public that generally fails to view women as being credible on such issues as the economy, budgeting, national security, foreign policy, and other issues deemed important for a president.

Likewise, Stephen Stambough and Valerie O'Regan had to contend with the small number of female governors while pursuing the same research questions we consider.[9] In their case study of women who sought the office, they also discovered sex role bias in gubernatorial races. As to the question of why female candidates for executive office fail to win more races, the experience of gubernatorial candidates is again worth noting. It has been suggested that such factors as poor campaigns, media bias against women candidates, and sex role stereotypes by the public that make it difficult for women to get elected have all contributed to the problem.[10] A list of women serving as governor prior to the 2002 elections is offered in Table 1.2.

The well-developed literature base on women and legislative office can also help answer the question of why a woman has yet to be elected president. This research points to a host of variables explaining the election of women to legislative office and other factors making it difficult for women to get elected.[11] The research is too extensive to be treated comprehensively in this introduction. However, in general it finds that women historically have been more likely to get elected in urban, more progressive districts but have faced sexism at the polls. Women seeking

Table 1.2 Women Governors, 2002

Name	State/Territory	Party
Jane Dee Hull	Arizona	Republican
Judy Martz	Montana	Republican
Ruth Ann Minner	Delaware	Democrat
Jeanne Shaheen	New Hampshire	Democrat
Jane Swift	Massachusetts	Republican
Sila Calderon	Puerto Rico	Popular Democratic

the presidency and governorships have had difficulty raising campaign funds, a double standard that might both prevent them from running for office and make it more difficult to get elected. Some studies have suggested that women have experienced negative perceptions from a portion of the electorate when running for office while raising young children, something that is not true for male candidates. Also, it appears that, once elected, women have not had the advantage of mentoring from senior male legislators, are unlikely to attain seats on the most powerful committees, and are even less likely to chair such committees. Historically, very few women have attained positions of power within the political parties or on important committees. The recent election of Nancy Pelosi (D-CA) to a leadership post in the Democratic House of Representatives is an exception, not the rule.[12] The good news is that such studies find that sexism at the polls has diminished markedly. In fact, some studies suggest that voters actually prefer women candidates. It remains to be seen, however, whether that is true of women seeking the White House.

Studies have also pointed to the existence of a gender gap, whereby women are more inclined toward such "nurturing" issues as education and health care, whereas men are more inclined toward such "force" issues as national security and crime prevention. At the same time, such findings may prove to benefit women running for the presidency. For instance, the literature on "shared issue concerns," whereby women have common sets of issues they support, suggests women may vote for a woman.[13] A female candidate for the presidency could thus expect to do well among women voters. Research also suggests that younger voters are more likely to vote for a woman.[14] The future looks promising for women candidates, as new generations of voters come to the polls with a more open mind toward candidates. That, coupled with the fact that women comprise the majority of the population and now account for the majority of voters, bodes well for women pursuing the presidency in the future.

The question has been raised as to whether the American public is ready to vote for a woman for president, in spite of public opinion polling that indicates roughly 92 percent of the public state that they would vote for a woman. It has also been suggested by none other than former president Gerald R. Ford that the first woman president is likely to be a Republican who initially gains the vice presidency. As is discussed in this book, a woman who happens to be a Democrat has the added burden of appearing too liberal and possibly too soft on defense to much of the voting public. A woman running as a Republican, however, would likely be perceived to be a liberal Republican and thus someone much closer to the center of the ideological spectrum. At the same time, the issue is likely to be raised that, rather than first ascend to the vice presidency, the first woman president should be able to prove herself electable directly to the presidency on her own merits.

One reason why no woman has yet been elected to the presidency is that to attain such high office, one must have an extensive political career and be serving in such highly visible offices as vice president, governor, or senator. The exception being, as the joke goes, "famous actors, athletes, and astronauts," who might have the luxury of running without extensive public service, which is usually necessary to attract sufficient funding, party support, and the attention of the media during a long, nationwide campaign. Until quite recently, few women had such public experience.

Among recent presidents, one finds this type of political resume. Lyndon B. Johnson, Richard Nixon, and George H. W. Bush all attained the presidency after first being the vice president. Vice President Gerald R. Ford assumed the presidency on the resignation of President Nixon, and Vice President Harry S Truman became president upon the death of President Franklin D. Roosevelt (FDR). FDR, Jimmy Carter, Ronald Reagan, Bill Clinton, and George W. Bush all came to the White House directly from the governor's office. Congressional experience, if it is of considerable duration or served in a position of power, has been another avenue to the Oval Office. Truman, Johnson, and John F. Kennedy had gained notoriety in the U.S. Senate, and Ford came from a leadership position in the House of Representatives. Dwight Eisenhower was the supreme allied commander during World War II and the latest in a line of well-known military leaders to reach the presidency that began with George Washington and included William Henry Harrison, Zachary Taylor, and Ulysses Grant.

It would appear, then, that a certain political career is necessary for a realistic run for the office. It has generally been the case internationally among women leaders that family connections help. Examples include Corazon Aquino, Sirimavo Bandaranaike, and Isabel Perón, who had virtually no political experience but had close prior familial ties to the office they attained. As more women attain the right type of high political positions, it would stand to reason that the pool of prospective, viable women candidates would grow. Prior to the 2002 elections, for instance, there were five female governors and thirteen female U.S. senators serving in office (see Table 1.3). That, in addition to several living former or present female cabinet heads, provides an impressive, diverse, and bipartisan pool of candidates for the presidency.

Table 1.3　Women in the U.S. Senate

Name	State	Party	Years
Rebecca Latimer Felton	Georgia	Democrat	1922
Hattie Wyatt Caraway	Arkansas	Democrat	1931–1945
Rose McConnell Long	Louisiana	Democrat	1936–1937
Dixie Bibb Graves	Alabama	Democrat	1937–1938
Gladys Pyle	South Dakota	Republican	1938–1939
Vera Cahalan Bushfield	South Dakota	Republican	1948
Margaret Chase Smith	Maine	Republican	1949–1973
Eva Kelley Bowring	Nebraska	Republican	1954
Hazel Hempel Abel	Nebraska	Republican	1954
Maurine Brown Neuberger	Oregon	Democrat	1960–1967
Elaine S. Edwards	Louisiana	Democrat	1972
Muriel Humphrey	Minnesota	Democrat	1978
Maryon Allen	Alabama	Democrat	1978
Nancy Landon Kassebaum	Kansas	Republican	1979–1997
Paula Hawkins	Florida	Republican	1981–1987
Barbara Mikulski	Maryland	Democrat	1987–present
Jocelyn Burdick	North Dakota	Democrat	1992
Carol Moseley-Braun	Illinois	Democrat	1993–1999
Barbara Boxer	California	Democrat	1993–present
Dianne Feinstein	California	Democrat	1993–present
Kay Bailey Hutchison	Texas	Republican	1993–present
Patty Murray	Washington	Democrat	1993–present
Olympia Snowe	Maine	Republican	1995–present
Sheila Frahm	Kansas	Republican	1996
Susan Collins	Maine	Republican	1997–present
Mary Landrieu	Louisiana	Democrat	1997–present
Blanche Lincoln	Arkansas	Democrat	1999–present
Maria Cantwell	Washington	Democrat	2001–present
Jean Carnahan	Missouri	Democrat	2001–present
Hillary Rodham Clinton	New York	Democrat	2001–present
Debbie Stabenow	Michigan	Democrat	2001–present

Women are now in the presidential pipeline. Roughly 28 percent of President George W. Bush's administrative appointments in 2001 were women, and Al Gore seems to have seriously considered a female running mate on his presidential campaign in 2000. Women have been on the short list for vice president in several preceding elections, and, in the 2000 presidential election, two third-party candidates chose women as their running mates: Reform Party nominee Pat Buchanan picked Ezola Foster, an African American woman, and Green Party nominee Ralph Nader picked Winona La Duke, a Native American. Women such as Mary Matalin and Karen Hughes have been playing more visible and important roles in recent presidential campaigns as chief advisers and campaign managers, and several women are frequently mentioned in the media as possible presidential candidates. Such anticipatory exposure is necessary for launching a serious bid. The list includes Senator Hillary Rodham Clinton, the former first lady; Senator Dianne Feinstein of California; Senator Kay Bailey Hutchison of Texas; General Claudia Kennedy; Jeanne Shaheen, former governor of New Hampshire; Kathleen Kennedy Townsend, lieutenant governor of Maryland; and Christine Todd Whitman, the former New Jersey governor and Environmental Protection Agency chief in the administration of George W. Bush (see Table 1.4).

Shoulders to Stand On

When a woman finally does get elected to the presidency, she will not have done it on her own. Rather, she will have benefited from the efforts of countless women before her whose efforts helped blaze the long and difficult trail to the White House. A starting point for this road to the presidency was the Seneca Falls Convention of 1848, although efforts to enfranchise women precede even this historic gathering. Convening in Seneca Falls, New York, Lucretia Mott, raised a Quaker, and Elizabeth Cady Stanton, the daughter of a judge who was brought up in a household of abolitionists, led what was at the time probably the most important meeting on the issue of the rights and status of women.[15] The roughly 300 conventioneers in attendance succeeded in reaching consensus on the rights of women to be educated, divorce, and own property after marriage, although they hesitated on declaring the right to vote. They also produced the *Declaration of Rights and Sentiments,* which was based on the Declaration of Independence and declared women worthy of such equality. Conceptualized in notions of justice, peace, and basic human rights, a fledgling women's movement now had leaders, an organizational structure, publicity, and a growing voice.

A common bond for many of those involved in the early efforts to gain basic rights for women was their shared commitment to the

Table 1.4   Presidential Appointments

Years	President	Cabinet Appointments		Total Appointments[a]	
		Appointments	Women	Appointments	Women
1968–1974	Nixon	31	0 (0%)	625	25 (4%)
1974–1977	Ford	12	1 (8.3%)	250	35 (14%)
1977–1981	Carter	21	4 (19.0%)	919	124 (13.5%)
1981–1989	Reagan	33	3 (9.1%)	2,349	277 (11.8%)
1989–1993	G. H. W. Bush	17	3 (17.6%)	903	181 (20.0%)
1993–2001	Clinton	29	12 (41.4%)	2,160	592 (27.4%)

Note: a. Requiring Senate confirmation.

antislavery cause. Many later suffragists learned the drill in the trenches of the abolitionist movement, where women were often the foot soldiers leading the cause. Northern abolitionist leader William Lloyd Garrison included many women in the ranks of the organizations he led.[16] Angelina and Sarah Grimké put their lives on the line speaking out against slavery in the very South where it existed. Clara Barton nursed soldiers during the Civil War, and others served as nurses and spies. Harriett Tubman did it all, spying in the Deep South, scouting for advancing Union troops, and helping to liberate slaves through the Underground Railroad, all the while risking certain death if captured. Harriet Beecher Stowe and the freed slave Sojourner Truth (formerly Isabella Baumfree) became household names.

Members of the "first wave" of the women's movement gained invaluable experience, political savvy, and organizational skills in the fight against slavery. But, more important, they emerged on the all-male stage of leadership and politics and succeeded in ending the institution of slavery.

After the passage of the Thirteenth Amendment in 1865 ending slavery, women continued to promote equality. When the Fifteenth Amendment to the Constitution—referred to as "Negro male suffrage"—was passed in 1870, some leaders of the women's rights movement such as Mott and Stanton took the bold position of opposing it on grounds that it did not extend the right to vote to women.[17] This conflict divided the movement and undermined support from some key abolitionists in the North. Further, Sojourner Truth, Mary Walker—who dressed as a man in an attempt to vote—and several other leaders tried to vote in 1872 and were arrested, again jeopardizing their own safety, reputations, and base of support. Susan B. Anthony was arrested, taken by the police, and brought to trial for trying to vote. Because she used the trial as a means to promote the cause, the trial was moved to a rural location in Canandaigua, New York, where she was not permitted to speak or testify until the very end of her trial. An all-male jury found her guilty.

After the trial, Anthony carried on her work, the National Woman Suffrage Association and other organizations continued to hold conventions, and other women attempted to vote in 1874 and subsequent years. The movement began by Mott and Stanton was continued after the Civil War by Anthony and others who formed women's political organizations and extended the goals of Seneca Falls to political enfranchisement. Throughout history, women have always been the foot soldiers in efforts to promote peace, justice, equality, the rights of children, and other important social causes. The movement to grant women basic political rights was thus, in many ways, simply an outgrowth of these earlier efforts, especially the abolition of slavery.

Throughout the later nineteenth and early twentieth centuries, the suffragists were joined by a seemingly unlikely array of women. Such diversity of voices, goals, and approaches, although giving the appearance of instability and disunity because of the divisions that occurred periodically in the movement, ended up being a strength. As a result, the movement to promote the rights of women supported a variety of issues, such as ending violence toward women and gaining basic family planning, and even included teetotaling advocates of eradicating public drunkenness, who would later succeed in amending the Constitution to ban the sale or manufacture of alcoholic beverages. An assortment of strategies were employed, from organizing at church and holding prayer meetings to practicing civil disobedience and being willing to go to jail.[18]

By the dawn of the twentieth century, suffragists were championing a variety of issues and focusing on strategies and tactics. Alice Paul and Harriot Blatch (the daughter of Elizabeth Cady Stanton) adopted strategies of civil disobedience from British suffragists, and the stakes were again raised. In the words of Emmeline Pankhurst, "deeds, not words," became the focus.[19] Many trade union women were brought into the fold, and highly visible parades with supporters from all over the country were organized, featuring students, laborers, artists, and homemakers marching side by side. The very institutions of male domain—the church, education, courts, marriage, politics—were challenged. Margaret Sanger added birth control and sexual liberation to the agenda. And by World War I, suffragists were organizing lengthy vigils in front of the White House, standing with placards and signs day after day in defiance of both war in Europe and the war against women. Hundreds were arrested during the war, an effort that again threatened and divided the movement. Suffragists were called traitors for "disrupting" the war. But their efforts caught the attention of the press and President Woodrow Wilson, who would soon change his position and support women's suffrage.

In January 1918, the House of Representatives passed a constitutional amendment for women's suffrage by one vote. Almost one and a half years later, it passed the Senate. In August 1920, it was ratified by the requisite number of states and became the Nineteenth Amendment to the Constitution. The boldness that always characterized the movement had finally succeeded, but the work was far from over.

In the 1950s and 1960s, women again emerged as the foot soldiers in the civil rights movement. Rosa Parks, Fannie Lou Hamer, and others emerged as leaders in the effort to register African Americans to vote, desegregate public spaces, and extend full political rights and equality to all races. Just as had been the case 100 years before, these women gained valuable political and organizational experience promoting racial equality and found themselves again fighting for sexual equality.

Betty Friedan's 1963 book, *The Feminine Mystique,* became the rallying point for a second wave of women concerned with equality of pay and educational opportunity, birth control and abortion rights, sexual liberation, and an array of other issues.[20] As has always been the case, the movement also included the causes of peace, racial equality, and such unresolved issues as the rights of children, from which Marian Wright Edelman emerged as the leader of the Children's Defense Fund. The National Organization for Women was established in 1966, in 1973 the Supreme Court passed the landmark ruling on abortion rights, *Roe v. Wade,* and a broad social and political agenda continued through the 1970s.

A setback for the women's movement was the failure of the Equal Rights Amendment (ERA), which was originally advocated in 1923 by Alice Paul and supporters of the National Woman's Party. It stated: "Equality of rights under the law shall not be denied or abridged by the United States or by any state on account of sex." Although it passed Congress in 1972, it failed to gain passage by the requisite three-quarters of the states before a rarely used sunset limitation, which had been imposed on the amendment, ran out. Although fully twenty states approved of the measure almost immediately, strong conservative opposition was organized, and the effort stalled. From 1977 to 1982, battle lines were drawn, money was raised, marches on the nation's capital were organized, and even first ladies entered the fray, with Betty Ford and Rosalynn Carter supporting and Nancy Reagan opposing the ERA. But by 1982, the required three-fourths of the states had failed to approve the measure.

But as with any movement, there are victories and failures, and the struggle endured. In the 1980s, a political action committee (PAC) called Emily's List (Early Money Is Like Yeast) was created and would become one of the largest and most effective PACs in the nation. The year 1992 bore fruit for the movement, earning the moniker "The Year of the Woman" because of the numbers of women pursuing and winning elected office. After this historic election, the number of women in the U.S. Senate went from two to six, the House of Representatives added nineteen women, going from twenty-nine to forty-eight, and women were elected to the governorships of Kansas, New Jersey, and Texas. A year later, in 1993, President Bill Clinton would appoint a record number of women to his administration.

Firsts
Throughout the long struggle for political equality, a number of "firsts" occurred that are worth noting, establishing broad shoulders on which

Madam President will one day stand. Jeannette Rankin became the first woman elected to Congress in 1916, winning a seat to represent the state of Montana, a state that had granted the right to vote to women in 1914. Rankin would go on to serve with distinction, taking bold positions, as had many women before her, against war and for the causes of peace and justice. For example, Rankin cast the only vote in Congress against World War I. In 1922, Rebecca Latimer Felton from Georgia became the first woman to serve in the U.S. Senate.

A decade later, Frances Perkins would make history as the first woman appointed to head a federal cabinet agency when President Roosevelt appointed her as secretary of labor in 1933. Perkins, a Mount Holyoke graduate, had been a part of the suffragist movement and involved in such important social movements as Chicago's Hull House. One should not be surprised, then, to find her occupying a prominent role in the promotion and implementation of FDR's New Deal social programs, labor rights, and a fair working wage. Roosevelt's administration also appointed Mary McLeod Bethune, the first black woman to hold a high federal office, to lead the Office of Minority Affairs of the National Youth Administration. It is fitting that these historic firsts for women were largely the result of the personal lobbying of First Lady Eleanor Roosevelt, herself a giant among women leaders.

The first woman of color appointed to head a cabinet was Patricia Harris, tapped by President Jimmy Carter to lead the Department of Housing and Urban Development (1977–1979) and then the Department of Health, Education, and Welfare. Aida Alvarez became the first Hispanic woman to head a federal agency when Clinton made her head of the Small Business Administration in 1997. The Clinton administration also achieved firsts by appointing women to lead major cabinet departments, such as Janet Reno, who was named attorney general, and Madeleine Albright, who was the first female secretary of state.

The Presidency

Female candidates for the presidency can take solace from knowing that others have gone before them. Upon the able shoulders of Victoria Woodhull they will stand. The first woman to seek the presidency, Woodhull was a flamboyant publisher and banker who campaigned for the office in 1872.[21] She found herself attacked as "Mrs. Satan" by her enemies and was placed under arrest, stopping her from campaigning on election day. Following in her footsteps was her supporter, Belva Lockwood, a teacher who had founded a coeducational school and was the first female lawyer permitted to practice law before the U.S. Supreme

Court. Lockwood ran for the presidency in 1884 and 1888 for the National Equal Rights Party.

Margaret Chase Smith, who had earlier blazed trails as the first female to serve in both houses of Congress, became the first woman to have her name placed in nomination for the presidency by a major political party, when she campaigned for the Republican nomination in 1964. The first woman to mount a campaign from the Democratic Party also earned the distinction of being the first African American woman to seek the office. After having been elected to Congress in 1969—the first African American woman member of that body—Shirley Chisholm, a Democrat, pursued the presidency in 1972. Like Woodhull and Lockwood before her, Chisholm's campaign was largely symbolic, and she failed to gain her party's nomination. That all changed in the following decade, when New York representative Geraldine Ferraro was selected in 1984 as vice presidential running mate on the Democratic ticket, opposite Walter Mondale. Ferraro, another champion of women's issues who viewed everything from education to the economy as a "woman's issue," became the first woman to be nominated as vice president. Since Ferraro's important "first," however, advocates of the first female presidency have seen only two prospective presidential campaigns. In 1987, U.S. representative Pat Schroeder, a Democrat from Colorado, after a long tenure in the House of Representatives, explored the option of mounting a presidential campaign. Elizabeth Dole, a former cabinet secretary in the administrations of Ronald Reagan and George Bush, ran as a Republican in 1999 but experienced the same inability to raise adequate funding as Schroeder and her predecessors. Table 1.5 lists those women who pursued the presidency and vice presidency.

Table 1.5 Female Presidential Candidates and Vice Presidential Nominees

Name	Year	Party
Female Presidential Candidates		
Victoria Woodhull	1872	Equal Rights
Belva Lockwood	1884	National Equal Rights
Margaret Chase Smith	1964	Republican
Shirley Chisholm	1972	Democrat
Patricia Schroeder[a]	1987	Democrat
Elizabeth Dole	1999	Republican
Female Vice Presidential Nominees		
Geraldine Ferraro	1984	Democrat
Winona La Duke	2000	Green
Ezola Foster	2000	Reform

Note: a. She explored a run for the 1988 race in 1987.

Whomever Madam President will be, she will have benefited from many considerable shoulders on which to stand. Each accomplishment of the women's movement and each woman elected to public office have moved the country that much closer to the election of a woman to the presidency. In turn, Madam President will, herself, provide perhaps the broadest shoulders upon which countless future female political leaders will stand.

About the Book

The following collection of chapters provides a summary discussion and analysis of the literature on women in politics, including gender bias, voting behavior, and the rather recent and still maturing field of study of women in executive office. Together, the chapters examine the prospects for, challenges facing, and significance of the first female presidency. The chapters are organized into four major sections, followed by a conclusion. Each section of the book closes with a profile of a different woman who pursued the presidency.

Part 1, "The Struggle for Political Equality," opens with a chapter by Max Skidmore, who assesses the strides women have made in the electoral arena and offers possible scenarios for a woman to become president. Anne Costain then looks at the role women's groups have played in paving the way for a women to pursue—and win—the presidency. Erika Falk and Kathleen Hall Jamieson consider the qualifications of several recent presidents, observing that few women have had similar qualifications (mostly backgrounds), and ponder why this is so. They offer a convincing case study of Margaret Chase Smith's 1964 presidential bid and suggest ways to make the climate more receptive to women candidates. These initial chapters lay the groundwork for an analysis of specific facets of the presidency from the perspective of a female candidate.

Part 2, "The Campaign," begins with Melissa Haussman's detailed examination of the presidential nomination process, with consideration given to the challenges faced by a female candidate. She is followed by Victoria Farrar-Myers, who dispels the myth that women candidates receive less funding than their male counterparts by using the case of well-funded House and Senate candidates. Her work poses a number of questions, such as why a well-funded woman candidate for president has failed to emerge. Dianne Bystrom then draws on studies of candidate gender and media coverage as well as political advertising to propose a communication strategy for women seeking the presidency. The section closes with a chapter from Carol Lynn Bower, who looks critically at the role of gender stereotypes in the public discourse surrounding women who seek the Oval Office, building on what has been established in the previous chapters.

The third part, "The Media, Voters, and Public Opinion," commences with Diane Heith's critical assessment of the press coverage of the campaigns of Geraldine Ferraro and Elizabeth Dole. She finds that the media continue to define the presidency in masculine terms, thus putting women at a disadvantage. Carole Kennedy discusses the importance of public opinion in a successful bid for the presidency, linking what we know and what the previous authors have established about gender stereotypes, campaigning, and the role of the media. Ann Gordon and Jerry Miller then examine the role of racial and gender stereotypes in voter assessments of candidate viability.

Part 4, "Governing," takes a look at the challenges Madam President will likely face once she has been elected. Lori Cox Han details the institutional constraints that the first woman president will find when she arrives at the White House. She argues that the office itself may define the nature of the first woman's presidency, rather than her presidency being a function solely of her gender. Similarly, Tom Lansford investigates several structural factors that lead to a remarkable consistency in U.S. foreign policy. There will be an opportunity for her to integrate women's issues into the foreign policy agenda, but Lansford weaves a fascinating and complex cast of forces, institutions, and actors with which she will have to contend. John Davis concludes this section with insights gained from interviews with numerous women involved in national security, as he explores the sensitive relationship Madam President will have with the nation's national security apparatus.

The book closes with a conclusion by Karen O'Connor, who reflects on the significance of the first woman president and the consequences for the nation, women, and the presidency of this historic event. The world has already experienced a number of female heads of state and heads of government, and history is no stranger to strong women leaders: generations of schoolchildren have read about Egypt's Cleopatra, Queen Isabel of Spain, Queens Elizabeth and Victoria of England, Empress Catherine the Great of Russia, and Joan of Arc. Yet, the United States has yet to elect a woman president. The occasion of the first female president's election will be one worth noting, because it will shatter possibly the most profound glass ceiling facing women. Perhaps then and only then will the old saying that "a woman's place is in the home" be replaced with the reality that a woman's place is in the house—the White House.

PART 1
THE STRUGGLE FOR POLITICAL EQUALITY

2

Breaking the Final Glass Ceiling: When (Not If) a Woman Becomes President

Max J. Skidmore

Sometime early in the twenty-first century, the United States will swear into office a new president who, for the first time in the country's history—a history of more than two centuries—will be a woman. She will be a seasoned politician. She will likely command wide support. She will have demonstrated the success of an arduous struggle to overcome a bias against women that long permeated an entire culture; a bias so strong that it included even figures as enlightened as Thomas Jefferson. "The appointment of a woman to office is an innovation for which the public is not prepared, nor am I," Jefferson could write some two centuries ago with no embarrassment.[1] We can dismiss such a view as archaic, but Jefferson went much further. On September 5, 1816, he wrote to Samuel Kercheval that women "could not mix promiscuously in the public meetings with men." If they were to do so, it would result in "deprivation of morals and ambiguity of issue." However outrageous the belief that a woman's children—her "issue"—would be of doubtful parentage if she were to mingle with men unchaperoned, it was widespread in Jefferson's day.[2] Given such harsh attitudes, one can only imagine his reaction if he could see a woman as his successor, assuming the highest office in the land.

Surprisingly, though, some women had voted in colonial America. Their status actually worsened following the American Revolution and throughout the course of the nineteenth century. "Women did vote for a time in Virginia, and in New Jersey for more than thirty years. But after the Revolution had been won, these tentative concessions were forgotten, and state and national constitutions were drafted without mention of the rights of women."[3] Even during Jefferson's time, though, there were

21

a few persons capable of rising above popular prejudice and questioning the restrictions upon women. Abigail Adams is well-known for her assertive correspondence with her husband, John, who relied heavily upon her political wisdom, and she did begin "to question the position of women in American society."[4] Calls for suffrage—let alone officeholding—for women were nevertheless decades away.

Somewhat later, in 1844, Margaret Fuller, one of the most powerful intellects in U.S. history, broke with tradition by becoming a writer for Horace Greeley's *New York Daily Tribune*. Then, in 1845, she scandalized society with the first of the great American feminist works—one that continues to be unequaled—*Woman in the Nineteenth Century*. Few of her readers, if any, were willing to be persuaded when she wrote of women: "But if you ask me what offices they may fill, I reply—any. I do not care what case you put; let them be sea-captains, if you will. I do not doubt there are women well fitted for such an office."[5]

Fuller was as farsighted as the most radical of the pioneering feminists, those who organized the Seneca Falls Convention in 1848—a conference that may well have been the birthplace of modern activist feminism. In any case, it clearly was an early step on the long journey that resulted ultimately in the first major accomplishment, suffrage for women. That step started society on the even longer journey that will culminate in the first woman occupant of the presidency. Yet so strong were the prejudices against women that Lucretia Mott, the gentle but determined Quaker who helped organize the convention with Elizabeth Cady Stanton, shrank in horror when Stanton proposed support for suffrage. "Elizabeth," she allegedly said, "Thee will make us ridiculous!"[6] She was under no illusion regarding woman's "place."

Early Struggles

Regardless of that "place," a daring and determined woman did run for president decades before women had the vote. Victoria Claflin Woodhull had accomplished many things, including creating the "first female-run Wall Street brokerage firm." She added to her list of accomplishments in 1872 by becoming the first woman to run for the U.S. presidency. Even women in the suffrage movement turned against her because of the outspoken radicalism of her views on marriage and the sexual liberation of women. As if that were not enough, she did her cause no good when she attacked sexual hypocrisy by publicizing the details of a sexual liaison that the prominent minister Henry Ward Beecher had with a parishioner's wife.[7]

A second woman made the attempt in 1884, running on the ticket of the National Equal Rights Party. Belva Lockwood received some 4,000 votes. She also became the first woman to argue before the Supreme Court after having pressured Congress to pass legislation permitting women to practice before federal courts. Nevertheless, eighty years passed "before another woman sought the presidency. Margaret Chase Smith, the first woman to serve in both the House and Senate, entered the Republican race in 1964, and dropped out after coming in fifth in New Hampshire, the first primary."[8]

Woman's place had not changed by 1873, a quarter of a century after the Seneca Falls Convention. The previous year, Susan B. Anthony had been arrested in New York because she had attempted to vote, arguing that the new Fourteenth Amendment had extended the vote to women.[9] That year, no less an authority than the U.S. Supreme Court recognized and verified what that place was and what it was to be when it upheld an action by the State of Illinois. Illinois had denied Myra Bradwell a license to practice law. Although Bradwell had passed the bar examination, she could not be admitted to the bar, said the state, because she was a woman. Rejecting Bradwell's claims that Illinois had infringed on her rights under the Fourteenth Amendment's privileges and immunities clause, the Court ruled against her. "Man is, or should be, woman's protector and defender," said the Court's opinion. "The natural and proper timidity and delicacy which belongs to the female sex evidently unfits it for many of the occupations of civil life. . . . This is the law of the Creator."[10]

One hundred years later, in the twentieth century, the Court issued a vastly different opinion. Writing for the majority in *Frontiero v. Richardson,* Associate Justice William Brennan called all laws that incorporated sexual classifications inherently suspect and condemned the attitudes that had led to the earlier decision.[11] Because of them, he said, American women throughout much of the nineteenth century were in a position similar to that of slaves in the South. He noted that even as he wrote in 1973, although there had been much improvement, women still faced discrimination.

Brennan was correct. The previous year Shirley Chisholm had attempted to secure the Democratic nomination for president. Even though she was black, African American men sought to prevent her from running. "They said I was an intellectual person," she said, "that I had the ability, but that this was no place for a woman. If a black person were to run, it should be a man." She said that she suffered far more discrimination in politics from being a woman than from being black. She managed to appear on the ballot in twelve primaries but received only a small percentage of the vote. She remarked that she decided to "take the plunge. I knew I wouldn't be president," she laughed, "but somebody had to break the ice, somebody with the nerve and bravado to do it."[12]

Reflecting on the Struggle

The twentieth century wound down to its tumultuous—one might well say ignominious—close as the country fumbled through a most awkward, mean-spirited, and bizarre election, one noted for its clear disregard of principle. The political system had left the "Year of the Woman" far behind, and there still had been no woman president. To be sure, women had come to hold high political office, and there had been substantial change. As Ann Richards, former governor of Texas, put it:

> I've reached the age where I can accept that our progress has been remarkable if I will just stop and look at it. My grandmother could not vote for a period of her life. Idiots, imbeciles, the insane, and women could not vote in Texas. Here, one generation later, I was the governor. So I know we're going to have a woman president. And it's not going to be just a popularity contest. This woman is going to be good, she's going to be smart, she's going to be prepared, and she's going to win.[13]

Yes, 1992, the Year of the Woman, had reflected that progress. Numerous women had been elected to public office around the country, including some notable successes in both houses of Congress. During the 1990s, some states charted new territory by filling both their Senate seats with women. States on both coasts—Maine and California—continue to do so. But women remain a small minority in elected office, including in the Congress. For the Year of the Woman to have been considered successful when so few women occupy elective office indicates how much remains to be done—in addition to choosing the first woman president.

The movement in favor of woman suffrage had gained momentum after the Seneca Falls Convention, but only very slowly. Wyoming entered the Union in 1890 as the first state in modern times to grant the vote to women. "By 1896, [it was] joined by Utah, Colorado, and Idaho. But the movement stalled there. While women in several states were granted partial suffrage—most often in school or municipal elections—not until 1910 was another state added to the full suffrage column."[14]

In the watershed election of 1912, neither the Republican candidate, President William Howard Taft, nor the great Progressive reformer Woodrow Wilson supported suffrage for women. Only the Bull Moose

Progressive Theodore Roosevelt—who lost to Wilson but came in far ahead of the incumbent Taft—did so.[15] Roosevelt had a long history of advocacy for women's rights. As a senior at Harvard in 1880, for example, he had chosen "The Practicability of Equalizing Men and Women Before the Law" as the topic of his senior thesis, and he argued in its favor.[16] He did not even "think the woman should assume the man's name."[17] As a member of the U.S. Civil Service Commission prior to becoming president, Roosevelt increased the number of women in government jobs by putting them for the first time on an equal basis with men. Later, as a member of the Police Commission, he also added women to the New York City Police Department.[18]

When Wilson became president, he intensified his progressivism, and (although neither man would have admitted it), he moved further in Roosevelt's direction. He came, for example, to support the vote for women, which ratification of the Nineteenth Amendment in 1920 finally ensured. He argued that a leader had to wait for the populace to follow. As John Cooper put it, "ironically, Wilson advanced that argument to justify his former lukewarmness toward woman suffrage."[19]

As late as 1917, though, only ten states had provided the vote for women. The House of Representatives rejected a proposed suffrage amendment, but times were changing. Political developments encouraged new roles for women: "In addition to the determined insistence of Anthony and other women's leaders, and to support from the Progressive movement, World War I was bringing women into public life to an unprecedented extent." President Wilson's support added to the momentum. "Before the year ended, New York became the first state in the east to give women the franchise."[20]

And so after a long and bitter struggle led by Susan B. Anthony and other courageous advocates, the Nineteenth Amendment barring sex as a criterion for voting finally became part of the U.S. Constitution. This success is in marked contrast to the fate of the Equal Rights Amendment about sixty years later in a presumably more enlightened time. A review of the arguments against both amendments will reveal that they were similar to a startling degree.

At the national level, the first woman to be elected to Congress was Jeannette Rankin, a Republican from Montana. She served one term (1917–1919) before ratification of the Nineteenth Amendment, just in time to vote against declaring war on Germany in World War I. She also served an additional term, from 1941 to 1943, where she cast the sole vote in the House against entry into World War II. Her election to Congress laid the groundwork for numerous women to follow her not only to the House but to the Senate as well. As the twentieth century ended,

Elizabeth Hanford Dole was briefly a serious contender for the Republican presidential nomination (Shirley Chisholm had predicted that she would not finally enter the race because "she doesn't have the temperament. She's too cautious"),[21] and the state of New York had elected a sitting first lady, Hillary Rodham Clinton, as U.S. senator. Although she surrendered the informal title of first lady after less than a month in the Senate, Senator Clinton became not only the first woman to be senator from New York but the first president's wife ever to be elected to Congress.

The first woman to hold a cabinet position was Frances Perkins, who became Franklin D. Roosevelt's secretary of labor in 1933. She not only led the way for others—including ultimately Madeleine Albright, who as President Bill Clinton's secretary of state became the highest-ranking woman in U.S. history in 1993—but she had enormous influence on policy and was one of the key players in developing the landmark Social Security program. President Ronald Reagan broke with tradition by naming the first woman to the U.S. Supreme Court, Sandra Day O'Connor. President Clinton later added Ruth Bader Ginsburg. The Court ended the century with women as two of its nine members.

But those well-publicized successes obscured the fact that women continued to represent only a small fraction of the whole. Moreover, not only had the country failed to choose a woman president by the time the twentieth century ended, but neither major political party—despite Elizabeth Dole's short-lived foray into the 2000 race as a Republican—had even nominated a woman as its candidate. There had been, however, one woman on the national ticket of a major party. In 1984, Democratic presidential candidate and former vice president Walter Mondale had selected Geraldine Ferraro as his running mate.

It would be difficult to overstate the importance of Mondale's choice. As Republican Tanya Melich, who later broke with her party because she perceived its treatment of women to be inexcusable, put it regarding the announcement of her nomination, "Ferraro won our hearts that night, and none of the ugly campaign that followed ever took us far from her. Not even in November, when the majority of American women joined American men in deciding that Reagan deserved a second term, did the optimism and promise that her candidacy gave us dim. A respectable part of America's male-dominated establishment now believed a woman could be president."[22]

It seemed that Ferraro's candidacy had shattered a taboo. Many women came to believe that perhaps at last a woman could be president. A letter that Ferraro received made the point graphically. "I'm thirty-six years old," the writer said. "I'm a Republican. For years something's burned inside me. Resentment about the way women are perceived in the world. Shame in halfway believing it. And now you've come along to say—never again do I have to feel this way. I am free. Thank you for my liberation. You have changed my life."[23]

Republican women activists, Melich said, used Ferraro's nomination to seek the attention of Republican leaders for the backing of women candidates. Among those activists, some threatened to jump ship and support Ferraro. A few actually did, including "Mary Crisp, Kathy Wilson, Californian Mary Stanley, who'd been a Reagan supporter until 1980, and Betsy Griffith, who had written a *Newsweek* op-ed column, which appeared early in the week of the Republican convention, in which she said the national party had given Republican feminists a choice either to 'keep quiet or to keep out.' Griffith switched," Melich said. As for herself, she thought at the time that she could accomplish more by remaining within the party, but she did join others in refusing to attend the Dallas convention.[24]

The result was a campaign of unusual ferocity, much of which, Melich wrote, could "be traced to the inner circle's willingness to turn over the party's positions on social issues to the Religious and New Right."[25] At the convention, women appeared in prominent positions to demonstrate a commitment to equality, but she noted that in the platform and after the convention, the agenda of the Moral Majority held sway: "the misogynists had written a mean-spirited platform limiting women's opportunities. U.S. Representative Trent Lott of Mississippi was the Platform Committee chairman. His committee included his New Right co-revolutionaries: Newt Gingrich, Henry Hyde, Phyllis Schlafly, Roger Jepsen, Vin Weber," and so on.[26] Melich described the campaign against Ferraro as an "attack of bigotry," which was "of a kind never before experienced by a vice-presidential candidate."[27]

The Reagan team examined Ferraro's life exhaustively and proceeded with such vigor that it was "as though Reagan's victory depended on destroying her." They did not need such tactics to defeat Mondale: "their assault on Ferraro was both gratuitous as well as cruel. A team had been dispatched to New York to track down dirt on Ferraro and leak it to the press." According to Melich, "pickets constantly harassed her with ethnic epithets and anti-abortion slogans," such as "Ferraro: Vice-President for Death," and "Ferraro, A Disgrace to Motherhood."[28]

Melich went so far as to charge that "allies of the Reagan team went after Ferraro with the same ferocity exhibited three hundred years ago by the 'good Puritans' of Salem." Initially, she said, the Reagan-Bush campaign denied any connection with the attacks, but "they were lying. The press found them out. The National Right to Life Committee admitted it 'was in constant contact with the Reagan-Bush people,'" an audiotape instructed demonstrators to identify themselves only as "concerned citizens," not as members of Students for Reagan, and the tactics were reminiscent of the "guerrilla groups" that Republican presidential campaigns had used for some time to sabotage the opposition.[29] The campaign against Ferraro extended to include attacks on her by several leaders of her own church.

In view of the treatment accorded the only woman ever to run on a major party ticket, some observers have suggested that when a woman does become president, it will be as a Republican. They note that it took a militant anticommunist, Richard Nixon, to renew relations with China. It took a Democrat, Bill Clinton, to succeed in reforming welfare. Similarly, when the time to have a woman as president comes, the candidate will be a Republican. Rather than give in to such simplistic formulations, let us assume that either party has a chance to have the first woman president.

Before it happens, the twenty-first century will be well under way. The speculative scenario that follows suggests a likely possibility:

When the crucial election arrived, one party found that it had a woman as its front-runner, but she had insufficient support in the primaries to ensure her nomination. The other party had a vigorous, youthful, and charismatic male front-runner who had swept the primaries and assured his nomination—but it had a woman candidate as well who had strong support. It had been almost a foregone conclusion that the party would place her on its ticket as its vice presidential nominee, and it did so.

The other party turned away from its female front runner, when its convention chose a former vice president to head the ticket. The new nominee was colorless and he had a history of serious health difficulties, but he had impressed the dominant wing of his party because he had impeccable party credentials, he was a candidate of demonstrated ability who had even overshadowed the president whom he had served, and he was not a woman. As a consolation to the defeated woman candidate, and to demonstrate that gender equity was "uppermost" in its concerns, the party placed her on the ticket as its vice presidential nominee.

Thus, it was assured that the new vice president would be a woman. This was the first time that such a possibility had even existed since the Ferraro candidacy of 1984.

When the new administration took office, observers tended to assume that the new vice president would be a strong candidate for the nomination eight years hence. The glass ceiling appeared certainly to be cracked, if indeed it was not actually broken.

A further scenario might have fate intervening, as follows: Shortly after the new administration assumed office, the country received a shock. After having been reassured numerous times by the official physician that his health was no issue, the president died suddenly. Several months had passed since his inauguration, so the tragedy would not enter the record books as a term shorter than James A. Garfield's six months, let alone William Henry Harrison's one month. But his death led to the swearing in of Madam President, the first in history.

Is such a speculation too contrived? Consider this: from the Republic's beginning until the presidency of George W. Bush, there have been forty-two presidents. Eight of these, or nearly one-fifth of the total, have died in office. An additional one resigned. Thus, more than one of every five has failed to complete his term. The fledgling Republic was fortunate in having more than a half-century pass before it had to face the sad fact of a presidential death. William Henry Harrison, who died shortly after assuming the presidency in 1841, was the first to die in office. Never again, as the following table shows, has there been such a lengthy period without a presidential death—until now (see Table 2.1).

From Harrison's death in 1841 until Kennedy's in 1963, a president died in office at least once every quarter-century. As of the year 2002, it has been more than four decades since this unhappy event has taken place. Already it has been the longest such period in U.S. history, except for the very first half-century after adoption of the Constitution. It is unlikely that such a fortuitous circumstance can continue indefinitely. Therefore, it seems not too far-fetched to consider a scenario such as the one above that places the first woman vice president in office at a time when she will be called upon to fill a presidential vacancy. After all, when she becomes vice president, the period without a president dying in office will be approaching in length that period between the founding of the United States and Harrison's death, if indeed it has not already exceeded it.

However it happens, many women of both parties will rejoice that a woman will be president—and many men will join them. One may hope

Table 2.1 Presidents Who Died in Office

	Year(s) Elected
William Henry Harrison	1840
Zachary Taylor	1848
Abraham Lincoln	1860, 1864
James A. Garfield	1880
William McKinley	1896, 1900
Warren G. Harding	1920
Franklin D. Roosevelt	1932, 1936, 1940, 1944
John F. Kennedy	1960

that the country as a whole will welcome her happily as well. The pundits will inevitably conclude that the glass ceiling is gone. The more curmudgeonly among them may argue that it had never existed. Other, more realistic, observers will be cautious in their predictions. The breaching of the glass ceiling will not signify that it has been shattered, that women no longer face disadvantages. More prudent observers will note that John F. Kennedy's election removed Roman Catholicism as an absolute barrier to election, but that as of 2002, no other Catholic had been elected.

Certainly, when a woman becomes president, the country will have passed a milestone—an enormous milestone. Once a woman has become president, it will be easier than before for another to attain the office. In all likelihood, though, until there have been several women presidents, a woman contender will continue to face more barriers than her male counterparts.

Until that day of equality—of political maturity—women candidates will be required to offer not merely good qualifications but superb ones to have any chance at success. Women will not truly have eliminated the glass ceiling until a woman candidate can remain in the running while being as lackluster as all candidates were in the election of 2000.

3

Paving the Way:
The Work of the
Women's Movement

Anne N. Costain

From the first public statement of a set of goals at the first women's rights conference in the United States (held in 1848 in Seneca Falls, New York), to its work in the antislavery movement in subsequent decades, to its dramatic actions a century later on the boardwalk in Atlantic City displaying garbage cans filled with bras, girdles, high heels, and other trappings of the beauty pageant culture, to the nomination of Geraldine Ferraro as the first woman vice presidential candidate of a major political party, the U.S. women's movement has been a force throughout most of the nineteenth, twentieth, and the early twenty-first centuries. The longevity, diversity, and scope of this movement have been critical in paving the way for the election of the first U.S. woman president.

Throughout their long history, women's movements, whether labeled suffrage, temperance, women's liberation, or antislavery, are linked in their consistent cry for democratic inclusion—politically, economically, educationally, and in the professions. The movement's democratic core is further underscored by its centuries-long commitment to nonviolent means of achieving social change, such as the movement's work to achieve universal suffrage and political enfranchisement. The election of the first woman president is a natural culmination of the efforts of women's movements.

The Political History of the Women's Movement

The First Wave
Rather than sketching the unbroken chain of women's rights activism that extends back to abolitionist protest, in this chapter I focus on historical

convention and on the three most intense "waves" of feminist mobilization and their legacies for electing the first woman president. The first wave is the woman's suffrage movement. When Elizabeth Cady Stanton, Alice Paul, Susan B. Anthony, and other prominent women's rights activists of the time realized that slavery would be ended and citizenship and the vote offered to males, regardless of race, but not to women, regardless of race, the battle to obtain the vote for women was under way. A seventy-year struggle ensued, capped but not ended in 1920 with the granting of national voting rights through the Nineteenth Amendment to the U.S. Constitution. Although reversing exclusion from the vote and consequently from full citizenship was an essential milestone on the long journey to the White House, other aspects of first-wave feminism were equally as essential.

Women collectively had to move from the private sphere into more public spheres of life to become viable political candidates. During the suffrage movement, dramatic breaks occurred, challenging the view that women should remain within their homes and leave political pursuits to men. In the crowds gathered at rallies sponsored by suffragists, such as Stanton and Anthony, many attendees must have come out of pure curiosity to witness a woman speaking in public. Such was the status of women at the time. Although many at these events were skeptics, it is equally likely that many male voters would have discovered that the well-reasoned yet impassioned speeches of the best-known advocates of woman's suffrage compared favorably with the stump speeches of male politicians of the period. It is not surprising that many of these woman suffrage advocates in the first wave of U.S. feminism, who flouted convention and lectured about politics in front of the public, legislative bodies, courts, and presidents, had grown up in the Quaker faith, which even then accepted and encouraged women to speak openly to public gatherings.

While women were stepping into more public roles, the predominant political strategy of suffrage organizations also pointed the way to the White House. The British suffrage model was adopted by the more radical suffrage organizations. They elected to blame the U.S. administration in power for failure to achieve ratification of the women's vote, even when its president and his political party favored extending the vote to women. This political tactic has been criticized as one more suited to the parliamentary model from which it arose—in which the prime minister leads a majority capable of delivering votes and consequent legislative victories—than to a presidential form of government. In hindsight, however, the failure of the U.S. women's movement to persuade the courts to interpret the Fourteenth and Fifteenth Amendments as granting women the right to vote, along with early refusals by the U.S. Congress to ratify the "Anthony" amendment granting suffrage, made it an appealing alternative. This presidentially focused strategy produced dramatic scenes of women picketing the White House, chaining themselves to its fences, and initiating hunger strikes in support of suffrage. The U.S. presidency, with its symbolic importance as head of government and of state, became a potent focus for transformative change, which was highlighted through this strategy.

The Second Wave

The second wave of the women's movement burst on the scene in the mid-1960s, emerging in the wake of the civil rights movement. Just as the first wave gained activists and inspiration from the antislavery movement, there is no doubt that this second wave took hope, encouragement, and vision from the civil rights movement. Early media accounts of the second wave mistakenly judged it as largely deriving from the civil rights movement and the protest wave of the 1960s and predicted its early disappearance.[1] Greater historical perspective would have recognized the continuity in its championing of the causes of inclusive democracy and nonviolent political change. It also reclaimed the desire to add the Equal Rights Amendment (ERA) to the U.S. Constitution (first introduced in Congress in 1923 at the urging of victorious suffrage crusaders by none other than Susan B. Anthony's nephew, who was a member of Congress). The political temper of the times, with government institutions responding more swiftly to the proposed ERA than to other components of the women's movement's agenda, led the ERA to become the emblematic issue of the second wave. Yet, in retrospect, the most significant events of the decades from the 1960s to the 1990s may well have been the nomination of Geraldine Ferraro as vice president and the congressional "Year of the Woman" in 1992, when an unprecedented number of women were elected to the U.S. Congress. These events both established the viability of women candidates for high elected offices and began to produce political women with the credentials to reach for the White House.

The ERA itself healed a significant rift between women's groups that had endured for more than forty years after the attainment of suffrage. During this period, suffragist Alice Paul and the National Woman's Party, which she led, had pressed for legal equality for women through an equal rights amendment to the U.S. Constitution, but the League of Women Voters and the more moderate suffrage groups had insisted that the vote, if women used it strategically, would allow them to gain all their goals as equal citizens.[2] The opposition of labor unions and consequently of many Democrats to the ERA melted away, as passage of the 1964 Civil Rights Act removed labor laws "protecting" women, which unions had supported. When these laws were repealed, there were fewer reasons for unions to oppose the ERA. By getting beyond these long-standing feminist divisions, a united second wave women's movement became possible.

As a political issue, however, the ERA remained surprisingly controversial. It attracted considerable media coverage, with 39 percent of all *New York Times* stories on women's issues during the 1970s featuring the ERA.[3] Yet comparing the balance between positive and negative coverage of equality (which in essence was coverage of the ERA) in the *Times* from the period from 1965 to 1985 reveals a much closer correspondence between the two than a similar comparison of other issues focusing on women as a constituency group.[4] A later set of *Times* articles (spanning the period from 1980 to 1996) reinforces these conclusions by showing that among the women's issues most frequently covered, civil rights and abortion had the closest balance between the numbers of positive and negative references, whereas education, jobs, and the economy were all portrayed much more favorably.[5]

In the 1980 presidential race, Republican candidate Ronald Reagan established sex as a major electoral cleavage through his outspoken opposition to the ERA, women's special needs, and the vision of social change presented by the women's movement. Prior to Reagan's presidency, the two major U.S. parties were divided over how to handle women's issues, with the split largely paralleling that between postsuffrage women's movement groups that was noted earlier. The question dividing political parties and groups was whether women fared better if they assumed the same rights and responsibilities as men or whether the biological and social differences between the sexes were sufficient to require laws tailored to meet women's and men's special needs. Since the administrations of John F. Kennedy and Lyndon B. Johnson in the 1960s, the Democrats had been moving away from their long-held emphasis on protective legislation grounded in women's special needs. They migrated toward the more "Republican" posture of equality and competition. Partly because of Reagan's outspoken opposition to the ERA, the Republican Party moved away from its long-held principle of sexual equality, just as a bipartisan consensus in favor of it was forming.

This dramatic shift captured headlines and public attention, giving birth to a political gender gap crucial to electing a future woman president. In this period between 1960 and the Reagan administration, the parties did more than just switch sides on these issues.[6] The year 1990 was not 1950. Although the parties are again divided over women's issues, on most issues women's groups today are not. Virtually all groups favor increasing the political, economic, and social participation of women so that it equals that of men. Simultaneously, legislation addressing child care, parental leave, prenatal care, and women's health have become realities. The Republican Party has clearly positioned itself as the antifeminist party since the 1980s, thereby losing women's votes but picking up support from white male voters. At the presidential level, from the 1980 presidential vote through the 2000 election, there has been a gender gap of at least 6 percent nationally, with women leaning toward the Democratic Party's candidate and men favoring Republican candidates.

Congress vacillated in its willingness to respond to women's equality or the special needs agenda. In the 1960s, the few laws passed addressing women were based on perceptions of their special needs. Most of these legislative actions were appropriations for the Women's Bureau in the Department of Labor, established in 1920 under pressure from moderate suffragists to address the needs of women workers. The sole laws premised on equality were the Equal Pay Act of 1963 and the Civil Rights Act of 1964. As important as these laws were—prescribing equal pay for women and men performing the same jobs and mandating equal hiring, firing, and terms and conditions of employment regardless of sex—each was part of a legislative agenda that was not centrally concerned with women. The Equal Pay Act responded to labor union pressure to stop companies from hiring women as inexpensive labor. Addition of sex to the 1964 Civil Rights Act was a tactical effort by southerners in Congress to bring about its defeat. There is some debate on this point because Representative Howard Smith, who introduced the amendment to the Civil Rights Act, is said to have been friendly toward the National Woman's Party. But in his speeches in the *Congressional Record,* he and his supporters clearly demean the significance of equality for women. He may well have been favorable toward the National Woman's Party because it was conservative on many issues other than women's equality.

In 1970, however, equality became the dominant focus of congressional legislation on women's issues. The egalitarian majority in Congress passed bills to give women equal access to financial credit, to admit girls to national military academies, to put women on federal juries, to open Little League programs to girls, and to make available federally supported educational programs to men and women alike. Yet by the end of the 1970s, even though Congress voted to extend the time limit for state legislatures to ratify the ERA, its own legislative focus had returned to women's difference. New laws created a supplemental food program for pregnant and nursing mothers, safeguarded the rights of pregnant workers, committed the U.S. government to improving conditions for women in developing countries, and provided federal funding for meals for women and children in battered women's shelters. With the final failure of the ERA to win ratification in 1982, the equality agenda was eclipsed.

The Third Wave

Third-wave feminism became a presence in the 1990s. It arose out of the better organized and more strongly institutionalized segments of the women's movement. The third wave combines grassroots activism, including protest politics, with a strong commitment to inclusion of socially as well as economically marginalized groups of women, including racial, ethnic, and gender minorities. It continues the same enduring themes always championed by the women's movement: democratic inclusion in politics, more public roles for women, and support for nonviolent change. This wave has helped to solidify the link between the Democratic Party and the women's movement, along with setting the stage for the broad coalition of groups needed to elect a woman president.

With the end of the Cold War, "softer" women's issues, such as education, family, and jobs, rose to the fore, displacing crime, drugs, and foreign policy as front-burner topics of national debate. Core constituencies of the Democratic Party, including African Americans, ethnic minorities, and northeastern voters, discovered more in common with the emerging focus of third-wave feminism on the interactions among race, class, and gender. Although the American South and Midwest became bedrock Republican strongholds, the shifting demographics of southwestern and western states, which had increasing numbers of Latino, Asian Pacific, and socially as well as economically libertarian voters, created a battleground where national Democratic candidates had greater opportunities to compete with Republicans by stressing economic growth, social diversity, investment in education, and protection of the environment. The recasting of foreign policy from enemy nation-states to domestic security concerns made it easier for women candidates to claim a special knowledge denied them when the arms race and international battlegrounds had been the focus.

How the third wave of the movement will incorporate the goal of electing the first woman president within the existing goals of the movement is uncertain. However, a number of organizations, scholars, and leaders in the women's movement have been working toward this goal, and the lessons, resources, and accomplishments of the movement have been employed toward putting a woman in the White House.

The Women's Movement and the Media

These themes and social realities would never have achieved the public awakening they did without an effective media strategy by the women's movement. The cultural shift allowing large majorities of the public to view a woman candidate as a potential president, rather than as a woman trying to do a job for which she may lack the training or even the capacity to perform successfully, took hundreds of years to bring about. The women's movement, in common with other social movements, had formed to promote change by educating the populace on these issues while challenging social and political institutions. For this process to happen democratically, the movement had to initiate a meaningful dialog among citizens. The media played an enormous role in influencing the content of political discussion in the United States.[7] Studies have persuasively demonstrated that media coverage does not necessarily tell citizens what to think but what to think about.[8] For public opinion to have changed sufficiently to elect the first woman president, the women's movement had to succeed in using the press to frame issues and solutions in ways that persuaded a large group of voters that a woman could serve effectively as president.

Scholars such as Thomas Rochon and Alberto Melucci make the argument that the key role of social movements is the diffusion of changes in values or norms.[9] The position of the media becomes critical since most people learn of events outside their direct experience through the mass media.[10] To assess this phenomenon, I and two collaborators created a composite list of all articles indexed under the headings "Women—United States" and "Women—General" that were published in the *New York Times* between 1955 and 1995.[11] Although this listing does not completely correspond to the three highly mobilized waves of the women's movement referenced above, it establishes a timeline showing the transmission of the views of the women's movement to the public by means of the press. The research divided the 3,251 articles into four decades: 1955–1964, 1965–1974, 1975–1984, and 1985–1995. Fifty articles were selected at random from each decade for examination in depth. The analysis involved both reading articles and using QSR Nudist, a content analysis and pattern recognition program, to evaluate them. The first period precedes the emergence of second-wave feminism, providing the opportunity to see what the residual message from the suffrage movement had become almost forty years after its peak. Periods two and three largely cover second-wave feminism. Period four blends into third-wave feminism, beginning three years after the downfall of the ERA.

Media coverage of women's issues in the first period focused primarily on the then growing phenomenon of married women and mothers entering the workforce. For instance, under the headline, "Mothers Replacing the Career Woman," the *New York Times* reported demographic data showing that a significant majority (60 percent) of employed women were then married, contradicting the perception of the time that women left the workforce after marrying.[12] Other stories probed why women worked and the variety of what was then considered to be nontraditional occupations in which they were employed. Nearly half of the articles discussed women's role within the family. A prescient survey conducted by the Young Women's Christian Association and analyzed by a family life consultant found that married, unemployed women under thirty-five with children were least likely to want to change their lives. However, women over thirty-five who were married and had children in school were discontented and desired part-time jobs.[13] This kind of finding motivated Betty Friedan's watershed book *The Feminine Mystique,* which is widely credited with giving voice to the problem "which has no name" and the second wave of the U.S. women's movement.[14]

When second-wave feminism emerged in the mid-1960s, it, the civil rights movement, and the ERA contributed to the expanded coverage the *Times* and other media sources gave to women's issues in the second period (1965–1974). Together these issues accounted for as many stories as those on women, work, and family life. The next period (1975–1984) saw the fruition of second-wave feminism. Seventy-six percent of the 1,705 articles from that period mentioned women's rights, overshadowing continuing coverage of work and family.

As third-wave feminism began to develop, work and family again dominated coverage. Fully 82 percent of the stories sampled dealt with women and employment and 70 percent with family. Clearly, the need to balance work and family accounted for many of the articles. In this most recent period, the earlier theme of tension between husbands and wives over the woman working outside the home was largely replaced by discussions of the pressure women were under to work full-time while also assuming primary responsibility for child care. The articles on family frequently dealt with the inadequacy of child care options.

The U.S. media, encouraged by the women's movement, educated the public concerning the widespread demographic changes that increasingly brought married women with children into the workforce. It published numerous accounts of the efforts to balance work and family. While giving significant coverage to the second-wave women's movement and its efforts to attain legal equality, the underlying theme throughout was the lack of adequate government solutions to problems of work and family. By emphasizing the post–World War II social reality of the changing position of women in the workforce and the strains it created both in family life and in the workplace, the coverage moved these issues to the fore. In most cases, women politicians had more firsthand experience in managing this balancing act than did males. Their knowledge gave them the opportunity to speak authoritatively to the public as workers and as educators of children.

The failure to bring about legal equality through the constitutional amendment route may even have made women's direct entrance into politics more inevitable. If the laws could not be trusted to treat women evenhandedly, all the more reason for women to make and execute the laws themselves. This concept might well motivate the first woman president.

With the media delivering the message, the public over a forty-year period increasingly came to understand that women were discontented, that they regularly mobilized into large social movements, and that among significant unresolved issues of concern to women and to society in general were families and work. When the United States entered a prolonged period in which domestic politics either overshadowed international affairs or international politics became local, as in instances of domestic terrorist threats, women had an advantage over men in running for elected office.

When Politics and Cultural Change Converge

More than a century-long social movement of, by, and for women changed laws, institutions, and lives in directions that are likely to pave the way for Madam President. Gaining the vote and full citizenship for women was just the first step. Women making gains in public discourse and participation in the public arena were additional crucial achievements. Additionally, the women's movement had from its earliest days identified the presidency as the U.S. institution that would eventually need to be won.

The second wave of feminism helped to mend the rift that had largely divided feminists into rival factions. Although the ERA was not ratified, the broad-gauged passage of laws acknowledging and improving women's place as a special interest, along with extensions of legal equality and citizenship, showed that desirable change could follow more than one path. The emergence of women's issues as defining ones in national elections and the positioning of the Democratic and Republican Parties based on their positions on issues like abortion, child care, and the ERA made it easier for women's (and men's) bloc voting to occur. Political campaigns used sex to target their messages and recruit candidates to both the Democratic and Republican Parties. Democrats came to accept that since women voters often supplied their candidates' margins of victory, women had to be represented on their tickets. Republicans learned that the post-1980 gender gap, which meant they had to attract higher and higher percentages of male voters to compensate for all the female votes they were losing, could be counterbalanced either by running Republican women candidates or men with experience in fields that would allow them to address women's issues in campaigns. The second wave of the women's movement itself turned largely to electoral and interest group politics after the agenda of legal equality lost momentum.

The third wave of the women's movement is working to create a majority coalition, campaign resources, and candidate recruitment that will put women into all levels of political office. It hopes to cement the alliances between core Democratic constituencies and feminist sympathizers.

The media, with prodding from the women's movement, has played a significant role in educating the population about the changing role of women in the United States. At the same time, they provided generally sympathetic coverage of second-wave feminism and its sustained struggle to pass the ERA. When that failed to happen, the press resumed its long and detailed exploration of the issues of women, work, and family. Government under male presidents took so long to address these conflicting pressures that women politicians gained prominence nationally through their advocacy of solutions to these unresolved issues.

One possible scenario for the future is for a Democratic woman candidate from the West, with a northeastern male running mate and strong ties to minority groups, to gain the opportunity to run a successful campaign stressing world-class, safe schools; stewardship of natural resources and the environment; a more competitive and inclusive workforce; homeland security guaranteed by stronger communities and renewed commitment to American traditions safeguarding free speech, freedom of movement, and procedural guarantees of due process; a more dynamic, technologically grounded economy; and stronger national policies to help families balance responsibilities of child care and child rearing with those of employment. The added support from women voters eager to see the first woman president elected, combined with successful service by earlier women performing as secretary of state, national security adviser, attorney general, and ambassador to the United Nations in both Republican and Democratic administrations, will do a great deal to blunt any backlash. There are few issues about which opposing forces could say, "It is hard to imagine how a woman could handle . . . " Examples exist of women either directing or implementing practically every facet of government activity.

Conclusion

The women's movement played an important role in taking women from private, domestic, noncompetitive roles to public, leadership, and partisan ones. The movement has paved the way for women to attain the ultimate position of public leadership: the presidency. It has been a long process, fraught with controversy about the qualifications women must have to succeed. Should they compete as men's equals and consequently use male models of success? Or should women bring to the table a different set of life experiences and expectations? Over time, women will do both. Some have outperformed men in highly traditional ways. Others, in both politics and the marketplace, found new ways to resolve old problems. As more women ran for office and voted, politics became increasingly "sexed," with gender gaps and "male" (e.g., military and foreign policy) and "female" (e.g., education and environmental protection) issues rising and falling in salience and popular appeal. These trends are especially apparent in national elections, namely presidential contests, and in public opinion about the qualifications and characteristics of the president. As glass ceilings shattered in multiple fields, the available pool of women with the experience to be presidential candidates grew. The groundwork has been laid, the stage set. The accomplishments of the women's movement created the backdrop for the eventual election of the first woman president in the twenty-first century.

4

Changing the
Climate of Expectations

Erika Falk and Kathleen Hall Jamieson

In 1996, during the Republican primaries, the chief executive officer of Titan Wheel International, Morry Taylor, stood side by side with Senator Bob Dole and argued that his credentials as a businessperson qualified him to be president. On the same stage was millionaire Steve Forbes. Neither Forbes nor Taylor had held elected office, neither had the traditional qualifications to serve as president, and neither was particularly charismatic or articulate. Yet each assumed that he was qualified and that the country would be interested in examining his case for the presidency. Why were there no women making a similar case?

In 1998, the Ms. Foundation inaugurated a new initiative called the White House Project, designed "to change the political climate so that qualified women from all walks of life could launch successful campaigns for the U.S. Presidency and other key positions."[1] It offered a list of potential presidential candidates to the nation and asked citizens to select their favorites. The list included, among others, Ann Fudge, president of Maxwell House; astronaut Mae C. Jemison; Wilma Mankiller, former head of the Cherokee nation; and Judith Rodin, president of an Ivy League university. None of these women had ever put themselves forward for nomination. However, if more women would ask themselves, "Am I as qualified as Taylor or Forbes?" one might see more women running for president, and as a result, the United States would be more likely to see a president who is a woman in the near future.

Among the top vote getters in the White House Project poll were Senator Dianne Feinstein; General Claudia Kennedy, who retired in 2000 with three stars; and former New Jersey governor and Environmental Protection Agency chief Christine Todd Whitman.[2] Perhaps these selections were not surprising because history tells us that governors, generals, or those who have served in both the House of Representatives and Senate are the likely contenders for and winners of the White House. However, there are few women with qualifications similar to those of men who have won the presidency, and those who are similar either have chosen not to run or have not been taken seriously by the press.

Since the first woman ran for president in 1872—Victoria Woodhull on the Equal Rights Party ticket—about fifteen women have gained the nomination of their party (all of them on minor party tickets). Many more (about 100) have sought but not obtained their party's nomination, including approximately fifty who have pursued the nomination of the Republican or Democratic Parties.[3] However, only two of these have held office in Congress (Senator Margaret Chase Smith and Representative Shirley Chisholm). No women governors or military leaders have publicly aspired to the Oval Office. Yet governors, military leaders, and senators are the type of people who tend to win the office of the presidency.

In this chapter, we explore why few women have the same qualifications as the men who run for president. We then examine the press coverage of the one woman who ran and had such credentials (Margaret Chase Smith) and note some ways in which the press was biased against her. In closing, we provide some suggestions for improving the climate to make it more receptive to women who are presidential candidates.

Qualifications of Recent Presidents

Four of the past five U.S. presidents were former governors. Before entering the White House, Jimmy Carter had served in the Georgia State Senate and, later, a single term as governor. Ronald Reagan had served as governor of California, Bill Clinton as attorney general and governor of Arkansas, and George W. Bush a term and a half as governor of Texas. One explanation for the absence of women presidential aspirants may be that few women have ever held offices that serve as a jumping-off point for such a candidacy. In the history of the United States, only nineteen women have sat in a governor's chair, thirteen of those since 1990. In fact, no woman was elected governor in her own right until 1974.[4] In 2002 there were just five sitting governors who were women, the largest number ever to hold office simultaneously.

Legislators have also ascended to the presidency in recent years. Richard Nixon, John Kennedy, and Lyndon Johnson all sat in both the House and Senate. However, women are scarce in the Senate, and it is even rarer for women to have held seats in both chambers. Only thirty-one women have ever served in the Senate, and only thirteen women are serving today—a record number to date.[5] Only seven women have ever served in both the House and Senate; six of them remain in office today (Barbara Mikulski, Barbara Boxer, Olympia Snowe, Blanche Lincoln, Maria Cantwell, and Debbie Stabenow).[6] The seventh, Margaret Chase Smith, ran for president in 1964.

The third route to the White House is through the vice presidency. Gerald Ford, George H. W. Bush, Lyndon Johnson, and Richard Nixon entered through that route, though Ford and Bush both had previously been members of the House and Johnson and Nixon members of both branches. Of course, no woman has ever been vice president, and only one has ever been selected as a vice presidential candidate on a major party ticket (Geraldine Ferraro in 1984).

The final path for recent (i.e., 1953–2001) presidents has included military leadership. Dwight D. Eisenhower was a five-star general and commander of Allied forces in Europe during World War II. Since discrimination against women serving in the military is still legal, the military is one of the more difficult avenues to national leadership for them. Women currently make up only about 14 percent of the armed forces. There have been nine five-star generals in U.S. history—all of them male.[7] Similarly, all the 618 four-star generals since the Civil War have been male.[8] The first and only three-star general who is female (Lieutenant General Claudia J. Kennedy) achieved that rank only in 1997.

However, it should be noted that many recent presidential candidates—several of whom have been successful—have run as "outsiders." Jimmy Carter, Ronald Reagan, Bill Clinton, and George W. Bush all cast themselves as outsiders, downplaying their political experience in elected office, and third-party candidates such as George Wallace and Ross Perot took this strategy even further. Accordingly, the differences in political experience between men and women and the general lack of women in upper levels of government might not be the liability it would otherwise appear to be. Yet, there is a difference between not serving in a high profile office and serving in such an office but downplaying it when it suits an outsider image.

Why So Few Women Have Similar Qualifications

Taking into account all the women who have ever had the same experience as our recent presidents (been governor, served in the House and Senate, served as vice president, or held the rank of five-star general), there have been only twenty-six, and one of them (Margaret Chase Smith) did run for president. Clearly, the most significant barrier to a successful candidacy of a woman is the fact that so few occupy the positions that tend to be entryways to the White House.

Ruth Mandel has pointed out that, in recent history, the relative scarcity of women in political office is not a reflection of lack of interest or involvement in politics.

> The overwhelming majority of politically-minded women had accepted their place as secondary and auxiliary to the real politicians and leaders—the men. The vast majority of women interested in electoral politics had worked at party housekeeping tasks or had joined campaigns behind the scenes. They staffed campaign storefronts, performed the well-known licking and sticking duties and organized candidates' evenings and fundraising parties.[9]

Although much less prominent as candidates, women have been very active in electoral politics. Next, we outline reasons that so few women occupy positions functioning as entryways to the presidency.

First, western culture's traditional association of masculinity with leadership and public roles and femininity with child rearing and housekeeping has also led many to believe that women would be incompetent in higher elected offices. The way in which poll questions about a woman president have been asked is indicative of the subtle way in which this belief has seeped into U.S. culture. For instance, in February 1937 a Gallup poll asked respondents (emphasis added), "Would you vote for a woman for President if she were qualified in every *other* respect?" The clear implication was that being a woman was a disqualifier of sorts. The phrase "every *other* respect" was dropped after 1939, but as late as June 2000, Roper Poll was still asking, "If your party nominated a woman for president, would you vote for her if she were qualified for the job?" thus revealing the cultural assumption that even a woman nominated by a party might not be qualified. Such assumptions are particularly problematic because women as well as men absorb them.

Second, women have been hampered in their efforts to assume political office by the political system, which is biased in favor of incumbents. About 95 percent of incumbents in the U.S. Congress win reelection, and most incumbents are men. Challengers win just about 5 percent of the time.[10] Accordingly, even if all challengers were women, the rate at which they would integrate the U.S. Congress would be slow. However, most challengers are not women. In fact, just 8 percent of candidates for the U.S. Congress are women.[11] Thus, the likelihood that a woman will seek the presidency is minimized by the relatively late entrance of women candidates into the electoral process combined with their slow advancement through the political system.

The third reason for women's diminished participation in political office reflects these factors. It is all the more important because in many ways, this process perpetuates itself: the relative scarcity of women in higher offices has meant women are less likely to have role models and mentors. At the same time, Mandel found that women were more likely than men to "attribute inspiration or assistance to their political careers to female role models, mentors, and the campaigns of other female candidates for whom they worked."[12] The importance of role models to political ambition was aptly demonstrated in a political cartoon that appeared during Prime Minister Margaret Thatcher's incumbency. In it a boy and girl discussed what they would like to be when they grow up. The boy said, " I want to be Prime Minister," but the girl retorted, "You can't be Prime Minister. You are a boy."

The fourth reason for the absence of women in the presidential queue is that women are less likely to be recruited to run for office than are men. Among the reasons identified by Ruth Mandel was the fact that "women are still less likely . . . to be part of the business community and leadership networks that breed potential candidates and ease their way into the system."[13]

However, not all the encumbrances are external. The fifth reason researchers point to as a major contributor to women's low rates of candidacy is "role conflict." Traditional social mores have tended to assign the task of child rearing and housekeeping to women, and to some extent it still holds true in society today. At the same time, during the twentieth century women became increasingly integrated into the workforce. These two factors have created what some feminists have identified as the "double burden." Not only are women expected to work as men do but in many families, they are also primarily responsible for raising and taking care of the children and housekeeping duties. This added burden may deter and delay women's political involvement. Among other effects, such conflicting demands have prompted women to delay entering the political field. Women began running for office in notable numbers only in the 1970s. Thus, they have had relatively little time to move into more powerful and prominent posts.

This point is further amplified by the fact that women are more likely to run for office after their family responsibilities have diminished. Mandel wrote, "Elected women are more likely than elected men to be widowed, separated, or divorced, and they are less likely to have young children at home. Furthermore, elected women are more likely than elected men to report that the age of their children was an important factor in their decision to run for office."[14] Because women are more likely to feel free to run after their children are grown or a husband has left, they make a later entry into elected office, leaving less time to reach the highest political ranks.

The final contributing factor may be the persistent belief that women have less chance of winning office than do men. In fact, studies show that when women run, they win just as often as men do.[15] However, most people do not believe it. The 1994 National Women's Political Caucus survey found that two-thirds of the respondents thought it was harder for women than men to get elected.[16]

Margaret Chase Smith and the Press

Thus far, we have noted that there are very few women in offices that have served as feeder positions for the presidency and have identified six reasons contributing to their scarcity: (1) traditional sex roles that lead many (including many women) to believe women are incompetent in the political sphere, (2) the strength of incumbency, (3) women's lack of role models, (4) discrimination in recruitment, (5) role conflict, and (6) a perception that women are less viable. These factors explain why women are uncommon in positions that have in recent history led to the White House. The tribulations of the one woman who defied these precepts, sat in both the House and Senate, and ran for the presidency provide a case study revealing some of the barriers imposed on women who do seek office.

Margaret Chase Smith entered the U.S. House of Representatives as a widow finishing her husband's term but was soon reelected in her own right and went on to serve in the Senate as well. She ran for the Republican Party nomination for president in 1964. Because Chase Smith was widowed and had no children for whom to care, she was not hindered by one of the major barriers that many women face. She ran for the House after her husband recruited her to run in his place just before his death, and when she aspired to be a Senator, she first ran for an open seat, greatly increasing her chances of winning.

When examining the press coverage of Senator Chase Smith, we found that there was less coverage, less serious coverage, and a minimization of her accomplishments. When we examined three newspapers from 1964, we found that, on average, Chase Smith had 7.5 articles per newspaper per month, whereas Nelson Rockefeller, the candidate closest to her in primary votes (running in the same race), had on average 25 articles per newspaper per month.[17] We also found that Chase Smith's coverage was less likely to mention issues than Rockefeller's. When we categorized each paragraph as being predominantly about issues or not, only 8.6 percent of paragraphs in articles about Chase Smith were about issues, compared with 25 percent of articles about Rockefeller.[18] Chase Smith was also more likely to have the title "senator" dropped for "Mrs." than

was Rockefeller to have "Mr." substituted for "governor." Senator
Chase Smith was identified as "Mrs. Smith" about one-third (32 percent) of the time when she was mentioned by name in the articles. The
parallel mistake of using "Mr. Rockefeller" instead of "Governor Rockefeller" occurred just five times out of 100. By removing Chase Smith's
honorary title in favor of a common one, the papers diminished her accomplishments and political experience in favor of her marital status.

We also found that Chase Smith was often treated as though she
were not running for president and was "really" interested in the vice
presidency. This occurred despite the fact that she repeatedly and publicly said she had no interest in the second spot on the ticket. Typical
of these mentions is this comment from the *New York Daily News:*
"Sen. Margaret Chase Smith of Maine—who said she'd like to run
for president, period, but is believed to be willing to settle for the vice-
presidential nomination. . . ."[19] More dismissive, however, is this example from the *Bangor Daily News:* "If Mrs. Smith made a good showing in the primaries, she would be in a position to seek the second spot
on the Republican ticket."[20] Thus, even under the supposition that
Chase Smith did well, the papers funneled her to the vice presidency
and not the presidency. These examples are not anomalies. In fact, mentions of Chase Smith as a vice presidential candidate occurred in 21 percent of the articles that mentioned her. Rockefeller was never cast as a
potential candidate for vice president (though, ironically, it was he who
would years later hold the position).

Another interesting feature of the articles is the way in which they
identified Chase Smith's candidacy as a "first" (though she was at least
the third). For example, Nellie Penley and Marie Sullivan frame Chase
Smith as a "first" in their column dated January 28, 1964. They note in
their first paragraph that "Senator Smith is the first woman ever to stand
as a candidate for nomination to the presidency."[21] Similarly, in a letter
to the editor, Chase Smith was described as the "first woman ever to
enter the presidential race."[22] By framing Chase Smith's candidacy as a
"first" instead of a continuation or extension of a long history of political activism and involvement among women in American politics, the
press may have promoted the idea that women are less normal and more
risky in the political sphere. This bias may have affected Chase Smith's
chances of winning, but more important, it may have deterred other
women from considering elected office.

The notion of women as unnatural in the political world was reinforced in other ways as well. One argument regularly advanced in the
press was that women were too emotional and irrational to hold office.
For example, in one vox populi, a man said, "Women are too illogical

and too emotional for high elective posts."[23] In another, a man retorted, "A woman is not emotionally or physically capable of assuming the obligations of the most powerful office in the world . . . we'd be in mortal danger with a female president."[24] When asked, "Would you be prejudiced against a woman running for president of the United States?" Stephen Eisman, another person on the street, gave a familiar reply, "Definitely! A woman is too emotional. She acts on impulse and she is often too sensitive to criticism."[25] The regular appearance of such attitudes in press treatments may perpetuate traditional attitudes about women's unfitness for office, but in addition, these attitudes are absorbed by women as well as men, perhaps convincing women that they are ill-suited to hold leadership positions.

Though the data presented here come from a single case study, these patterns in the press coverage may collectively contribute to making women appear less normal in the political sphere by giving them less coverage, dropping their political titles, and repeatedly framing them as firsts. This phenomenon is also analyzed by Diane Heith in Chapter 11. The press coverage may also contribute to making women appear less suited to the presidency by portraying them as irrational and emotional and by dismissing their presidential ambitions as actually vice presidential ones. Although these attitudes may reflect societal beliefs, they also reinforce them adding to the climate that makes political office and women seem incompatible.

Suggestions for Changing the Climate

Having looked at several of the reasons why there has not yet been a woman president and some patterns in the press accounts of one woman who did run, we now propose a few suggestions to help change the climate for women.

1. *Support term limits.* Term limits (even with long terms) would help women more rapidly infiltrate the Congress. Women who run for open seats have a 50 percent chance of winning, whereas those running as challengers have a 5 percent chance. Instituting term limits would eliminate one of the institutional barriers that reinforces men's political dominance while providing an opportunity for women's greater involvement.

2. *Increase the number of women running.* Once space is created for women, more women will need to put themselves forward as candidates. To help increase the numbers of women candidates we must raise awareness among girls, women, political fund-raisers,

and party elites that when women run, women win just as often as men do. The parties should make recruitment of candidates who are women a priority.

3. *Raise awareness of press biases.* It is unlikely that most media professionals are aware of the fact that women who run experience press bias. Confronting journalists and editors about bias may help reduce it. As the press begins to give the same column inches to women as they do to men, and as conventions that minimize women's political competence begin to erode, political women will seem more normative.

5

Profile:
Shirley Chisholm, Blazing Trails

Robert P. Watson and Ann Gordon

REPRODUCED FROM THE COLLECTIONS OF THE LIBRARY OF CONGRESS

Born on November 30, 1924, in
  Brooklyn, New York
B.A. (cum laude) from Brooklyn
  College in 1946
M.A. from Columbia University in
  1952
Elected to New York State Assembly
  in 1964
Served in 91st–97th Congresses
  (1969–1983)

With her election to the House of Representatives in 1968, Shirley Chisholm became the first black woman to serve in Congress. She represented New York's 12th district, a poor area of Brooklyn that was majority black and Puerto Rican, as well as Jewish, Polish, and Ukrainian.[1] With the slogan "unbought and unbossed," she campaigned on a shoestring budget. As she recalls it:

> Soon after the primary . . . a woman rang the doorbell, and when I answered it she pushed an envelope into my hand. "This is the first, Chisholm," she said. There was $9.69 in the envelope, and I learned that she had collected it from a group of people on welfare at a bingo party. I sat down and cried. My campaign was financed that way, and out of my own pocket.[2]

Shirley Chisholm won election with 70 percent of the vote and went on to serve seven terms.[3] She introduced some fifty pieces of legislation to address her concerns about education (she had been a teacher), unemployment, housing, day care, and other issues.[4] She was also proud of her speech against the Vietnam War, made on the floor of the House shortly after she was elected. The decision to speak out came when the Nixon administration cut funding for Head Start and urged Congress to spend more money on defense—in the very same day.

> I am deeply disappointed at the clear evidence that the number one priority of the new administration is to buy more and more weapons of war, to return to the era of the Cold War and to ignore the war we must fight here, the war that is not optional. There is only one way, I believe, to turn policies around. . . . We must force the administration to re-think its distorted, unreal scale of priorities. Our children, our jobless men, our deprived, our rejected, and starving citizens must come first. For this reason, I intend to vote "no" on every money bill that comes to the floor of this House that provides any funds for the Department of Defense. Any bill whatsoever, until the time comes when our values and priorities have been turned right-side up again, until the monstrous waste and the shocking profits in the defense budget have been eliminated and our country starts to use its strength, its tremendous resources, for people and peace, not for profits and war.[5]

The Presidential Campaign

In 1972, Shirley Chisholm sought the Democratic nomination for president of the United States. She recalled in her memoir that the idea came from students who urged her to run when she visited college campuses. In addition, black politicians and civil rights leaders thought it was time for an African American to run for president. But Chisholm found out that for many that meant a black *man*. She was accused of "messing things up," and her loyalty to "black causes" was even questioned: "they hinted that I would sell out black interests if they came in conflict with those of women."[6] However, Chisholm persisted and entered the race, ultimately spending $300,000 dollars and campaigning in eleven primaries.[7] Though her candidacy was serious, Chisholm was realistic about her chances.

All the odds had been against it, right up to the end. I never blamed anyone for doubting. The Presidency is for white males. No one was ready to take a black woman seriously as a candidate. It was not time for a black to run, let alone a woman, and certainly not for someone who was both. . . . I ran because someone has to do it first. In this country everybody is supposed to be able to run for President, but that's never really been true. I ran because most people think that the country is not ready for a black candidate, not ready for a woman candidate. Someday . . . [8]

Democrats George McGovern, Eugene McCarthy, and Hubert Humphrey also took her seriously and saw her candidacy as a potential threat. She was even asked by party leaders to withdraw.[9] In the end, McGovern won the nomination, but not before Chisholm garnered 152 votes and had her say on the convention floor.

Once I was in the campaign, I had to stay all the way to the end, all the way to that night at the convention. Nothing less would have shown that I was "a serious candidate." If there had been only ten delegates ready to vote for me on the first ballot, instead of more than 50, I would still have stuck it out. The next time a woman runs, or a black, a Jew or anyone from a group that the country is "not ready" to elect to its highest office, I believe he or she will be taken seriously from the start. The door is not open yet, but it is ajar.[10]

Life After Congress

After she left Congress in 1983, Chisholm taught politics and women's studies at Mount Holyoke College in Massachusetts. She has been awarded more than thirty-five honorary doctoral degrees. She was even nominated to be ambassador to Jamaica by President Bill Clinton.[11]

Representative Chisholm was honored by Congress in July 2001 with a resolution that recognized her contributions. Representative Barbara Lee of California said she registered to vote because of Chisholm. In her tribute to Chisholm, Lee said, "Ms. Chisholm's mission to include women, children, African-Americans and other minorities in public policy opened the door to a whole new debate lacking in Congress during that time. She is a remarkable woman who paved the way for many of us."[12]

PART 2
THE CAMPAIGN

6

Can Women Enter the "Big Tents"? National Party Structures and Presidential Nominations

Melissa Haussman

In the summer of 2001, the Republican and Democratic Parties each announced women-focused initiatives that could help women get nominated for president.[1] The presence of a viable candidate pool of women who possess electoral experience in the state legislatures, statewide elective office, or Congress (13 percent in the latter and 24 percent as a state legislative average) is another hopeful sign. In 2002, five states have women governors who were elected, at least partially, on the typical "chief executive" criterion of economic management ability.[2] With the parties' awareness of women's majority status as voters and increasing representation in electoral office, it seems reasonable to expect a woman's nomination by a major party within the next few presidential election cycles.

Some may question whether parties still matter in the presidential nominating process. To a certain degree, at least regarding presidential elections, the debate concerns different party levels.[3] Some commentators find their evidence for a declining role in the increased importance to candidates of media, money from nonparty sources, and more evident "self-starter" routes to candidacy. Still others argue that the selection of nominees through the primary process since 1972 has all but destroyed state party leaders' control over delegate selection.

On the other side, theorists point to the parties' service-oriented turn since the 1970s and their importance to candidates as evidence of continued party leverage. One key area parties can still influence is candidate access to crucial resources, including money, consultants, and advertising.[4] This influence is most overtly demonstrated during the general elections. Many studies of the service-oriented parties have focused primarily on congressional elections.[5] Regarding presidential elections, however, some scholars take the view that the 1979 amendments to the Federal Election Campaign Act (FECA) indicated a watershed for the relationship of parties and candidates. These amendments allowed the national parties to send money to their state and local counterparts, primarily for the use of "organization-building" activities. Ironically, these amendments, combined with the beginning of public presidential campaign funding and spending restrictions in 1972, helped to create a situation in which the "party-building" money, or "soft money," began to be used for the expensive extras in an election campaign, such as advertising. Nelson Polsby and Aaron Wildavsky have noted that the financial situation of presidential campaigns has become one in which "public money is now the floor, not the ceiling."[6]

William G. Mayer argues that the "new" era of presidential campaign financing began in 1980, under the rubric of these changes.[7] The changes in the sources of money, he argues, drove the accompanying changes in the presidential nomination process. The continued importance of party is seen in that being within the "mainstream" of one's party and having connections in the state and national committees helps a candidate to achieve the needed credentials as a "serious contender" in the pre-primary and primary stages and then to access indirect "soft money" and direct party contributions in the general election. The pre-primary stage, also called the "invisible" primary, takes place during the year before the primary season starts. The recent figure is that $20 million must be raised before the primaries begin in order to signify the readiness of a potential presidential contender.[8] Also, potential primary contenders need to visit the crucial first caucus and primary states, Iowa and New Hampshire, at least a year before the primaries to test support in those waters and later to be able to make a credible showing there. A paradox in all this is that although the need for money is at its most acute during the prenomination campaign, party organizations cannot directly provide it during that time.[9] Until the general election, the "most important financial source to the candidate is the individual contributor."[10]

How may it be shown that party organizations still remain relevant to presidential nomination contestants? There are a number of ways at each stage of the process. During the "invisible primary" season in the year before the primaries begin, a party outsider has a much worse chance of getting contributions and media attention since the new rules combined for the first time in the 1980 presidential race, Mayer argues.[11] The pre-primary year is characterized by well-known presidential scholars as the "year of the test" by press and party activists, who are judging the candidate's strength. Although voters may not be watching, "the press and party activists clearly are," with some of their impressions "clearly filtering through to the voters."[12] During the "exploratory year," "the news media pay attention to signs that candidates are hiring competent campaign staff . . . and are establishing a beachhead in early battlegrounds . . . [and] doing respectably in straw polls conducted at various party meetings around the country, polls that everyone says 'don't count.'"[13] Therefore, the party organizations appear to have retained at least a sub rosa role in filtering party preferences about various candidates to the media, campaign professionals, and voters before the primary season starts.

It is also true that one party's primaries are more important than the other's during each presidential election. Polsby and Wildavsky have argued that the ground rules governing presidential nominations are far more important in the party not currently controlling the White House (in 2004, the Democrats), since "challenges to a sitting president from within his own party are doomed to failure."[14] To paraphrase Paul Allen Beck, parties become the greatest innovators in their organizational structure when they do not hold the presidency.[15] Although the position of state party leaders has declined because they have been "reduced to making deals to support one or another candidate at the time of the state primary or caucus . . . thus the candidate's job is to attract support from state party leaders by looking like a probable winner as early as possible."[16] A model developed by Mayer shows the linkage between doing well in the pre-primary stage and then in the primaries (as of 1996): "in five of the last six contested nomination races, the pre-Iowa front-runner ultimately won the nomination . . . each of these candidates was at least 15 percentage points ahead of his nearest rival in the last poll before Iowa."[17] It may be seen that party straw polls and informal signals carry some influence in the primary process. Also, of the "eight nomination races held between 1980 and 1996, three were won by the incumbent president, and three were won by major national party leaders." The other two contests, won by former Governors Dukakis and Clinton, involved in the former case, a well-liked governor with strong ties to his state party, and in the latter case, the former Chair of the national Democratic Leadership Council and the U.S. Governors' Association. As Mayer sums up, no outsider has been nominated for president by a major party since Jimmy Carter in 1976.[18] Yet another way state party structures remain relevant is in their power to structure delegate allocation rules, within certain limits established by the national parties.

From the 1970s through the early 1990s, the Republican Party had a 3 to 1 lead over the Democrats in funds available, which by the turn of the century had been reduced to about one-half that amount.[19] One reason for Democratic ability to reduce that differential, at least until the 1980s, was their ability to "convert resources" into "money and control over information."[20] It was particularly evident during the 1930s, 1940s, and 1960s, when the Democrats controlled the White House and "contributors wanted access to the winner." Since that time, it is held that Democratic presidential candidates have been able to depend on "free" labor provided by union affiliates, something that Republicans cannot obtain. Also, the presence of Democratic organizations in "large cities with strategic impact on the electoral college" helped gain access to resources for presidential candidates. Finally, the larger national membership base of the Democratic Party has enabled it to convert party support into money. Since the 1970s, though, it has been shown that Republicans, through comprehensive strategies of fund-raising and technological innovation, have narrowed that gap, converting party support into contributions so as to compensate for having a smaller membership.[21] Recent estimates of national party spending on presidential general elections are $299 million in 1984 and $880 million in 1996.[22] Figures for "hard" money spending by both parties in the 2000 presidential election are roughly $690 million, somewhat lower than 1996.[23] The disparity between the two parties was fairly large, with the Democrats spending about $265 million in hard, regulated money, versus the Republican figure of $426 million. Soft money spending by each of the national parties was about equal, between $240 and $250 million.[24]

The argument advanced in this chapter is that political party structures remain important to a presidential nomination bid. Their importance is less overt during the invisible primary and the primary season, and sometimes scholars have to do investigative work to find out exactly when and how they matter. Party structures and networks do matter at those stages and are shown to clearly matter during the presidential general election regarding direct ("hard") and indirect ("soft") money. It is a crucial test for women's futures to examine both the presidential nomination "seasons" and the structural rules and changes each party has adopted for itself. We then turn toward an examination of the current women's organizations working within each party, as well as some of the "outside" activism. Changes in campaign finance laws due to take effect in 2002 will be covered as well.

National Party Structures

In between conventions, the two national committees are the governing entities of the party. Structural comparisons are descriptive both of the founding ethos of each party (the Democrats in 1796 and the Republicans in 1860) and how the party's "culture" becomes replicated in institutional relationships. The Democratic National Committee (DNC) is about four times larger than its Republican counterpart, deriving from its larger number of "members," including voters and individual financial supporters. Republicans assign each state and territorial party three seats on the national committee, which are held by the Republican state party chair and a man and woman from the state committee. The Democratic committee uses a more complicated formula involving different constituencies. Representation on the Democratic National Committee is determined by the population and level of party support in each state. Other members are drawn from the following pools: present officeholders, members of affiliated groups, and at-large members from the "target groups" codified since 1972, including racial minorities, women, and young voters.[25]

In electing its national chairperson, each party tends to follow different sets of rules depending on whether it currently controls the presidency. Typically, the party controlling the White House will follow the president's wishes as to national party chair. When a party is out of office, it appears to be freer to make its own choices as to whom to appoint national leader, although this choice can also be subject to constraints. In 2001 the national party chairs, Terry McAuliffe of the DNC and former Montana governor Marc Racicot of the Republican National Committee (RNC), both had strong presidential "fingerprints" on their appointments.[26]

Since the Republican Party recognized earlier than the Democrats the importance of the "service-based" model to help candidates, its structural changes will be discussed first.

Republican Party Structural Reforms

For Republicans, the meaning of the modern, service-providing party organization has been one in which the national committee, in effect, exists largely to help the state and local committees and their candidates. Begun under National Committee chair Ray Bliss in the 1960s, the national committee worked to help the state and local committees with the "nuts and bolts of party organizational work."[27] This model was expanded under William Brock in the 1970s, who led the party to master two new developments of the time: using new sources for money, which in turn depended on new campaign technologies, including the use of computer-based donor lists. Particularly under Brock's chairmanship, the Republican National Committee in the late 1970s started to identify multistate networks from which to solicit money.[28] In the early years, a key figure in this effort was direct-mail pioneer Richard Viguerie. A major part of this shift to the nuts and bolts of electoral campaigning was designed to stem the party's significant loss of seats in the U.S. House in 1974, after the Watergate scandal. Polsby and Wildavsky note that "by the late 1970s, direct mail was bringing in 75 percent of the RNC's receipts, and it did not take the Democrats long to catch on."[29]

In the 1970s, the Republican Party began to provide "recruitment and training of candidates, research, public opinion polling, data analysis, computer networking and software development, production of radio and TV commercials, direct mailing, expert consultants, and legal services," in addition to the other party-building activities ratified by the 1979 FECA amendments and general financial support to campaigns.[30] The national Republican Party has operated since its beginning according to the precept that it would not interfere with state committee activities or prerogatives. This decision has meant that when the national committee is approached for help or decides that interacting with another level of the party would be beneficial, it has had to do so quite carefully. One such example is that in 1984, the committee decided to change its policy of working only with the state parties when asked and to send assistance to "650 key counties, containing a majority of the nation's voters."[31]

The modern Republican Party from the 1970s onward is described by Beck as following the model of a confederation, in which state and local units have a large degree of decisionmaking autonomy. Prior to the 1970s, the Democrats shared this model, but since 1972 they moved to empower the national committee to oversee the conditions of state delegate apportionment in the interests of promoting equity among Democratic target constituencies.[32] An example of the strength of Republican adherence to the confederal model is shown in the following. In 1996, Republican National Committee chairman Haley Barbour appointed an eight-member Task Force on Primaries and Caucuses to address the increasing problems of "frontloading" the primary season. Interestingly, the "task force approach was a new mechanism for the Republicans, since it assumed the RNC to be in a position of leadership vis-à-vis the state parties, rather than a relatively passive instrument of the states and a clearinghouse for information."[33] Additionally, since only the Republican National Convention is allowed to change candidate nomination rules, the task force had to guard and publicize its advisory character.

Ultimately, the recommendations made were to offer incentives to states to move their primaries back in the schedule through a system of awarding bonus delegates to compliant states. For example, states holding their primaries and caucuses from March 15 to April 14 would only get bonus delegates equal to 10 percent of their original state delegations. The incentive would grow as the primary dates were moved back:

those holding primaries and caucuses from April 15 to May 14 would get a 15 percent add-on to the original delegation size, and those in the final period from May 15 through the third Tuesday in June would get a 20 percent delegate add-on.[34] A powerful internal argument against this change was that "only Democrats use bonus delegates" and that this shift would violate the traditional Republican method of apportioning primary votes on a winner-take-all basis.[35] However, the third stage of the primaries would not likely have much effect, since in a predominantly winner-take-all system of primary votes, the Republican nomination is typically decided fairly early in the season. The recommendation encouraging states to spread out their primary system did make it through the Republican amendment system, albeit with the "delegate add-on" reduced by half, going from the rules committee to the national committee and ultimately to the national convention.

Even as Republicans were trying to encourage a "spreading out" of the primary season, they adopted a paradoxical rules change for 2000 to shorten the presidential primary window on the front half. Thus, although some reforms were taken to stem the frontloading process, another reform was undertaken expressly to allow for that frontloading, allowing states to move forward past the traditional one-month window after the Iowa caucus and New Hampshire primaries. It could be speculated that one reason for this was to achieve the effect of the Democratic "Super Tuesday" shift in 1988, to allow more conservative states to hold primaries early and thus help a more conservative nominee. An early adapter to this model was South Carolina.

In the 2000 presidential nomination period, the clear front-runner as early as 1998 was George W. Bush.[36] He was a fairly unique presidential contender in moving the invisible primary up to two years ahead of the start of the primary season and in currently holding the record for presidential fund-raising. In terms of changes to the primary calendar that have occurred, "several California officials argued that an early California primary [in March] combined with the [New England] Yankee primary, first used in 1996, could tilt the balance in favor of a 'moderate' Republican." So far, this has not happened, although it is important to note that the shift of the California primary to March has a large effect on primary voting, since 40 percent of Republican delegates and 50 percent of the Democratic ones are now picked on that day.[37] Although the California and the Yankee primaries could help a moderate Democratic woman become nominated, they are unlikely to serve this function for a Republican woman of this mold because the Republican platform is still officially antiabortion. Therefore, a Republican woman moderate on abortion would not be nominated, and if she were antichoice, the largest women's political action committees (PACs) would deny their support.

It appears that intraparty Republican changes must be couched in the terminology of an "incentive," or an "idea whose time has come" and often contrasted with what is described as the Democratic "mandate" approach. During the 1996 discussions about the Republican proposal to award "bonus" delegates as an incentive to change the primary season, the discussion emphasized that the Republicans were using the "carrot" approach, as opposed to the Democratic "stick." The Democrats were described as being more centralized and prescriptive, with the national committee having the power to influence states on changing their primary nomination procedures. The Republican process, however, was described as "incremental and bottom-up."[38] Although the Republicans did not change their nomination process as much as the Democrats did, to a certain degree they were either "forced" into the primary schedule by state legislatures or chose to talk about increased participation as a goal in itself. The other point is that the term *mandate* is still anathema to a party that prides itself on market values, opportunity, and liberty. Because one has to do investigative work to uncover the roles of both party networks during the prenomination stage of the presidential election process, one sometimes has to do investigative work to find out, lacking explicit rules, how "informal" party culture within the Republican Party shapes the expectations and opportunities for women's roles.

Other evidence of RNC deference to constituent units is that the Republican senatorial and congressional committees are given much latitude. Within the national and (Capitol) "Hill committees," there are numerous functional specializations. Two of them are the executive and finance divisions of each committee, whose functions are more or less self-explanatory. The largest component is the political and campaign committee within each of the party's three national committees (the senatorial and congressional committees and the RNC), which is most subdivided within itself. It includes subdivisions relating to PACs, voter mobilization, legal issues, congressional candidates (for open seats, incumbents, or challengers), and candidates from various regions.[39] The other divisions of the national committees include communications, which helps to produce campaign ads (and especially in the Republican Party, below market cost); research, including opposition research for candidates; and "coalition development."[40]

Democratic Party Reforms

In becoming more noticeably heterogeneous from the 1960s onward, Democratic Party reforms have often addressed related issues of inclusion.

This effort began in the 1960s, when the party took actions against southern delegations to the national convention, who labored under the misimpression that an all-white state delegation represented the state's Democratic constituency. Starting in the 1960s, the mechanisms for internal Democratic reform have involved increasing national committee control over state committees, so as to secure compliance. In so doing, the Democratic National Committee has become more prescriptive vis-à-vis its state units.[41] In addition, since the national committee and convention have tended to significantly change the delegate selection or apportionment rules for almost every presidential election since 1972, the national party has frequent interactions with the state committees.

The most noticeable wave of modern Democratic Party reforms was the McGovern-Fraser Commission, catalyzed by the fractious 1968 national convention in Chicago. After the commission made its recommendations, the party leaned toward using primary elections as presidential nominating mechanisms. Also, primary electors, committees (national, state, and local), and state and national conventions were required to become more representative of Democratic target groups such as minorities, young voters, and women. It has been noted by party scholars that the Democratic Party's reforms were based more on the internal procedural reform path until 1980, when the more outward-looking "service to candidates" model was developed.[42]

Beck has suggested that, in certain ways, the national Democratic Party can take more centralized actions vis-à-vis the states, given its history since the 1960s of requiring states to change presidential delegate selection and apportionment rules. In 1974, the Democratic Party adopted a provision for the supremacy of national party law in its charter.[43] The two national party organizations have essentially moved along different trajectories since the 1970s; while the Republicans have become more confederal, giving greater latitude to state committees, the Democrats have become more federal in structure, giving more enforcement power to the national party. The national Republican Party has been able to enforce its will on the state and local parties mainly through the provision of campaign expertise, services, and money, rather than through rules changes. Another crucial difference between the workings of the two national parties is that Republicans can only effect rules changes at the national conventions. Democrats can and have given their national committee and sometimes their commissions "the power to recast nomination rules between conventions."[44] A recent example of this was the mid-term Democratic National Committee meeting in January 2002, at which time a primary season rule was changed to imitate that used by Republicans in 2000, allowing states to move themselves forward in the primary process into the once-untouchable month-long window after Iowa and New Hampshire.

Given the internal party questioning during the McGovern-Fraser changes and the consistent loss of presidential office by Democrats throughout the 1980s, Democratic soul-searching ensued. The result was to again change the presidential primary vote and delegate allocation procedures and to work toward a more "mainstream" set of issue stances that ostensibly could elect a Democratic president. In 1972, the rules allowed governors, members of Congress, and DNC members not otherwise chosen as delegates to attend the national convention as nonvoting delegates. By 1980, the Hunt Commission, named after North Carolina moderate governor Jim Hunt, began its work by stating with then current DNC chair Charles Manatt that there was a need to "give party professionals and elected officials an enhanced role at the convention." The accord reached between the 1980 and 1984 elections included "core" elected officials from each state (governor, members of Congress, state party officials, etc.) as unpledged superdelegates, with an additional "add-on" amount possible if more slots were needed to represent other important Democratic officials (such as mayors of cities with more than 250,000 inhabitants).[45]

Another shift, designed to have an effect on the timing and overall "weight" of certain states' votes in the primary process, was the institution of the Democratic "Super Tuesday" primary in 1988. It is widely viewed as having been designed to ensure that a moderate Democrat acceptable to the South would gain many votes and delegates needed for the nomination. Although it did not work that way in 1988 because of a crowded nomination field that lasted longer than usual, the resulting nomination of a moderate has been achieved since then.

The 1985 creation of the Democratic Leadership Council (DLC) under former House Democratic Caucus director Al From was another much-noticed event.[46] Those helping to start the council were Governors Chuck Robb and Bruce Babbitt, Senators Sam Nunn and Lawton Chiles, and Representative Richard Gephardt. Early on, the council was seen to be tilted toward southerners. Although its membership broadened throughout the 1980s to include people such as Paul Tsongas, the southern representation was still important, with Governor Bill Clinton as its head before his election to president in 1992. After 1988, half of incumbent congressional Democrats and half of the Democratic governors were members.[47] The initial DLC annual budget was $500,000; by the 1990s, this figure was at least $42 million. Regarding the nonelected "sustaining memberships" in 1991–1992, of which there were 100, Jon Hale notes that over half of these members were contributors from corporations, and another dozen came from professional or trade associations. Other organizations represented were from the energy, health care, insurance, pharmaceutical, retail, and tobacco sectors.[48] Some have viewed the beginning and continued influence of the DLC as the "corporatization" of the Democratic Party.[49] The DLC's mandate included expansion of fund-raising and membership efforts to reach those under forty; extension of membership to state and local officials and creation of DLC chapters in the states; the creation of a think tank, the Progressive Policy Institute (PPI), and a new publication, *The New Democrat,* "to spread the message to all Democratic elected officials and supporters."[50] As is now widely recognized, the DLC dominates issue packaging within the party. Although some have speculated that may change following the defeat of Al Gore, it seems highly unlikely that the national party will turn back to its liberal activist days of the 1970s. There are too many built-in incentives to continue the present system, both for those in national office and in key positions in the national party, including the DNC chair.[51]

Following the Republican success at direct-mail fund-raising and the provision of many new services to candidates, the DNC began to take on a service ethos from about 1980 under Chairman Charles Manatt. Although starting from a financially inferior position, the party began to increase its fund-raising efforts and the money and services provided to state and local parties. The next DNC chairman, Paul Kirk, retained and built on the service-party model.[52]

In addition to the DNC, other national party committees include the two Capitol Hill committees, Democratic Governors' Association, Legislative Campaign Committee, College Democrats of America, and Young Democrats of America (like the Young Republicans, they are part of the national committee structure). Another component of the national Democratic structure is the Women's Leadership Forum (WLF).

Women's Policy and Electoral Committees in the National Parties

This part of the discussion traces the presence of women in the national committee structure, both during and between national conventions. One of the earliest official commitments to gender equality was the "Fifty-Fifty Rule," adopted by both the Democrats and the Republicans, stating that men and women must be equally represented on all nationally appointed party committees. This mandate is carried out via the different national committee selection mechanisms of the two parties and, in certain instances, is said to trickle down to state and local party

committees as well.[53] Currently, there are fifteen women Republican
state committee chairs.[54] Each state committee sends one male and one
female delegate to the national committee. The DNC has a rule that
each state committee chair and vice chair must be of opposite sexes to
achieve gender balance. Thus, the Democrats have fifteen women state
committee chairs and thirty-five women state committee vice chairs.[55]
These numbers constitute significant increases over their 1996 levels,
especially since "in the post-reform party system, the post of state party
chair now serves as a stepping stone to elective office for both men and
women."[56]

In 1952, when state committee chairs were added to the RNC, it
tilted the balance on the national committee even more toward a male
majority. Currently, the RNC requires that one-third of its membership
be female.[57] In 1960, the Republicans added the requirement that half of
all convention committee members be women; this requirement does
not apply to delegates because "the Republican party has traditionally
regarded the selection of delegates as a state matter."[58] The Democrats
added the rule requiring equal gender representation among convention
delegates in 1971. Following the rise of women delegates at the Democratic National Conventions, there was a noticeable increase in women
at Republican conventions from 1972 to 1980 to about one-third of the
overall number of delegates.[59] It must be noted that the two parties did
not simply have an epiphany at one point regarding the necessity of including women in reasonably proportional numbers at the national conventions. It was the result of hard work by the National Women's Political Caucus (NWPC) since its founding in 1971, "an important political
battle . . . that succeeded in doubling and tripling women's representation in the post-party reform era."[60]

Both national parties have the rule of gender balance at the chair
level; so if a woman is chair, a man will be vice chair. So far, each party
has had only one woman as chair of its national committee: Jean West-
wood of the Democratic Party and Mary Louise Smith of the Republican Party. It has been noted that they were figureheads, in that they
were appointed before the second-wave women's movement had become institutionalized. Even more significantly, neither was treated to
the same perks as all other (male) national party leaders have enjoyed,
and each one was removed after the election, instead of being kept on as
chair "during the crucial party-building years between conventions."[61]

The route to chairmanship of the national party depends on whether
the party controls the White House or not, and so too does the number
of women delegates to the Republican National Convention. Following
a Republican culture described by Jo Freeman as having "whom you

know" rules for advancement, "in 1984, the proportion of Republican women increased to a record 44 percent largely through the intervention of President Reagan's campaign manager, Ed Rollins, who personally called each state party." Curiously, it was the same Ed Rollins who nearly derailed Christine Todd Whitman's first gubernatorial campaign in New Jersey when he "disclosed" the practice of providing money to certain constituencies so as to dampen turnout. After the 1984 convention, when there was a contested primary in 1988, the "proportion of women delegates" at the Republican National Convention returned to about one-third.[62] A similar comparison was made between the uncontested Republican primary in 1992 and the contested one in 1996.

Since women's presence in elected office is continually increasing, by 2002 they constituted more of the Democratic superdelegates as well. Democratic women currently comprise two of the nation's governors, fifteen chairs of state committees and thirty-five vice chairs, and fifty-four members of the U.S. Congress.[63] The addition of these unpledged delegates to the required floor of 50 percent of pledged delegates means that women constitute an important voting bloc for issues still decided at the national conventions, such as platform and rules changes. Also, the women superdelegates can be an important group to lobby on behalf of presidential contenders in the years before the convention.

The two oldest "women's divisions" within the Democratic Party structure are the "women's bureaus," begun after national suffrage was granted in 1920.[64] They are by no means activist organizations, and their emphasis for most of the twentieth century was on integrating women into the party (i.e., mobilizing the vote) to work on behalf of male candidates.

The "highest" Democratic women's policy committee within the national party structure, listed as a national committee, is the Women's Leadership Forum, begun in 1993. The WLF website states that during the 2000 election cycle, it "raised a record-breaking $7 million, and exceeded its goal of engaging over 100,000 women in electoral and grassroots activities." It also has as its stated goal the formation of a network of elected and activist women across the country and currently has "20 state and regional chapters and a membership of over 6,000 women."[65] Since 1993, the WLF has raised "nearly $30 million for the DNC," although no breakdown is given as to how much of that went to women candidates. Also within the national committee structure is the Women's Campaign Council within the Democratic Senatorial Campaign Committee (DSCC), formed in 1992. During that election cycle, it raised $1.5 million, which was distributed among ten women candidates for the Senate. Since then, it has worked to expand the membership and national visibility of the organization.[66] Current and former DNC staff consider the Women's Campaign Council to be the most important body in efforts to elect more women Democrats, including at the presidential level.

Other "allied" women's groups are the National Federation of Democratic Women and the Women's National Democratic Club (formed in 1922). Although they are usually viewed as more low-key networking organizations for women Democrats, the federation announced the creation of its PAC in December 2001. As its website states, "it has been established to provide financial support for Democratic women, Democratic candidates and other Democratic committees nationwide . . . and state and local offices" (evaluated on a case by case basis).[67]

In the Republican Party, the National Federation of Republican Women (NFRW) is the oldest women's group that has conducted sustained activity on behalf of women. It was given official RNC status in 1988 by being granted a voting seat on the twenty-eight-member council governing the party between national conventions (and therefore RNC meetings).[68] The NFRW describes itself as "the education arm" of the national party. Its website describes it as a "grassroots organization with nearly 95,000 women and 1800 unit clubs nationwide."[69] The NFRW lists its interests as policy development within the party, including issues related to children, women, work, healthcare, and so on. Another interesting activity the group mentions is its ability to generate a "Comprehensive Advocacy Alert," in which a national hotline is quickly set up "by the NFRW president to generate support or opposition for an issue that concerns the members of the Federation." It can also be done in response to a request by a member of Congress, a member of the Executive Committee, or a state federation president. First, the NFRW president contacts the Executive Committee members, who start the chain, as the website states—*"until every Federation member has been reached"* (emphasis in the original).[70] Members are requested to follow up a call to the relevant officials (the phone numbers, addresses, and websites for the White House and Congress are provided) with a fax or email. Another step suggested is to "call a local and then a national radio show," with Rush Limbaugh's show given as the example. This strategy of mass phonebanking, faxing, and emailing has been used by high-profile interest groups, such as the National Rifle Association, since the 1980s, as well as by Republican campaign committees. It will be interesting to see if this strategy is used in the future on behalf of women candidates or to modify issues on a gendered basis. Another important function of the women's federations in both parties is conducting and arranging campaign schools with well-known consultants. This has been a growth industry in both parties, for the Republicans since the 1980s, and for the Democrats, a bit later.

Another important element of women candidates' electoral success has been creation of women's PACs, whether partisan, bipartisan, or nonpartisan. Two of the most long-standing actors include the Women's Campaign Fund and the National Women's Political Caucus, which has a co-chair from both parties. Both of these groups, particularly the latter, have been active with both parties, but they have had to be active rather surreptitiously within the Republican Party, given that party's distrust of "multiple allegiances." Examples are given of NWPC support for rules change attempts to keep proportional representation in the Democratic presidential nominating allocation process, of working within the Republican Party for the Equal Rights Amendment (ERA) in 1976, and of trying to modify the Republican abortion plank in 1992.[71] Given the continued importance of the Republican National Convention as a policymaking body, it is important for women's groups to have continued representation there, no matter how difficult it is to achieve.

The Women's Campaign Fund has been active on an ongoing basis with issue development at the national conventions as well.[72] As the oldest women's PAC, formed in 1974, the fund has been a generous donor; in 1992, it gave $1.9 million to women candidates, outshadowed only by EMILY's List, which donated $3.5 million. Other well-known national women's PACs gave the following amounts: the National Organization for Women (NOW) PAC, formed at the tail end of the ERA struggle in 1980, gave $691,000, and two committees of the NWPC gave just under $300,000 to women candidates.[73] All these PACs have been extremely active in shaping and conducting women's campaign schools as well. The Women's Campaign Fund also notes on its website that it is available to help take potential women candidates around the District of Columbia to meet other PAC leaders.

PACs that are explicitly partisan include EMILY's List, formed in 1985 to help pro-choice Democratic women candidates, and WISH List, based on the same criteria for the Republicans. EMILY is an acronym for "early money is like yeast" in "making the dough rise." WISH is an acronym for "women in the Senate and House." NOW PAC is not explicitly partisan but overwhelmingly helps Democratic women candidates who must be pro-choice and pro-ERA. Another PAC, the Susan B. Anthony (SBA) List, based on the single issue of being pro-life, was formed right after 1992, "in response to the Year of the Woman." This PAC claims to have knowledge that Susan B. Anthony, feminist pioneer, was also strongly antichoice. It was indignant that "all the new women elected in 1992 were pro-choice," which led to a female congressional representation of "all pro-choice women except two" (Helen Chenoweth and Ellen Sauerbrey). Following the pioneering "bundling strategy" of EMILY's List, the SBA List claimed success in ousting many of those women in 1994 and, in 1998, "helping to return eight pro-life incumbents to Congress."[74] The SBA List was able to be informally integrated into the "new party" establishment of the Republicans under Newt Gingrich. What this shows is that when the party chooses to integrate a certain perspective advanced by women's PACs, noticeable results may be achieved.

A final word on the question of whether the two national parties now acknowledge that women's candidacies are potential winners is that many legislative studies of women have shown that, at least for the U.S. Congress, when similar types of races are compared—for example, a race for an open seat or a race against an incumbent—men and women win at similar rates. Most accounts weight the unusual number of open seat races as the main factor for the Year of the Woman in 1992. It would have been interesting if the two parties had been ready for women to run in the last major sweeping out of incumbents, in 1974–1976. Also, the two parties have given women congressional candidates more money, on average, than men in similar races (with the exception of Republican women incumbents in 1994). It was also true that throughout the 1980s, women candidates received a higher average amount from the Republican Party than from the Democratic Party, both because the Republicans had much more money at the time and because the party had an official strategy during the 1980s of trying to counter the gender gap by electing more female candidates.[75]

Therefore, it is clear with regard to the national parties that "where there is a will, there is a way." It is true with regard to recruiting women candidates, supporting them with technology and money, and supporting a particular issue stance. One can only wonder when the will to put the resources that have been used for Congress since 1992 will be used to nominate and elect the first woman president.

The National Parties and Women Voters

Within a few weeks of each other in the summer of 2001, both parties announced initiatives to work on getting out women's votes in future elections and educating voters on party issues affecting women. The Democratic Party calls its effort the "Women's Vote Center," and it is coordinated with and by the Women's Leadership Forum at the national committee level. The new project was described as being based in the political and communications wings of the DNC and was designed to get the word out to active and potential women voters. It would thus "educate, engage, and mobilize women voters throughout the nation." As the newly appointed DNC chair, Terry McAuliffe, noted, "we know that when women vote, Democrats win—and with their help, we will make a difference in the lives of American working families."[76] This program appears to have a forerunner in the EMILY's List project "Women Vote!" that was established after record numbers of women did not vote in 1994 and prominent women Democrats were narrowly elected or reelected.

The project of encouraging women's turnout is called "Winning Women" in the Republican Party and is being coordinated by the vice chair of the national committee, Ann Wagner. It appears that the RNC vice chair, a woman, is allocated special responsibility for women's programs. The Republican Party instituted a similar effort a decade ago.[77]

Although these initiatives are helpful in that they mobilize more women to vote, thus helping the two national parties, they also gloss over a key problem. Study after study has shown that women voters do not necessarily tend to vote for women candidates more than men, so that mobilizing more women voters may help women candidates, but there is no confirmed statistical relationship. That is why, for example, any studies of the "gender gap" show that women and men have voted for different parties (women favor the Democratic Party and men the Republican Party) since 1980. Similarly, more women than men supported Republicans during the 1940s and 1950s.[78] In short, the gender gap is primarily about the different nature of support for the two parties. It may or may not involve the candidate's gender in a particular election. This "party support gap" is based on which of the two parties manages to frame its issues so as to appeal to women, whether it be the pro-ERA stance or "strong leadership of Eisenhower" through the 1950s or the fight to keep social and education programs funded that created the Democratic-leaning gap among men since the 1980s. Both national parties seem to be weighting this strategy very heavily, probably with an eye toward congressional and future presidential elections.

Women as Party Outsiders?

An excellent scholar of women's relationship to the parties, Denise Baer, believes that in the postreform party system operative since the 1970s, the rules for gaining influence for women are harder to interpret. For example, in the "prereform" days, she notes that women were able to become party activists through their previous work in women's organizations. Although official rules in both parties have opened up the organizations to women's participation, Baer warns that women's roads still traverse many minefields. For example, "informal associations" have become more important within the parties, and when they are linked to lines drawn among hardened factions, as they increasingly are, women are likely to be drawn into these battlegrounds. Thus, "the more active women are within the party, the more opportunity they have to be recruited via party-linked factions and groups—a fundamentally decentralized and 'privatized' process beyond the reach of party rules."[79] The result is that to gain more influence within the party organizations, women must demonstrate that they represent the organized women's movement, which is an increasingly difficult task in these purportedly "post-second-wave women's movement times."[80]

Partially because of the ever-shifting nature of alliances within the party structures, women's organizations have quite often used a bipartisan strategy, similar to that of many corporate PACs, in the desire not to shut out any potential ally.[81] Both parties have demonstrated since women received the national vote in 1920 that sometimes women are more important to them than at other times; no party has held a monopoly on being either the "good" or the "bad" guy. One example is that in 1985, the "DNC under Paul Kirk disestablished the [National] Women's [Political] Caucus."[82] It has since been reestablished.

Similarly, many people both formerly and currently involved with the DNC are very positive about current DNC chair Terry McAuliffe's commitment to making the Democratic Party more gender-friendly to women voters and candidates. They view him as a "twenty-first-century man" and believe that the DNC can aspire to greater heights of electing more women under his leadership. His tenure would appear to bode well for a woman's presidential run in the future.

A Few Words About Money

Currently, one of the largest roles for parties is that of "funnels" for soft money, receiving money from different sources, often business ones, and providing funds to state and local parties to offset candidate spending limits in particular states if they have taken public funding and are subject to those limitations. Another role for the parties, particularly since the 1990s, has been that of funding "issue advocacy" ads on behalf of a certain candidate, as long as the ads do not explicitly advocate voting for the party's presidential candidate or voting against the other party's candidate. According to legislation signed by President Bush at the end of March 2002, the tradition of issue advocacy ads and "soft money" contributions to the national parties will become illegal after the 2002 congressional election. The final disposition of this legislation remains uncertain, pending litigation by the National Rifle Association, among others, arguing that its free speech rights will be limited by the abolition of these soft money provisions. Individuals will still be able to make soft money donations to state and local parties, subject to a $10,000-per-year limit.

If this legislation is allowed to stand, pending probable scrutiny by the Supreme Court, what does it mean for presidential candidates? Immediately, one jumps to the conclusion that allowing this law to stand may bode well for women presidential candidates. For example, Elizabeth Dole had virtually no promises of soft money support, even from her husband, a former RNC chair who presumably could have delivered on such a promise, if she chose to stay in the race until the primary season began. Soft money is how corporations and parties basically "bet" on their particular candidate to win. With the reduction of its role, the playing field for obtaining money should be more equal than it has been.

Evidence of women's ability and willingness to make "hard" money contributions toward favored candidates includes the fact that over 50 percent of Elizabeth Dole's hard money contributions came from businesswomen over forty. Under the new campaign finance regime, individuals are allowed to increase their contributions to $2,000 per candidate per election, up from the current $1,000. That is hardly a significant amount in and of itself, but if it were multiplied by 100,000, it could easily add up. Evidence from the 2000 presidential election, from fund-raising reports released at the end of first quarter of 1999, is that "when candidates are ranked by total dollars they received from women giving at least $200, Gore placed first at $2.6 million, Bush was second at $2.3 million, and Bradley was third at $1.2 million."[83] It is apparent that there are women who are willing and able to contribute significant "hard" (regulated, reported, and limited) money to presidential candidates. Also, women have fund-raising expertise; candidates Al Gore, John McCain, and Elizabeth Dole had female finance directors, and nearly half (40 percent) of the members of Elizabeth Dole's national finance team were women.[84]

Therefore, if soft money is permanently excised from the national fund-raising picture, then perhaps public funding will again become the ceiling of presidential finance, as it was intended to be, not the floor, as it has been recently called. This type of system would benefit the relative newcomers to the electoral system, both women of all races and men from racial minorities. Since many talented women fund-raisers exist and individual women and women's PACs have continuously increased their donations to women, the signs have never been more positive that other sources will emerge to help a woman presidential candidate in the absence of soft money.

Conclusion

Given the changes that have taken place since the 1970s within the two
parties' national structures, interesting opportunities for women have
opened up to work within the nominating structures to contest for the
presidency. The changing of the primary calendar for both parties is extremely important; for Republicans, the combination of the California
and Yankee primaries in early March could help elect a moderate, but
there is the question of how to deal with the socially conservative wing
of the party. This structure could also help a "new Democrat," such as
Ellen Tauscher or Jane Harman from California. Both parties have
shown interest in being publicly recognized for doing all they can to
help maintain or increase the numbers of women in Congress at their
current record level and to increase the number of women governors,
since that office is now an important stepping-stone to presidential
nomination. With regard to Congress, women's increased presence is
not simply important with regard to descriptive and policy representation in Congress; it is also important because in parties that are now
driven strongly by new technologies "doled out" at the national level,
such as access to PACs and the congressional wings of the national
committees, women members of Congress are in the right place from
which to run for presidential nomination. Since many of the structural
factors seem to be lined up in the right direction, one can only hope that
the strategic factors line up similarly soon.

Many eminent parties and elections scholars point to party organizations as the "intervening variable," or linkage point, between society
(voters) and political institutions. They have noted, as has been noted
here as well, that parties exist in a "feedback" loop with other political
and social changes. For example, in the wake of great social change,
such as the civil rights movement, the Vietnam War, or the loss of a
presidency because of a scandal-based resignation, the two parties have
undertaken reforms. Similarly, the context within which and the means
by which one party undertakes change often drives a convergence toward a new norm; such examples can include changed primary seasons,
adoption of a service-based model of party organization, new fund-
raising tactics, or an interest in representing more women on state and
national party committees. These new norms continue the feedback loop
toward more change; women candidates work to raise ever more money
for their campaigns and seek, via party committees, to have more platform influence, for example. Although some have stated that "conventional wisdom" holds that the first woman president will come from the
Republican Party, since she will supposedly be viewed as less "liberal"
by the U.S. electorate, that remains to be seen. If there is still an

xassumption within either of the two parties that women are "not yet ready for prime time" exposure as presidential candidates, it is time to root out that assumption as archaic. Women candidates win at equal rates to men.

The discussion about when the party organizations, both state and national, appear to be most important to the presidential nomination and election process also contributes to this outlined framework for electing a woman president. For example, in the prenomination period of the invisible primary and the visible primary season, party activists and organizers relay, either formally or informally, their opinions about various candidates' chances for a win to crucial opinion shapers in the media, which then affects the candidate's ability to gain money and votes during the primaries. The parties are now in the position to do this for a woman candidate in the early stages of her presidential campaign. Also, during the election campaign, the parties can throw their considerable weight behind women candidates to ensure their election. If the right combination of party issue stances and the gender of the candidate lines up in the right way, the United States will soon be able to proudly claim its first woman president.

A War Chest Full of Susan B. Anthony Dollars: Fund-raising Issues for Female Presidential Candidates

Victoria A. Farrar-Myers

Susan B. Anthony dollar coins were released in 1979 and seemingly relegated to use by mass transit systems thereafter. They were beautiful to look at and collect, but the world was not ready for a dollar coin. It is an interesting analogy for the notion of a woman president—everyone wants one as a curiosity, but few are certain whether the time is right for one to serve. But just as a dollar coin existed before and was reintroduced in a new form, so a well-funded woman will emerge in the near future. But why has a well-funded woman not yet emerged? More important, what would it take for a well-funded woman to emerge and be a viable candidate, at least financially, for the presidency?

In 1999, Elizabeth Dole announced that she would be running for the 2000 Republican presidential nomination. However, after only a few short months of seeking funds and trying to get her message out, Dole announced, prior to any primary voting, that she was getting out of the race; her explanation—a lack of money. Although some claimed more than just a lack of money was the reason Dole did not succeed, many scholars indicated that "even falling short, Dole's effort may have inched the country closer to the day when a woman can be elected president. She ran a steady—albeit distant—second to Texas Governor Bush in national polls, and bested Democratic Vice President Al Gore in theoretical match-ups."[1] One political analyst, Elizabeth Sherman of the University of Massachusetts, commented, "On balance, you have to say it's absolutely a net gain. Elizabeth Dole, no matter how you look at it, is a trailblazer."[2]

Further, according to many, "Dole's greatest legacy may be turning the extraordinary—a woman running for president and being taken seriously—into something rather more ordinary."[3] In the end, however, Dole's campaign highlighted the fact that although "a serious female candidate can excite the imagination, she can't ignore the basics: [according to Dole,] 'You absolutely have to start earlier and build the organization to turn the public's interest into real, tangible assets' . . . capturing the public's imagination is great . . . but you've got to have a very strong foundation of assets in terms of money and message to carry it through."[4] Dole's message was lost or appeared to waver, and she faced the prospect of "being outspent by a multiple of 75 to 80 times by George W. Bush and Steve Forbes."[5]

Many perceive money to be the key reason a woman has not been a serious contender in presidential politics.[6] Dole's pronouncement certainly could only add credence to this belief. Many seem to believe that women lack credibility because they fail to develop the necessary fundraising networks, have difficulty attracting a broad base of support, or are unable to achieve a high-level leadership position prior to pursuing the White House. Are these perceptions truly the reality that a female presidential candidate would face? On closer examination, it appears these perceptions might be too hasty.

In terms of forming key networks, women's groups have sprung up on all sides of the political spectrum—whether it is EMILY's List[7] for Democrats, the WISH List[8] on the Republican side, or even the White House Project.[9] These organizations assist women by recruiting candidates, training them, assisting them in campaigning and voter turnout, and providing key networks of financial support. Most of these organizations have concentrated on recruiting women into politics and therefore have spent much time on newcomers or challengers. Many credit these organizations with aiding the increase of women in politics. Some women who initially used these organizations for seed money and the like have even grown beyond needing their assistance—a feat that speaks highly of these groups' effect on getting women elected.[10]

Women candidates and incumbents are beginning to attract broadbased levels of support. Women officeholders are serving on key foreign policy committees and other typically "male-dominated issue committees" in Congress.[11] That has led to women breaking out of the typical "women's issue" focus and allowed them to appeal to business PACs, labor organizations and their PACs, and more traditional money sources.

Further, public opinion appears to have become more supportive of the notion of a female president. As Gallup Poll surveys, which have tracked this issue since 1958 (see Figure 7.1), indicate, well over 90 percent of respondents in 1999 indicated that they would vote for a well-qualified woman candidate who was nominated by their party; this percentage is more than double the level of support this proposition received in the 1958 survey. Further, the Roper Center at the University of Connecticut conducted a telephone public opinion survey, which found that 86 percent of the 1,000 registered voters polled nationwide, would prefer, were not uncomfortable, or were undecided about voting for a female for president. Only 14 percent said that the idea of voting for a female for president made them uncomfortable.[12]

Changes in voting patterns and political participation are also becoming an issue for assisting women candidates in attracting broad-based levels of support. "Ever since 1980, women have outvoted men in every national election. Since women outnumber men in the population at large, when they vote in greater proportions than men the numbers add up to a difference of millions (for example, in the 1996 national elections, over seven million more women than men voted)."[13] Furthermore, as several studies have found, women are not only voting in greater numbers but also are donating more to political campaigns.[14] Although this increased level of participation does not always translate into more votes for female candidates, the political pressure this voting bloc brings on the political discourse has made it more fashionable to appoint, promote, and recruit women.[15]

As has been discussed elsewhere in this book, in terms of high-level leadership positions, women are making strides in both parties, particu-

Figure 7.1 Gallup Poll Results Regarding Support for a Woman Presidential Candidate, 1958–1999

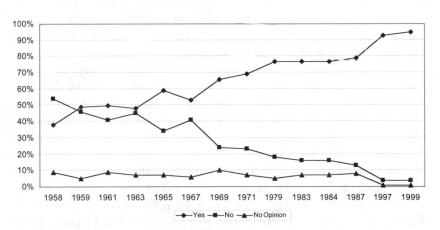

Source: Frank Newport, David W. Moore, and Lydia Saad, "Long-Term Gallup Poll Trends: A Portrait of American Public Opinion Through the Century."

Note: Response to survey question: "If your party nominated a generally well-qualified person for president who happened to be a woman would you vote for that person?"

larly in the House of Representatives. In the 107th Congress, the number of female House members hit fifty-nine. In addition, the first woman was elected to a leadership position when Nancy Pelosi (D-CA) became Democratic Whip. Other women, like Representative Jennifer Dunn (R-WA), have made inroads in the Republican Party. On the other side of Capitol Hill, the 107th Congress sees thirteen women serving in the Senate.[16] Despite this record number of women senators, however, they have not yet achieved leadership positions comparable to those held by women in the House.

The evidence from network formation, public opinion, and voting patterns, as well as the successful women officeholders, seems to fly in the face of the explanation that these factors have prevented a woman from winning the presidency. Clearly, money is the factor that has barred a woman from running successfully for the highest office in the land. Given this assertion, in this chapter I will explore the reasons that a well-funded woman has not emerged, the factors that would enable a well-funded woman to emerge, and what characteristics might be culled about a potentially viable candidate.

Why Has a Well-Funded Woman Not Yet Emerged?

Several women have run or explored running for the presidency, but none has succeeded.[17] In searching for an answer, many determinants have been offered as possible explanations. First, U.S. political culture has only in the later half of the twentieth century started to come to terms with women working outside the home and seeking parity with men in terms of political office. After all, many blame women's late start in politics on the granting of suffrage to women so belatedly in the United States.

More than the above, many point to the fact that the presidency has been particularly difficult for many to perceive being held by a woman because of the norms that have arisen around the office.[18] First of all, it has always been held by a man, whose wife (bachelor James Buchanan aside) has always served as "first lady." These norms sent many into a tailspin at the prospect of Elizabeth Dole winning and having to change the respective roles of the spouses. In addition, the United States is also just coming to terms with successful women leaders in business, yet another step toward enabling women to appear viable for political office. Further, although women have been accepted as political figures, much has been made of their differing style and their attention to traditional "women's issues." This imagery has done nothing but perpetuate an image that prevents parties, the electorate, and women themselves from seeking the presidency.

It seems, however, that times are changing. Women are seeking out political office and leadership positions within political parties. The public, as noted above, seems to have come around in its thinking. So, if the culture is changing, the status of women is improving, the role of women in politics is expanding, and women are perceived as a desirable voting bloc, why have we not seen the first woman president?

What Would It Take for a Well-Funded Woman to Emerge?

Running for the presidency requires, among other things, money, name recognition, party and public support, and a popular issue agenda. Using male examples of who emerges—senators, members of the House, and so on—one can begin to assess the prospects of a woman being able to raise the money necessary to be a viable presidential candidate.

Keep in mind, though, the image Elizabeth Dole left the electorate with in 1999—that a woman cannot run because she cannot raise enough money. Is this explanation true? Although many perceive it as only part of a more complicated story, its resonance with other women might prove a barrier anyway. Therefore, it is important to delve more deeply into the question of money and see if women are really being held back or if there is some reason to hope after all.

To examine a woman's ability to raise enough funds to wage a viable campaign for the presidency, one needs to consider women's fund-raising abilities at those lower positions that typically are proving grounds for presidential candidates—that is, governors, senators, and members of the House of Representatives. Do significant differences exist between the fund-raising practices of successful men and women candidates for these offices, or do women and male candidates face similar campaign finance issues? The lessons that can be drawn by examining the differences between the two genders at these lower offices will have implications now and in the future for the prospect of attaining a financially viable woman presidential candidate.

Publicly available state-level campaign finance data for gubernatorial elections are sporadic. Thus, one cannot easily compare the fund-raising issues faced by women governors and their male counterparts. The availability of federal-level campaign finance data through the Federal Election Commission and resources such as the Center for Responsive Politics allow a thorough comparison of the differences and similarities in campaign finance matters for men and women running for Congress.[19]

At the congressional level, in recent years women have proven to be just as effective fund-raisers as men for elected offices other than the presidency. For example, Figure 7.2 shows the average expenditures for winning candidates for the House of Representatives in the 2000

Figure 7.2 Average Expenditures for Winning House Candidates, 2000

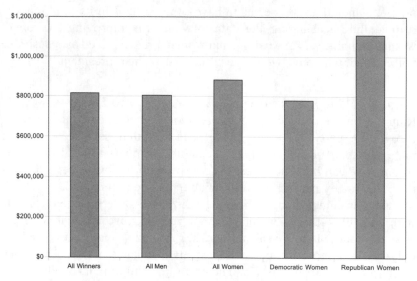

Source: Compiled from data available at http://www.fec.gov.
Notes: N (Democratic Women) = 40. N (Republican Women) = 18.

election.[20] During 1999–2000, the average winning candidate, men and women alike, spent approximately $816,000 to gain victory. Dividing the winners by gender, however, shows that the average winning female House candidate spent over $882,000, whereas the male candidates paid out, on average, approximately $806,000. In other words, successful women candidates outspent their successful male counterparts in the House by nearly 10 percent. In terms of partisan differences, the Republican women in the House maintained the traditional money advantage that Republicans have over Democrats, as they spent on average in excess of $1.1 million in 2000—over 35 percent above the average for all winning House candidates that year. Democratic women, however, average just over $780,000 in expenditures.

In the Senate, the basic story starts the same as for the House (see Figure 7.3). For the three election cycles from 1996 to 2000—covering all 100 seats in the Senate—the average winning candidate spent slightly over $5.1 million. During this period, the average winning female candidate expended over $7.8 million, whereas the average winning male Senate candidate spent approximately $4.75 million. The amount for the female senators, however, is heavily weighted by Hillary Rodham Clinton's successful senatorial campaign in New York in 2000. Clinton, still serving as first lady at the time of her election, spent over

Figure 7.3 Average Expenditures for Winning Senate Candidates, 1996–2000

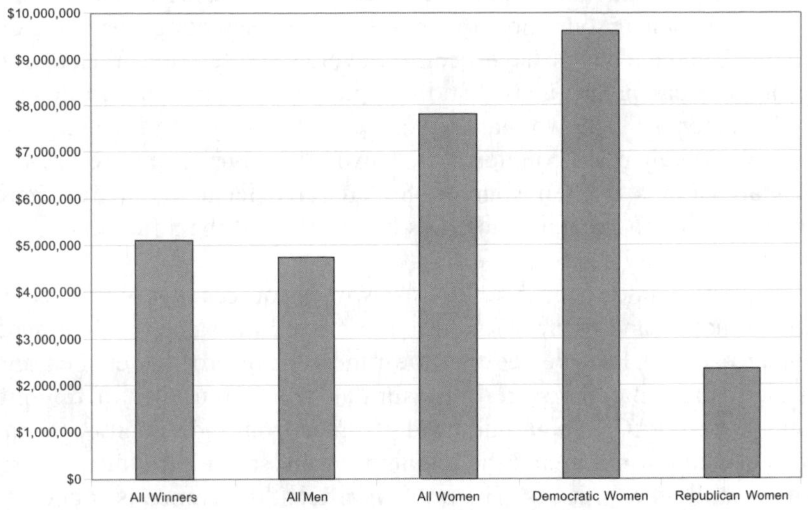

Source: Compiled from data available at http://www.fec.gov.

Notes: N (Democratic Women) = 9. 1996: Landrieu (LA); 1998: Boxer (CA), Lincoln (AR), Mikulski (MD), Murray (WA); 2000: Cantwell (WA), Clinton (NY), Feinstein (CA), Stabenow (MI).

N (Republican Women) = 3. 1996: Collins (ME); 2000: Hutchison (TX), Snowe (ME).

$29 million to win her election. This amount is more than her husband, Bill Clinton, raised in individual contributions during his 1996 presidential reelection campaign ($28.2 million); it compares with the individual contributions raised by Al Gore ($33.8 million), Bill Bradley ($29.2 million), and John McCain ($28.1 million) in their fund-raising efforts during the 2000 presidential primaries.[21] As one of twelve women in this analysis, Clinton significantly drives up the average expenditure for successful women in the Senate. If she is excluded from the analysis, the average winning woman candidate spent over $5.8 million—still 14 percent above the overall average and 23 percent above the average winning male in the Senate during this period.[22]

Interestingly, the traditional partisan differences in fund-raising are reversed when examining women in the Senate. The Democratic average, including Hillary Clinton, is over $9.6 million. Without Clinton, the average falls to approximately $7.15 million but is still buoyed by the campaigns of Barbara Boxer ($13.7 million in 1998), Maria Cantwell ($10.9 million in 2000), and Dianne Feinstein (almost $10.2 million in 2000). The Republican women senators elected between 1996 and 2000, however, spent on average only about $2,350,000. These three women were the two senators from Maine (Susan Collins, $1.6 million in 1996; Olympia Snowe, nearly $2.0 million in 2000), and Senator Kay Bailey Hutchison ($3.5 million), who faced minimal competition in her 2000 reelection bid.

These comparisons show that successful women congressional candidates in recent years have been on average better fund-raisers and spent more campaign funds than the typical male candidate. In this regard, women have shown that they can play the campaign finance game as well as their male counterparts. Now, let us turn from the uses of campaign funds to their sources. Specifically, let us compare where these successful women candidates have obtained their funding vis-à-vis their male colleagues.

Figures 7.4a through 7.4c break down the sources of women's campaign funding, and Figures 7.5a through 7.5c do the same for their male counterparts.[23] Here we see that the fund-raising profiles of men and women House members are quite similar, with a plurality of funding coming from PACs, about one-third of funds from individual contributions of $200 or more, and the remainder from small individual contributions and other sources. The only significant difference is found between Republican women and men. The average Republican woman House member's fund-raising profile is very close to the overall average, with 46 percent of her funds coming from PACs and 33 percent from large individual donors. Republican men, however, equally split their fund-raising between PACs and large donors (about 39 percent each).

The real differences between the fund-raising profiles of men and women show up in the source of PAC funds. Figures 7.6a through 7.6c break down the average source of funds from PACs for House women in 2000. Figures 7.7a through 7.7c provide the same information for a number of randomly selected incumbent House men equal to the number of incumbent House women reelected in 2000. In this analysis, male House members received a greater percentage of their funding from PACs related to business interests than their female colleagues did (an overall average of 71 percent for men and 56 percent for women). This variation stems largely from differences between Democratic men (54 percent from business PACs) and Democratic women (44 percent). Women, however, received a greater percentage from labor-related PACs than their male counterparts. As for single-issue or ideological PACs, they represented a consistent 8–10 percent of a House member's source of PAC funds, regardless of the member's gender or partisanship.

In the Senate, women candidates have relied more on individual contributions and received a significantly lower percentage of funds from PACs than their male colleagues, as seen in Table 7.1.[24] In terms of funding from PACs, male senators receive significantly more from

Figures 7.4 and 7.5

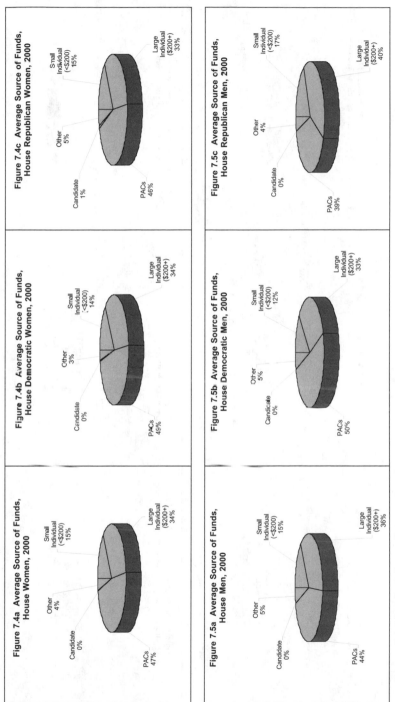

Figure 7.4a Average Source of Funds, House Women, 2000

Other 4%
Candidate 0%
Small Individual (<$200) 15%
Large Individual ($200+) 34%
PACs 47%

Figure 7.4b Average Source of Funds, House Democratic Women, 2000

Other 3%
Candidate 0%
Small Individual (<$200) 14%
Large Individual ($200+) 34%
PACs 49%

Figure 7.4c Average Source of Funds, House Republican Women, 2000

Candidate 1%
Small Individual (<$200) 15%
Large Individual ($200+) 33%
Other 5%
PACs 46%

Figure 7.5a Average Source of Funds, House Men, 2000

Other 5%
Candidate 0%
Small Individual (<$200) 15%
Large Individual ($200+) 36%
PACs 44%

Figure 7.5b Average Source of Funds, House Democratic Men, 2000

Other 5%
Candidate 0%
Small Individual (<$200) 12%
Large Individual ($200+) 33%
PACs 50%

Figure 7.5c Average Source of Funds, House Republican Men, 2000

Candidate 0%
Small Individual (<$200) 17%
Large Individual ($200+) 40%
Other 4%
PACs 39%

Source: Compiled from data available at http://www.opensecrets.org.
Note: Data are for incumbents who won reelection in 2000.

Figures 7.6 and 7.7

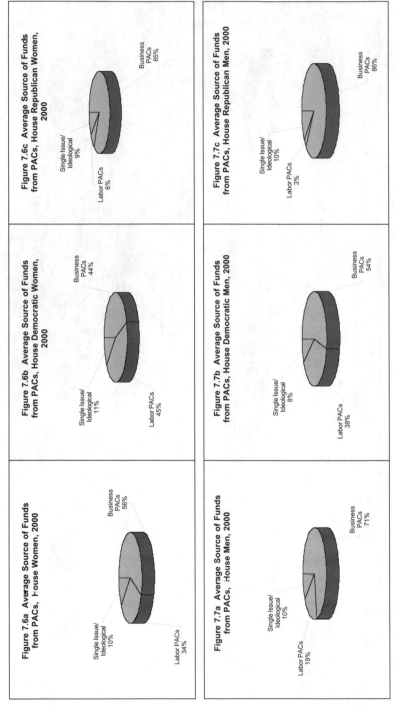

Figure 7.6a Average Source of Funds from PACs, House Women, 2000

Business PACs 56%
Single Issue/ Ideological 10%
Labor PACs 34%

Figure 7.6b Average Source of Funds from PACs, House Democratic Women, 2000

Business PACs 44%
Single Issue/ Ideological 11%
Labor PACs 45%

Figure 7.6c Average Source of Funds from PACs, House Republican Women, 2000

Business PACs 85%
Single Issue/ Ideological 9%
Labor PACs 6%

Figure 7.7a Average Source of Funds from PACs, House Men, 2000

Business PACs 71%
Single Issue/ Ideological 10%
Labor PACs 19%

Figure 7.7b Average Source of Funds from PACs, House Democratic Men, 2000

Business PACs 54%
Single Issue/ Ideological 8%
Labor PACs 38%

Figure 7.7c Average Source of Funds from PACs, House Republican Men, 2000

Business PACs 86%
Single Issue/ Ideological 10%
Labor PACs 3%

Source: Compiled from data available at http://www.opensecrets.org.
Note: Data are for incumbents who won reelection in 2000.

Table 7.1 Average Source of Funds by Gender, Senate, 1996–2000 (in percent)

Source	Women	Men
Individuals	65.3	55.8
PACs	18.6	34.6
Business PACs	(71.6)	(87.9)
Labor PACs	(12.8)	(4.5)
Single issue/ideological PACs	(15.7)	(7.6)
Candidate	7.8	0.0
Other	8.3	8.8

Source: Compiled from data available at http://www.opensecrets.org.
Note: Numbers in parentheses are percentages of the PAC total.

business PACs than women senators (87.9 percent versus 71.6 percent). Although the number of cases involved in the table is insufficient to draw definitive conclusions, on their face, they reflect differences in the fund-raising profiles between Senate men and women.

What Lessons Can Be Drawn from Women's Fund-raising Experiences?

One possible explanation that does not directly relate to the gender of the candidate is that PAC contributions are based more on the seniority rather than the gender of the candidate. Although this issue is beyond the scope of this chapter, small amounts of evidence do support this idea. First, PACs generally are known, all else being equal, to favor making contributions to incumbents rather than challengers and to more senior members than junior ones. Second, of the twelve women examined here, half were first elected to the Senate between 1996 and 2000, four were elected for a second term, and two were elected for a third term. Of the men analyzed, three were first elected between 1996 and 2000; four were elected for a second term, three for a third, and two for a fourth.[25] Third, if one examines a sample of House members, both men and women, first elected in 2000, they averaged approximately 30 percent of their funds from PACs (as opposed to the mid-40 percent for incumbent members), with the bulk of the funds coming from individual contributions. Thus, if this explanation holds true, then as women continue to become more entrenched in the Senate, the differences in their fund-raising profiles—generally and from PAC sources—from those of men in the Senate may begin to dissipate, much as appears to have happened in the House of Representatives.

This analysis now leads to the question at hand: what lessons can be drawn from women's fund-raising experiences for congressional seats for the prospect of a viable woman presidential candidate? Women in these lower offices—offices that are often in the path that men take to the White House—have become as adept as, if not better than, men at raising and spending funds while running for Congress. Moreover, particularly in the House, women are generally as able to obtain funding in similar percentages from similar sources as their male colleagues. In the Senate, women may lag somewhat behind men in terms of obtaining funding from more institutional sources, such as business PACs. But the important lesson is that in the House and to a large degree in the Senate, there are no substantive differences in campaign financing between successful women candidates and successful male candidates. The fundraising profile is simply that of a winning congressional candidate. Thus, the logical extension of the data is that, given some time, the success of women learning to become viable and successful congressional candidates likely may translate into similar success in presidential campaigns.

Conclusion

What does this all mean? First of all, the message that a woman has not become viable because of financing seems to be invalidated by these data from recent congressional election cycles. Does this conclusion mean we will get a woman to successfully run for the presidency in 2004? Although this chapter seems to suggest that the traditional economic structural barriers to a woman running for the presidency are beginning to dissipate, it still does not preclude residual cultural norms surrounding the office from sidetracking any efforts in the near future. The fact that the Senate still does not have many woman leaders and a relatively small (albeit growing) proportion of women overall suggests a few more election cycles are needed before a woman can take the next step to the White House.

The possibility of getting another woman vice presidential candidate seems more likely in the short-term future (in 1984, Geraldine Ferraro was the first female vice presidential candidate). With the growth of the gender gap, both the Democratic Party, which has benefited from it thus far, and the Republican Party, which has suffered from it, have a vested interest in appealing to the majority of the electorate. Many felt 2000 would be the year, but perhaps 2004 might be.

Regardless of this, what else is preventing a Madam President? Cultural norms are beginning to be affected by Hollywood and the efforts of candidates like Elizabeth Dole.[26] However, there still seems to be somewhat of a need for female candidates not to miss the lesson Dole's campaign provided. They still need to focus on the key obstacles that anyone trying to get elected to this high office faces: campaign organization, timing, and building support for a key agenda.

Women also need to realize, as Republican pollster Bob Teeter points out, that "Men and women would be much tougher in judging a woman candidate for president than for senator or governor." In addition, women also need to realize that, as some argue, women might have to face the fact that their own gender might be a liability, not the factor that gets them elected. Some, like one top Republican strategist, point out, "It's been a longtime secret among political consultants that women hate women candidates. Women are bred to compete. It's the old thing: you get 11 guys, you've got a football team. You get 11 women, you've got a riot."[27]

Although women are gaining on men in terms of fund-raising ability, the battle for obtaining the presidency is far from won. A woman candidate must heed the advice above and seek to build a credible vision that moves voters to look beyond gender and into judging the candidate on her merits. So what other characteristics does a potential woman presidential candidate need? Some argue a "Margaret Thatcher" type might be successful, but that issue will be left for others to debate. Hopefully, what I have demonstrated in this chapter is that women have already proven that voters and donors respond to them favorably.

Senator Mary Landrieu said it best about women's prospects for elected office when she stated, "We'll have equity when gender is no longer an issue. . . . When we're really measured on the basis of brains and talent, we'll do just fine."[28] It is in these words and in the findings that money no longer needs to be a barrier that a future female candidate for president may find hope.

8

On the Way to the White House: Communication Strategies for Women Candidates

Dianne Bystrom

"Communication is the heart of the modern political campaign," Judith S. Trent and Robert V. Friedenberg note in their classic textbook, *Political Campaign Communication.* "Without it, there would be no campaign."[1]

From the time a candidate contemplates her candidacy to the day of the election, she will be engaged in some aspect of communication, including interpersonal communications with party officials, campaign staff, the media, and voters; public speaking at rallies, news conferences, and debates; print materials such as direct mail appeals, brochures, posters, yard signs, and news releases; radio, newspaper, and television ads; and websites.

Although campaign communication comprises all such appeals, in this chapter I focus on two major ways by which women presidential candidates can communicate their image attributes and issue positions to the voters—coverage by the media and appeals to voters through television advertising. Candidates can attempt to use the media to present persuasive information about their campaigns, but they cannot control their coverage. Candidates can control, however, how their images and issues are presented to voters in their political ads.[2]

In this chapter I draw upon previous research on women political candidates—including studies on their media coverage, the content of their television advertising, and voter reactions to their campaign messages—as well as the results of voter surveys on presidential image and issue preferences to propose a campaign style and strategy for women seeking the presidency. In communicating with both the media and voters, women candidates must overcome stereotypes about their viability and leadership abilities.

Candidate Communication with the Media

According to political communication researchers, the mass media are powerful and important sources of information in a political campaign, not necessarily because they influence voting behavior but because they draw attention to the candidates and their campaigns. "Moreover, candidates have found that they can efficiently reach potential voters only through the mass media" and thus must focus their campaigns around the news events and issues the media are likely to cover.[3]

In crafting a media relations strategy, candidates need to consider where people get their news and information as well as what sources are more associated with political knowledge. According a recent Gallup poll, people get their news and information from a variety of daily sources.[4] Local television news shows (57 percent), nightly network news programs (55 percent), local newspapers (53 percent), and newspapers (50 percent) top the list. Of these sources, local television news was most trusted, with 64 percent of those surveyed relying upon it, followed by CNN (trusted by 59 percent); local radio news (53 percent); and public television news, television news magazine shows, discussions with family and friends, and nightly network news (all trusted by 51 percent).

Researchers have found some news and information sources to be more correlated with political knowledge. For example, Michael X. Delli Carpini and Scott Keeter found that reading weekly news magazines and the newspaper are most correlated with political knowledge, followed by listening to the radio and then watching television news.[5] Gender differences also have been found by researchers studying political knowledge and media use. For example, men are more likely than women to gather political information from newspapers, news magazines, political television talk shows, political radio talk shows, and the Internet. Women are more likely than men to obtain political information from local television news, morning television shows, and talking with others.[6]

Differences have also been found in the media coverage of female and male political candidates. Women presidential candidates should consider these findings—and the media biases they may face—in designing a media relations plan and strategy.

Media Coverage of Women Candidates

Extensive studies by Kim Fridkin Kahn examining the newspaper coverage of women candidates running for election in the 1980s found that this medium not only stereotypes female candidates by emphasizing "feminine traits" and "feminine issues" but also accords them less coverage that often focuses on their viability as candidates.[7] Studies conducted since Kahn's work have both confirmed many of her findings and given some hope that media coverage of women candidates might be improving. For example, Kevin Smith found that female and male U.S. Senate and gubernatorial candidates in 1994 received about the same quantity and quality of coverage, except in open races.[8] And, in his study of 1998 gubernatorial candidates, James Devitt found that although male and female candidates received about the same amount of coverage, women received less issue-related coverage than did men.[9]

The 2000 campaign provided not only an opportunity to study the media coverage of women running for governor and the U.S. Senate but also the short-lived presidential candidacy of Elizabeth Dole. A study of newspaper coverage of women and men running for their party's nomination for U.S. Senate and governor in the 2000 primary races found that these women received more coverage than men in terms of quantity and that the quality of their coverage—slant of the story and discussion of their viability, appearance, and personality—was mostly equitable. Still, these women candidates were much more likely to be discussed in terms of their role as mothers and their marital status, which can affect their viability with voters.[10]

However, three studies examining the newspaper coverage of Dole—the first woman to seek a major political party nomination for president since former U.S. Representative Patricia Schroeder's short-lived consideration in 1987—during seven months in 1999 found that she received less equitable coverage in terms of quality and, especially, quantity as compared to her male opponents.[11] Although polls consistently showed Dole as a distant runner-up to George W. Bush for the Republican nomination for president, she not only received significantly less coverage than Bush but also less coverage than Steve Forbes and John McCain, who at the time were behind her in the polls.

In terms of the quality of coverage, all three studies found that Dole received less issue coverage than Bush, Forbes, or McCain. However, according to the two studies that considered the types of issues mentioned, Dole's issue coverage was balanced between such stereotypically masculine issues as taxes, foreign policy, and the economy and such stereotypically feminine issues as education, drugs, and gun control.[12]

The findings regarding Dole's image coverage were mixed. One study found that Dole received significantly more personal coverage, including descriptions of her personality and appearance, than the male candidates studied.[13] Another study found that the media did not pay much attention to her appearance but did make reference to her personality in three-fifths of the articles studied.[14] The third study, limited to media coverage in Iowa, found that Dole was less likely than Bush to be covered in terms of her image, including appearance and personality.[15]

Although these studies show that media biases toward women candidates still exist, it does appear that coverage is becoming more equitable. A promising development for future women presidential candidates is that Elizabeth Dole's media coverage in 1999 was more balanced and less stereotypical than that found in earlier studies, particularly in the range of issues mentioned and the lack of attention to her appearance and personality. (This theme is further assessed in Chapter 11.) Still, Dole received less coverage than male candidates, even those running behind her in the public opinion polls. Women candidates should be aware of such media biases, and develop strategies to build relationships with the media. Reporters and political consultants have some advice.

Communicating with the Media

In a recent campaign workshop for women interested in running for public office in Iowa, veteran political reporter David Yepsen of the *Des Moines Register* offered some advice for "surviving the media." His "ten rules" included do not lie; be polite, helpful, courteous, and open; return calls immediately; and provide maximum disclosure of information with minimum delay—"if you have to endure a story you don't like, then get it all over at once."[16]

Yepsen also advised candidates never to say "no comment." "If you can't answer, say so," he said. "If you don't know the answer, say so and offer to get the answer." In addition, he advised candidates to think before they speak—not to ad lib—and to use short, declarative sentences. For those burned with a bad news story, Yepsen told candidates that "tomorrow is another day" and to "stay cool." And if a correction is desired, candidates should call the reporter before working their way through the supervisory chain. Finally, Yepsen advised a "proactive strategy" in which candidates get to know the reporters who write stories for their target audiences, tell their stories, become sources, and practice for media interviews.

Political consultant Ed Zuckerman, who worked on the campaigns of U.S. Senators Barbara Boxer of California and Patty Murray of Washington, admits that women candidates have more trouble than men in working with the media. Women candidates need to become media savvy, knowing when to talk or keep their mouths shut, he says. Candidates need to realize that reporters are a conduit to the people and have a job to do and deadlines to meet.[17]

Political consultant Cathy Allen, who has crafted a successful career working with women political candidates, advocates finding messages that establish female authority in nonthreatening terms. And pollster Celinda Lake believes that the media, although still biased, are showing increasing interest in women candidates, which can be used to their advantage in both newspaper and television coverage.[18]

Women presidential candidates, then, can develop ways for themselves and staff members to work strategically with the media. They need to be aware of existing media biases but take advantage of the "novelty" of their campaigns to get their stories—and issues—out to voters through the media. And although they need to work with the media to get their messages out, women candidates also can take control of their communication to voters through direct, nonmediated appeals, such as television advertising.

Candidate Communication with Voters

In presidential campaigns, candidates communicate with voters interpersonally; through speeches and debates; and through newspaper, radio, and television advertising and websites. Of these, television advertising is the most prominent. In fact, television political advertising has been acknowledged in recent years as the single most frequent exposure voters have to candidates during a political campaign.[19]

The importance of television advertising to today's political campaign is underscored by the significant financial resources devoted to such communication. For example, political parties and candidates for local, state, and federal office spent $400 billion on television commercials in the 1996 election, up 34 percent from 1992.[20] Studies examining the influence of political advertising on voter perceptions of candidates and their issues and images show that this money may be well spent.[21] For example, a study of the 1992 U.S. Senate races in California found that commercials influenced perceptions of candidate recognition, favorability, electability, and voting preference.[22]

In devising communication strategies for their television advertising, women candidates should consider the perceptions of voters as well as the context of the campaign. Recent surveys of voters and research on campaign commercials provide some guidance.

Voter Preferences and Perceptions

Recent surveys indicate that voters say they are more likely to support a woman candidate for president. (For more information on public support for women candidates, see Chapter 12 by Carole Kennedy.) In a study conducted in 1989, 54 percent of men and 80 percent of women said they would support a woman for president.[23] Ten years later, 83 percent of men and 84 percent of women say they would vote for a woman president.[24] Perhaps most notably, the greatest change in attitudes has come from male voters. However, although most Americans believe the nation is ready for a woman president, two-thirds of both women and men voters surveyed said the "right woman just hasn't come along yet."[25]

Despite the seeming widespread support for a woman's candidacy for the presidency, the 1999 survey by Deloitte and Touche also revealed underlying attitudes and persistent stereotypes that "serve to undermine women's chances for election to high political office."[26] For example, on the top-rated issue of law and order, a slight plurality of voters believed that a male president candidate would do a better job than a female president. Although 44 percent said there would be no difference on how well a man or woman president would handle the economy—the number two issue—more (31 percent) thought a man would do a better job than a woman (22 percent).

However, voters believed a woman president would do a better job than a man president on the next two most important issues—social concerns, such as education, poverty, and homelessness, and personal qualities. Men, however, were favored over women on the traditionally "hard" issues of foreign policy and governmental problems, such as balancing the budget.

In addition, the majority of voters associated men, rather than women, with the top image characteristic they desire in a president—leading the nation during a crisis—and were more likely to believe that men would do a better job in making difficult decisions, the second-rated trait. However, a woman president was favored on the third- and fourth-rated image traits—trustworthiness and honesty—more so than a man president. On other image traits, a woman president was favored on the ability to understand ordinary people and moral character; a man was perceived as more competent on preparedness to go to war and having a military record. Both women and men were considered equal on intelligence and the ability to forge compromise and obtain consensus.[27]

Perhaps more troubling, voters' stereotypical perceptions of the abilities of women versus men to serve as president extended beyond these issue and image considerations. According to the Deloitte and Touche survey, the majority of U.S. voters said that the personal and family situations of a presidential candidate would have "no effect" on their vote. But they also gave more scrutiny to a woman's personal situations than a man's. For example, 17 percent said they would be less likely to vote for a woman presidential candidate with a child under five years old, and 30 percent said they would be less likely to vote for a woman candidate if she were pregnant. Only 6 percent said they would be less likely to vote for a male presidential candidate with a young child, and 5 percent would be less likely to vote for him if his wife were pregnant. Having children aged six through eighteen had less of an effect on voting preferences.[28]

Interestingly, voters—9 percent of those surveyed—would be more likely to vote for a woman presidential candidate without children than the 5 percent who said they were more likely to vote for a male presidential candidate without children. Marriage was seen as an asset for both female and male candidates, with 20 percent less likely to vote for an unmarried woman and 17 percent less likely to vote for an unmarried man.

Finally, this and other surveys reveal information related to hypothetical voting behavior of women and men for female and male presidential candidates. For example, the women voters surveyed in the 1999 Deloitte and Touch poll were about nine points more likely than men voters to say a woman president would do a better job on all seven issues considered. Men voters, however, were three points more likely to say a male president would do a better job than a woman on these issues. Women surveyed also were significantly more likely than the men surveyed—by a margin of 54 percent to 41 percent—to say they would be positively inclined to vote for a female presidential candidate.[29]

As is discussed in the Appendix of the book, in an online survey conducted in 2001 by the White House Project and America Online, 85 percent of the 46,000 respondents said they were "willing" to vote for a woman for president and 59 percent said they were "very willing." Their top choices were former first lady and current New York senator Hillary Rodham Clinton (39 percent), talk show host Oprah Winfrey (25 percent), former New Jersey governor and current Environmental Protection Agency administrator Christine Todd Whitman (20 percent), National Security Adviser Condoleezza Rice (11 percent), and California Senator Dianne Feinstein (5 percent).[30]

These surveys showed different levels of optimism about when a woman might be elected president. In the 1999 Deloitte and Touche survey, most respondents (49 percent) anticipated a woman president in the next ten to twenty-five years.[31] In the 2001 online survey, respondents were more optimistic about a woman candidate's chances, with most (45 percent) indicating that Americans would elect a woman president by 2008.[32]

Communicating with Voters Through Television Advertising

Several researchers have argued that television advertising—and the control it affords candidates over campaign messages about their images and issues—is even more important for women candidates, whose speeches and comments are often framed in stereotypical terms by the media.[33] Using the "videostyle" construct developed by Lynda Lee Kaid and Dorothy Davidson[34] in 1986, researchers have studied the verbal, nonverbal, and production components of the political commercials of women and men running for the U.S. Senate and governor to compare and contrast their communication strategies.[35]

These studies have shown mixed results. For example, early videostyle research on 1990 and 1992 mixed-gender U.S. Senate campaigns found that female candidates used about the same percentage of negative attacks and talked about mostly the same issues and images as male candidates. However, these female candidates also smiled more, made more eye contact, spoke more often for themselves, appeared head on, dressed more formally, and invited viewer participation and action more than male candidates.[36] A 1999 study of spot ads from the 1996 mixed-gender U.S. Senate and gubernatorial races found a new trend emerging: females stressed male traits such as toughness even more than male candidates, ran more negative ads, and actually stressed warmth and compassion less than male candidates.[37]

A study of the videostyles of mixed-gender U.S. Senate campaigns from 1990 to 1998 found that female candidates had increased their use of negative attacks, as compared to their male opponents, over the decade.[38] Female candidates also continued to dress more formally and smile more than men. However, the issues that female and male candidates mentioned in their television commercials seemed to be more attributable to the "context of the election year" than the gendered videostyle of the candidate. For example, both women and men focused on education, the environment, and senior citizen issues in 1990; the economy, health care, and taxes in 1992–1993; taxes and crime in 1994; taxes, senior citizen issues, and education in 1996; and taxes, the economy, and senior citizen issues in 1998.

In addition, the study of commercials from the 1990–1998 mixed-gender U.S. Senate campaigns found that female and male candidates emphasized similar images in their television commercials.[39] They both emphasized mostly stereotypically masculine traits such as strength, aggressiveness, performance, and experience, balanced with such stereotypically feminine attributes as honesty, sensitivity, and understanding. That is, both men and women seem to be presenting themselves as tough but caring—at least when running against each other.

The researchers concluded that the presence of a female candidate in a political campaign could change the image and issue discussion of her male opponent. That is, when women run for political office, their male opponents are called into a campaign dialogue that includes attention to issues associated with women and their societal concerns—such as education, health care, and senior citizen issues—as well as presentation of stereotypically "feminine" attributes.[40]

Although the majority of research comparing female and male candidate television advertising focuses on the content of the commercials, a few studies attempt to assess voter reactions to the communication strategies employed. For example, an experiment on two 1992 U.S. Senate campaigns and the 1994 gubernatorial campaign in California— all of which pitted a woman against a man—concluded that women candidates were more effective in communicating with voters through commercials that focused on such stereotypical female issues as women's rights, education, and unemployment than such stereotypical male issues as crime and illegal immigration.[41] The researchers advise women candidates to "consider their constituents' stereotypes when designing their advertising strategies"[42] but to "pick the characteristics which will resonate best with voters based on the issue environment during that particular campaign season."[43]

However another study, comparing responses to negative commercials from 1990 and 2000 mixed-gender U.S. Senate and gubernatorial campaigns, found that female candidates received more election "votes" only when they were evaluated higher on both stereotypically masculine and feminine characteristics.[44] Male candidates were given more flexibility: in some races they received more election "votes" when they emphasized a balance of "masculine" and "feminine" traits and in another race when they focused on "masculine" characteristics.

Based on surveys of voters and the findings of previous research, women presidential candidates should be advised to emphasize both stereotypically feminine and masculine images and issues in their television commercials. Voters will perceive a woman presidential candidate as more honest and trustworthy than a man and as just as intelligent and able to forge compromise and obtain consensus. However, a woman presidential candidate will need to emphasize her ability to lead the nation during a crisis and to make difficult decisions.

Issue emphasis will vary with the context of the campaign. In recent presidential elections, the economy, education, and health care have been the top issues. Women are rated about the same or more favorably by voters on these issues. However, women are considered less able to handle such issues as law and order, foreign policy, and governmental problems. In elections when these issues emerge at the top of voters' concerns, women presidential candidates will need to demonstrate their competence on such issues.

Conclusion

The first woman to be elected president will need to overcome a variety of obstacles on her way to the White House. Biases—by voters and the media—toward women candidates still exist but seem to be slowly fading. A woman presidential candidate needs to be aware of these stereotypes in devising a communication strategy that both emphasizes her perceived image and issue strengths—honesty and trustworthiness and dealing with social concerns—as well as establishes her credibility as a tough and decisive leader able to handle such issues as crime, foreign policy, and the economy.

Or, as noted in the book *Running as a Woman: Gender and Power in American Politics,* a woman candidate must tackle "the fine line of ambiguity and stereotypes that voters and tradition superimpose on her. She must craft a message and public persona that persuades party, pundits, and the public—and not necessarily in that formerly preordained order—that she can be as clear and independent a decision maker as any man, but more caring and trustworthy."[45] A woman presidential candidate can do this through both her relationships with the media and, especially, with her television political advertising.

In dealing with the media, a woman candidate and her campaign staff should develop a proactive strategy by getting to know the reporters covering their campaigns and returning their telephone calls in a timely manner. A woman political candidate should prepare for her interviews; think before she speaks; and use short, declarative sentences in responding to questions. She should avoid saying "no comment" and either say she cannot answer the question or offer to get the answer. She should avoid being drawn into commenting on only stereotypical "feminine" concerns by leading the interview back to the issues most important to the campaign. If the candidate's campaign staff believes she is getting less equitable media coverage in terms of quantity and quality, they should call the reporter and describe their concerns. Political reporters seem to be getting more sensitive to charges about gender bias.

A woman presidential candidate also should rely on well-crafted and carefully produced television commercials to present her issues and images to the public. She should emphasize the issues important to the campaign—including stereotypically masculine issues, such as the economy, crime, or foreign affairs as well as stereotypically feminine issues, such as education and health care, where she has perceived competence. She should emphasize a "tough but caring" image, by mentioning her honesty, trustworthiness, and compassion as well as toughness, strength, and leadership.

Previous research shows that women can effectively use negative advertising, which has become a staple of modern presidential campaigns.[46] Observations by political consultants as well as the results of research show that women can be effective when communicating on television. As pollster Celinda Lake has said, "television likes women" because they can be more colorful, animated, and engaging than men.[47] A study of 1996 presidential ads found that Bob Dole's most effective ad was the one featuring his wife, Elizabeth Dole. This ad, "From the Heart," impressed both old and especially young voters. It received neutral responses from both Democrats and independent voters and overwhelmingly positive responses from Republicans. As one older male voter commented, "She made a nice impression. I wish she would run for Senator or President someday."[48]

Elizabeth Dole did run for president, although briefly, in 1999 and for the U.S. Senate (from North Carolina) in 2002. Her presidential candidacy- -as well as the increasing numbers of women running for the U.S. Senate, House of Representatives, and state governorships—have helped pave the way for other women candidates, including those considering a campaign for president.

Also helping to pave the way for women presidential candidates are men—including male candidates for governor, U.S. Senate, and president—who have emphasized stereotypically masculine *and* feminine issues and images in their communication in recent campaigns. In addition, women such as Madeline Albright, Janet Reno, and Condoleezza Rice—who have been appointed to serve as U.S. secretary of state, U.S. attorney general, and national security adviser- -have helped establish the credibility of women on foreign affairs, law and order, and national security issues.

The media and voters also seem more accepting of women political candidates. Media coverage of women political candidates is becoming more equitable, especially in terms of the range of issues associated with women and the decreasing attention to woman's appearance and personality. Voters indicate they are more willing to vote for a woman presidential candidate and, in fact, believe a woman will be elected president as soon as 2008 or at least by 2024.

9

Public Discourse and Female Presidential Candidates

Carol Lynn Bower

> This is one of the inherent duties of a president, to speak for the country with a strong forceful voice, recognizing that yours is the only one that might be heard on that subject, in a definitive way. . . . There is no alternative to the president's voice.
>
> —*Jimmy Carter*[1]

The president's voice can hold lives in the balance, can hold nations at bay, and can hold a world in silence, waiting for a stance to be taken. The person behind that voice won the right to its discourse in the ultimate political test performance—winning a U.S. presidential election. To triumph in the election, that voice had to find a style and strategy that would secure the favor of a sizeable percentage of the voting public. To date, that voice, with only a few exceptions, has been masculine.[2] But it will not always be a male voice dominating the public discourse. As more women are elected or appointed to state executive or national offices, the female voice becomes louder and gains more credibility. The final test of the female voice to inspire belief and trust will come when that voice is heard emanating from the Oval Office. To move from behind a gubernatorial or congressional desk to behind the presidential desk is a momentous step, but no longer an unthinkable step for a woman. In this chapter, I examine how that step could successfully be constructed in the public discourse. I explicate how gender socialization creates communicative boundaries and the consequences, or "double binds," a woman faces when she crosses the boundaries between private and public domain. Additionally, strategies for overcoming or reframing the stereotypes into winning political discourse will be developed.

Socialization

Socialization establishes, along gender lines, cultural personality norms for children who will participate in mainstream activities. These normative expectations are associated with traditional masculine and feminine stereotypes, which are made up of gender role characteristics or traits.[3] Socialization divides stereotypical behavior into two distinct domains—the private and public. Women are taught as children that their lives should be centered in the private domain, which includes caring for the family and home.[4] For women to enter the public domain in either the business or political arenas, they must deal with the stereotypical expectations both of the men who reside in the public domain and the women who do not choose to challenge the stereotypes.

Robert Cialdini states that stereotypes exist as a way for the human mind to deal with an increasingly complicated and fast-moving environment in an efficient manner. Stereotypes are short cuts that mean human beings do not have to repeatedly "recognize and analyze all aspects in each person, event, and situation we encounter" on a daily basis.[5] Philip Zimbardo and M. R. Leippe add that stereotypes can be formed into a "set of cognition[s] that constitute mental schema about the target group" and that once formed, "stereotypes exert powerful influences on how pertinent information is processed."[6] Kay Deaux and Brenda Major posit that it is almost impossible for anyone to be "sex blind," and when a male and female first encounter each other, their initial cognitive response centers on sex identification—"he is a man" and "she is a female"—to the exclusion of other information that could counteract the invocation of gender stereotypes.[7] To the contrary, Curt Hoffman and Nancy Hurst maintain that gender stereotypes exist as a means to rationalize the placement of men and women into appropriate social roles.[8]

Women are expected to be "associated with femininity, including passivity, nurturance, dependence, and empathy" and are "discouraged from developing characteristics associated with a masculine sex-role identity—aggressiveness, dominance, ambition, and independence."[9] Yet, for women to fully enjoy the possibilities of the public domain, they must be able to demonstrate their ability with masculine personality traits, since the male stereotypical traits dominate in most public venues. Therefore, a woman who runs for political office must display a "balance of masculine and feminine traits in order to convey an 'acceptable' image."[10]

Gendered Communication and Public Discourse

The balance of masculine and feminine stereotypical traits can be created and then maintained communicatively through the manipulation of the masculine and feminine styles of discourse. What is demonstrated in their communication is an individual's gender identity, with specific linguistic and rhetorical attributes showing that "women and men operate from dissimilar assumptions about the goals and strategies of communication."[11] Research with children who are playing shows distinctive sex traits being socialized. Boys play in larger groups, are competitive, have specific goals, and play by rules, whereas girls play in smaller groups that are less structured in terms of roles and rules. Boys achieve status by being dominant, but girls become adept at the interactive process. Each gender displayed three specific rules of communication. Boys communicate to assert themselves, attract and maintain an audience, and gain and then keep the focus on themselves. Girls communicate so they can be relational, not critical of others, and attentive to others.[12]

Deborah Tannen likens the sex type differences in communication to talking cross-culturally between two distinct gender cultures and likens conversations to negotiations in which men and women have different goals.[13] For men, life is a "struggle to preserve independence and avoid failure," whereas in women's view, life is a "community, a struggle to preserve intimacy and avoid isolation."[14] These styles construct a communication asymmetry that is about power and the imbalance of it. In summary, whereas the masculine style of communication is defined as being instrumental and competitive, scholars tend to define the feminine style of communication as being expressive and affiliative.[15]

The current understanding of gendered communicative styles and public discourse from the perspective of elective office have benefited from such studies as Bonnie Dow and Mari Tonn's, who analyzed the rhetorical techniques of former Texas governor Ann Richards. This work demonstrates that feminine style has become a part of mainstream political discourse while also being a "critique of traditional grounds for political judgment" and a means to advance "alternative modes of political reasoning."[16] Richards's acclaimed keynote address at the 1988 Democratic National Convention is infused with an alternative mode— the "comic" mode—including numerous personal anecdotes laced with a big-time Texan, stinging sense of humor. Dow and Tonn argue that beyond the simple inductive power of the feminine style, it can act in two additional ways: "first, it creates an implicit standard for political judgment that is based on the primacy of experiential knowledge and inductive reasoning; second, it explicitly critiques the validity of claims that cannot meet this standard."[17] Dow and Tonn call these extrapolations the "philosophical value" of the feminine style while labeling other traits as the "strategic value."

Jane Blankenship and Deborah Robson expand the feminine style by identifying five traits or characteristics, including "basing political

judgments on concrete, lived experience; valuing inclusivity and the relational nature of being; conceptualizing the power of public office as a
capacity to 'get things done' and to empower others; approaching policy
formation holistically; and, moving women's issues to the forefront of
the public arena."[18] Their research demonstrates that the feminine style
is finding acceptance across gender boundaries. The assumption of the
double bind issue is put into a modern political context, as the authors
point out that women who stride into traditional male territory are expected to employ the language of the dominant group but are then stig-
matized for using their harsh speech.[19] Blankenship and Robson advance
the concept of "bi-cultural [ism]" for those "individuals, who utilize both
masculine and feminine styles of discourse."[20] Their study is at the forefront in the comparison of the feminine style in the discourse of women
and men who were political peers after winning their elected positions.

Double Binds and the Consequences
of Communicating Female Leadership

Sue Tolleson-Rinehart and Jeanie Stanley point out that the "*new* acceptance of women in office emanates from *old* gender-role stereotypes
about what women and men do. . . . The readiness to accept a
'woman's' political leadership is new; the belief that women will be different is not."[21] Kathleen Hall Jamieson discusses the difficulties faced
by women who are in public domain leadership positions (see Chapter
12 of this book for a similar discussion). These difficulties arise out of
the conflict between women participating in the public venue and the
gendered construction of their "proper" role or place in society. These
conflicts are the double binds that women find when they have "over-
stepped prescribed boundaries" and "confronted situations constructed
to ensure that they were guilty until proven guilty."[22] In other words, the
modern woman who wants to succeed in a leadership role is first required to demonstrate male and dominant behaviors as a manager, and
then she is chastised for not being a lady. If she then attempts to modify
her style to be more traditionally feminine, she finds she is not taken seriously any longer. Jamieson defines five double binds, including si-
lence/shame—women should be silent in public, and if they speak up
for their rights, then they should be ashamed for wanting their rights;
sameness/difference—women should seek equality while being biolog-
ically different and seeking special protections for their differences;
aging/invisibility—as they get older, women do not get wiser or stay attractive, they become invisible; womb/brain—women are identified as
bodies, not minds, as wombs, not brains; and femininity/competence—a
stereotype that arises from the human "tendency to think in dichotomies

characterized as masculine/feminine and then set in a hierarchical relation to one another with the masculine thought superior and the feminine inferior."[23]

Massachusetts governor Jane Swift dealt with the womb/brain double bind when she became the first female governor to give birth while in office. Immediately upon being tapped for the chief executive's office because of the appointment of then Governor Paul Cellucci as U.S. ambassador to Canada in 2001, Swift was forced to field concerns about her ability to be the governor while being pregnant with twins.[24] She was both vilified and sainted for thinking that she could or should be able to "fulfill her responsibilities to the public and still be a good mother."[25] Swift was admitted to the hospital with labor pains one month after taking office and faced immediate criticism for conducting business on the phone, as if no other governor had ever used a phone before. Swift's handling of the public discourse about her pregnancy exemplifies how many female politicians tend to deal with double binds— refusing to comment on the gendered criticism while reiterating that they can handle the job.

Arizona governor Jane Dee Hull demonstrates how this tendency can work successfully. Hull, like Swift, ascended to the office after a male governor left, although in Hull's case, she succeeded J. Fife Symington after his federal convictions for bank and mail fraud.[26] In 2000, the Republican acting governor ran for the office in her own right against former Phoenix mayor Paul Johnson. The race was at times heated and divisive, but Hull, a former teacher, invoked her schoolmarm image to repeatedly deflect attacks on her competence and integrity. In refusing to engage in a public defense of her political history, Hull reinforced an image that her opponent was immature, negative, and disruptive.[27] This strategy for coping with the double bind of femininity/ competence paired with a need in the state for stability led to an overwhelming victory for the short-time incumbent.

Reframing

To better understand the relationship between gendered stereotypes in public discourse and the rhetorical construction by women of political candidacy traits, it is important to understand how the double bind is redefined by those women so as to produce political viability. Jamieson suggests several ways to defeat double binds. A first step is to "reframe" the double bind so others will see it for what it really is.

> Reframing invites an audience to view a set of options from a different perspective and confront the fact that the options offered are false— whether they present a no-choice choice, self-fulfilling prophecy,

no-win situation, double standard, or an unrealizable expectation. . . . At its base, reframing meta-communicates. It steps back to critique the conventional rhetoric used to describe women's options. At one time or another, most contemporary female politicians have recounted a version of the classic no-win situation that first identifies women in relation to men and then discredits any choice they can possibly make or any circumstance in which they can possibly find themselves.[28]

A second method for dealing with the competence issue is to "confound the stereotype." Jamieson's example is the 1990 senatorial debate between Christine Todd Whitman and Bill Bradley. When Whitman responded with strength and competence to a tough, technical question about a military plane, she busted the stereotype to which Bradley was playing. Whitman, as a woman, would be expected to be strong on soft issues such as education, welfare, and health, but she handled well a challenge on a traditionally male-dominated hard issue. The resultant research showed that Whitman "gained *more* approval from the [focus] group than she did when she spoke in areas traditionally identified as within a woman's sphere."[29] "The need for female candidates to establish that they are both tough and caring can be satisfied by sending tough cues in verbal form and caring cues nonverbally or vice versa."[30]

Political Candidacy Traits

Reframing of double binds needs to involve a clear understanding of the goal, which should be reframing a negative stereotype into a positive candidate personality trait. One of the first studies to look at the salient personality traits of a candidate as perceived by the electorate found that among voters during the Reagan presidency, "Judgments of presidential character appear to be organized around a small set of correlated but distinct themes: competence, leadership, integrity, and (perhaps) empathy."[31] The first two themes, competence and leadership, would be instrumental qualities and would, therefore, be more clearly aligned with male personality traits. Integrity and empathy are expressive or relational traits and would be categorized as feminine personality traits. Hence, this study, although not explicitly stating it, shows that a mixture of masculine and feminine traits were valued in male presidential candidates. Besides being thought of as having higher levels of integrity than their male counterparts, officeholding women are expected to be more accountable and responsive.[32] Additionally, Susan Carroll specifically looked at masculine and feminine personality traits in women candidates and found that a vast majority of women candidates blend the male and female traits. These women are "psychologically androgynous."[33] In other words, the females in the study were more effective as candidates because they had developed a public image that displayed both male and female personality traits, conveying both instrumental and relational or expressive styles.

One study conducted subsequent to the Geraldine Ferraro campaign but prior to the 1992 election found that "female candidates can employ tough messages without being rebuked by startled voters" and that "voters may infer that tough, aggressive women still possess latent (stereotypical) warmth."[34] These findings provide support for the psychologically androgynous woman candidate and the integration of masculine and feminine personality traits by women candidates in their public image. The implication is that, for the personality trait of competence, women candidates do not have to focus their image on the feminine traits because voters will infer competence on those feminine issues regardless of the extent of the message content. Additionally, this study shows that women can talk tough on the hard issues and not face negative voter perception.

A significant result of this research was that female candidates are still stereotypically perceived as being warm even when delivering a strong, aggressive message. However, Leonie Huddy and Nayda Terkildsen suggest that women candidates need to demonstrate their masculine traits in their public image since they should not assume that the electorate will presume those masculine traits already exist.[35]

Stereotype/Trait Strategies

A pattern of dualities based on the socialization of private and public domains emerges in the confluence of communication and political science research. The private domain is the site of the feminine style of communication and the stereotypes involving femininity, childbearing, and relational or emotive qualities, whereas the public domain locates the masculine style of communication and the stereotypes involving masculinity, competitiveness, and instrumental or rational qualities. Extending the equation used in constructing the double binds, such as femininity/competence or womb/brain, the following model can be extrapolated: private/public, female/male, feminine style/masculine style, relational/instrumental, and emotive/rational. The candidacy traits could be similarly organized: integrity and empathy/competence and leadership. Female politicians are assumed to possess the first set of traits (integrity and empathy) while needing to demonstrate the latter set of traits (competence and leadership). Hence, a generalized relationship is created that accounts for both the communicative and political aspects of public discourse as it is manifest for a female candidate—that relationship being stereotype/trait.

The importance of this construction is that it can specifically orient the direction of the female candidate's public discourse. Successful political women need to define which stereotypes they must address in their public discourse to form the public image that accounts for their candidacy traits as well as create a public sense of movement between the stereotype and trait. The Chavez-Mikulski Senate race in Maryland in 1986 demonstrates how attending or not attending to this construction can result in success or failure. Republican Linda Chavez and Democrat Barbara Mikulski ran head-to-head in one of the few all-female national contests. Chavez's public discourse focused on her acceptance of the political patriarchal order as outlined by the head of the GOP ticket, Vice President George Bush, a pseudo-incumbency strategy that stressed the maintenance of the status quo. Mikulski's public discourse, however, focused on demonstrating her ability as an effective leader, able to employ male candidacy traits while espousing policy issues in keeping with the patriarchal party mandate. Mikulski created an alternative but publicly acceptable femininity that established competence at the same time.[36] It was a particularly telling public image achievement since Mikulski was a single woman. She accomplished this public discourse feat by combining feminine-style language with masculine-style language to reframe the stereotype, such as in her description of a politician as a "social worker with power."[37] This construction allowed her to redefine the familial and maternal connection with the electorate instead of with a husband and children. Mikulski created movement between the stereotypes and the traits as she redefined them both. Chavez did not—she remained steadfastly in the stereotype side of the equation. Mikulski won in 1986 and continues to win.

This construction can also encompass political campaign strategies. There are three general categories of strategies employed: incumbency, challenger, and challenger/incumbency. Most female candidates are the challenger in the race, but all female candidates are the challenger in the public domain system of politics, whether they are an incumbent or not. Yet, it is in the assumptions of incumbency that many of the political traits, such as leadership and competence, are demonstrated, and it is by projecting the sense of having incumbency that a female candidate can reframe the stereotypes to project the traits. Arizona governor Jane Dee Hull ably showed the power of the duality of the challenger/incumbency strategy. Although only in office for a short time before having to mount her election campaign, Hull used incumbency to construct a successful transmigration between the stereotypes and traits such as competence and leadership, while at the same time voicing challenger discourse such as optimism for the future and speaking to traditional values instead of calling for a change of values.[38]

Other incumbency strategies can work well in a female candidate's public discourse. The use of surrogates can be highly beneficial, especially as the visible or vocal elements of negative broadcast advertising. A female candidate could evoke adverse consequences if she was seen as being too negative about her opponent. However, if a male surrogate was the image or voice of the negative comments, then the female candidate can disavow the direct effects while incorporating the positive public opinion outcomes. Another surrogate incumbency strategy could involve using a surrogate male public speaker to develop a patriarchal and conservative discourse for the female candidate who is seen as being liberal.

Conclusion

The key to understanding the public discourse of a female presidential candidate is to understand that her rhetoric is that of evolution without creating the impact of revolution. She is faced with the daunting task of changing the stereotypical views of the electorate without their having the understanding that they or their expectations are being changed. In this sense, her public discourse must be more persuasive and precise than that of her male counterpart. But additionally, this construction of a public female image incorporating the qualities of both the private and public domains allows for more strategic options by integrating the best of both worlds.

As more women work their way up the political ladder, gaining experience and creating the impression of incumbency, the public discourse will be expanded to encompass the new public image. This growth is evident throughout society, but nowhere more dramatically than with the investiture of television as the family information dispenser. From the infamous Nixon-Kennedy debates to the shot of Vice President George Bush glancing at his watch in the 1992 debate against Bill Clinton, politicians have learned the deadly pitfalls of the medium, which is both intimate and impersonal at the same time. Again, it is a duality that benefits the female politician, for the woman is stereotypically thought to be intimate and willing to share her feelings, whereas the man embodies the impersonal. So it is the male politician who, to remain viable, has had to evolve dualistically; incorporating in his public image the traits that embrace the intimacy and narrative or feminine style of television.[39]

Maintaining the delicate balance of duality is not a new phenomenon for women. However, being strategic about that duality and how it

is expressed in the public domain is a phenomenon for women, especially female candidates, that lacks depth of history and experience.
Knowledge and skills related to female public discourse are central to
controlling and manipulating the political rhetorical image, and it is
along that rhetorical pathway that the female presidential candidate will
find her way to the Oval Office.

10

Profile: Pat Schroeder and the Campaign That Wasn't

Robert P. Watson and Ann Gordon

REPRODUCED FROM THE COLLECTIONS OF THE LIBRARY OF CONGRESS

Born in Portland, Oregon, on July 30, 1940

B.A. (magna cum laude) from the University of Minnesota in 1962

J.D. from Harvard Law School in 1964 (one of only fifteen women in a class of more than 500)

Served in the 93rd–104th Congresses (1973–1996)

Patricia Schroeder was elected to Congress in 1972 and served Colorado's 1st congressional district for twenty-four years in the House of Representatives. She was elected at a time when committee chairs were all-powerful, and it posed quite a challenge for her. She was initially pleased to be put on the powerful Armed Services Committee, until she met the chair. F. Edward Hébert did not want her on the committee, nor did he want Democrat Ron Dellums of California on "his" committee. Schroeder recalls:

> Hébert didn't appreciate the idea of a girl and a black forced on him. He was outraged that for the first time a chairman's veto of potential members was ignored. He announced that while he might not be able to control the makeup of the committee, he could damn well control the number of chairs in his hearing room. . . . He said that women and blacks were worth only half of one "regular" member, so he added only one seat to the committee room and made Ron and me share it.[1]

Two years later, reform swept through Congress. Committee chairs had to be elected by a majority of the party. Hébert was replaced, and after two years of sitting "cheek to cheek," Schroeder and Dellums had their own seats. Fittingly, by 1992 Dellums became chair of the committee.[2]

A Distinguished Record in Congress

In Schroeder's first month in office, the Supreme Court passed *Roe v. Wade*. Throughout her career, Schroeder was an advocate for abortion rights. She sponsored legislation making it a federal crime to block access to abortion clinics.[3] "I was and, am, like many women, both pro-life and pro-choice. Obviously I wanted a family—I had struggled to have babies, and my children are the source of my strength. But I feel that every woman has to make her own decision about family size, depending on her circumstances, religious beliefs and medical advice."[4] In 1985, Schroeder introduced a bill to help families—the Parental and Disability Leave Act. She also sought to help military families with the passage of the Military Family Act in 1985. The Parental and Disability Leave Act became the well-known Family and Medical Leave Act that was passed in 1993 and signed by President Bill Clinton.[5]

Schroeder also worked on important legislation for women's health. The need for such legislation became apparent to Schroeder when she read "the results of these NIH-funded [National Institutes of Health] studies and realized that they always referred to men eating fish, men drinking coffee, men taking aspirin, men jogging, men aging. . . . I wondered: Does 'men' mean 'men and women'? I was sure it must. Why would NIH ignore half the nation's taxpayers?"[6] Together with Olympia Snowe and Henry Waxman, Schroeder asked the General Accounting Office to look into whether women were participants in health studies. They found that women were excluded and that, unbelievably, even breast cancer studies had been conducted on men.

> NIH had just completed the largest study ever conducted on aging—with 75,000 men. The study did not address . . . issues of particular concern to women. We asked why women were not a part of the study

since women have a longer life expectancy than men and constitute a higher percentage of the aging population. NIH told us it was easier for research subjects to use the men's restroom facilities.[7]

Schroeder's leadership on the issue was rewarded when the Women's Health Equity Act was finally signed into law by Bill Clinton after being vetoed by George Bush.

Run, Pat, Run

When Gary Hart dropped his bid for the Democratic nomination in 1987 due to scandal, it made Schroeder consider the office.

> I had consented to be Vice Chair of Gary Hart's campaign. And so in a way I had kind of cleared my calendar to do that . . . and was very involved in going around and representing Gary and looking at the other candidates and debating some of them when he couldn't come. . . . When the Donna Rice event blew that out of the water . . . I thought . . . 'I could do this too.' I think one of the things women often do is they're quick to run in to be a surrogate for someone without thinking well if I can be a surrogate I can probably be the candidate.[8]

In the summer of 1987, Schroeder began to explore a presidential campaign. She was realistic about the race, noting that she began looking into the possibility of running six months after the other candidates had entered the race. There were other obstacles as well. Schroeder found press coverage of her potential candidacy frustrating.

Regardless of the message her campaign tried to project, journalists selected out only those themes that were consistent with their expectations about what a woman candidate should be.

> When there are that many candidates the press tries to pigeonhole each one. We would very carefully try to make sure we had events in all communities—very broad-based, and very inclusive. And yet what people would say to us is why are you only talking to women? And I'd say "What?" . . . that would be all the TV would be showing. Here's the woman's candidate and today she spoke to this woman's group. Now, that was one of maybe ten speeches, but that's the one they picked out because that's the one that fit . . . and then the problem became I would have many men saying, "how come you don't want men to vote for you?" And I'd say, "Wait a minute. Where did you get that idea?" [They would say:] "Well because you only talk to women." [Schroeder would reply:] "Well no I don't." But their reality was that's all they saw on TV, therefore they assume that's all that you must be doing. . . . Your slot was the woman's slot and that's what they [the

press] were going to do. And unfortunately male voters would trans-late that you didn't want them . . . that you were just running for women.[9]

The press also had a tendency to focus on her appearance. "You'd give a speech on nuclear power and the first question would be 'why are you wearing green?'" Despite problems with media coverage, Schroeder felt her exploration had been successful. A *Time* magazine poll in August 1987 ranked Schroeder as third in the field of candidates. Still, she did not feel that she had the funds needed to be competitive. So in September, amid chants of "Run, Pat, Run," she told supporters she would not continue to pursue the nomination.[10]

Life After Congress

After serving twelve terms, Schroeder left Congress with an undefeated record. She served as a professor at the Woodrow Wilson School of Public and International Affairs at Princeton University and is now president and chief executive officer of the Association of American Publishers (AAP), which is a national trade organization. Schroeder continues her interest in politics as well. She leads the New Century/New Solutions think tank for the Institute for Civil Society in Newton, Massachusetts, and cochairs the Democracy Online Project's National Task Force.[11]

PART 3
THE MEDIA, VOTERS, AND PUBLIC OPINION

11

The Lipstick Watch:
Media Coverage, Gender,
and Presidential Campaigns

Diane J. Heith

Portraits of the candidate dominate modern presidential campaigns. In particular, media portrayals of the candidate can have significant influence on the course of the campaign and ultimately voter attitudes.[1] Traditionally, party labels mattered. But in this candidate-centered environment, they are no longer the driving factor determining voter choice.[2] From framing to priming to focusing on the game—or on the horse race—the language the media use influences public attitudes. In the presidential campaigns of 1984 and 2000, a new label was added to the traditional presidential candidate descriptors: gender.

As is discussed throughout this book, in 1984, Geraldine Ferraro became the first woman vice presidential candidate as the Democratic nominee alongside Walter Mondale. Running in the 1999–2000 nominating season, Elizabeth Dole became the first prominent female campaigner to seek the Republican presidential nomination. Dole was also the first prominent woman to run for the presidency since Shirley Chisholm in 1972.

Unsurprisingly, the label "first woman" factored into Ferraro and Dole's campaign coverage. Indeed, the first of any demographic group to run for the presidency or the vice presidency will receive intense scrutiny.[3] John F. Kennedy's Catholicism and relationship with the Pope was a critical component of the 1960 campaign coverage, for instance. Previous investigations of Senate campaigns found that gender differences in coverage tended to advantage males.[4] Were Geraldine Ferraro and Elizabeth Dole disadvantaged by gender coverage in their respective runs for office?

Gender was a significant label in the coverage of both Elizabeth Dole and Geraldine Ferraro. However, Elizabeth Dole received considerably more gender-based coverage than did Geraldine Ferraro, and this coverage hurt her chances for the Republican nomination. Dole's coverage contained a greater negative gender component, not because of some devolution in attitudes between 1984 and 2000 but because the presidency, in contrast to the vice presidency, is defined in masculine terms.

The Context of the Races

In 1984, Walter Mondale earned the Democratic nomination via a tough battle against Gary Hart, Jesse Jackson, John Glenn, and Alan Cranston. However, no intraparty scrum could possibly compare to the Herculean task facing Mondale in the general election: a race against popular incumbent Ronald Reagan. The first test of a presidential nominee and an opportunity to make inroads is the selection of the running mate. In this, Mondale and the Democrats benefited because "the choice of Ferraro . . . had . . . given them a boost."[5] Despite the excitement surrounding the choice of the first woman vice presidential candidate, the Mondale campaign never came closer than ten points to the Reagan-Bush team in the polls.

In contrast, as the first woman to seek the 2000 Republican nomination since Margaret Chase Smith in 1964, Elizabeth Dole initially appeared to be in a comfortable position. An early Gallup poll in 1998 revealed that George W. Bush was only slightly ahead of her.[6] But Elizabeth Dole's candidacy went downhill from there and was devoured early, along with the other Republican hopefuls (with the exception of John McCain), by the Bush juggernaut. On August 14, 1999, Dole received 14 percent of the voting in the Iowa straw poll. Her third-place finish did attract some media attention, "but she failed to capitalize on her success . . . she also suffered from fund-raising that never exceeded one-tenth of the Bush intake."[7] It was the "invisible primary," the competition for funds with George W. Bush, that ultimately ended Dole's bid for the White House.[8]

The failed bids of Mondale-Ferraro and Dole can be explained by traditional campaign assessments. The Mondale-Ferraro campaign suffered from numerous missteps, ranging from the national party chairman debacle to Ferraro's husband's financial problems to the lack of a coherent plan for winning.[9] The explanations cited for Dole's truncated bid range from her inexperience in running for elected office to the lack of endorsements and poor organization.[10] However, despite these traditional explanations, the news coverage of these "first women" also vitally influenced the outcome of these runs for office.

The Demographic Connection

The moment a woman, Jew, African American, or any other nonwhite, nonmale candidate enters a political race—in particular the presidency—demographics become an issue. With both candidacies, reporters naturally linked Ferraro and Dole's gender to discussions of voters' gender. Gender usually enters into campaigns as a group watch, that is, the candidate does well (or poorly) with group X. Similar links are made to the poll numbers of any demographic group: African Americans, Asians, Latinos, or even poll-driven innovations such as "soccer moms." In 1984, gender was a significant concern for the Reagan administration. For example, "substantial time and effort was also devoted to watching the newly identified 'gender gap.' Polling revealed that Reagan suffered on: the 'war issue . . . RR's personal style . . . [and the] economic issue among working women.' The Reagan White House was very concerned about the creation and persistence of this gap, and therefore monitored it regularly."[11]

However, with a woman in the race, reporters' coverage shifted from discussions of gaps to discussions of gender representation and audience presence. In 1984, 14 percent of Ferraro's articles cited the presence of either female audiences or female voters. By 2000, with a woman running for president, 52 percent of the articles covering Elizabeth Dole's candidacy mentioned the gender of the audience or voters. The press implicitly linked voting to gender, in contrast to voting discussions considering male candidates.

In both the Ferraro and Dole candidacies, the gender issue appeared to be helping, at first, according to the media and pundits. For Ferraro, most believed that gender would cross cut party divisions. "A *New York Times* survey finds that a woman on the national ticket shifts a large number of women voters to the Democratic Party [because] . . . every woman who has taken a lower salary than a clumsier male colleague, or held the head of a vomiting child at 3 A.M. while her husband slept, or watched her living standards and self-esteem shatter after a divorce" will vote for her.[12] The newspaper linkage between the candidate's gender and voter's gender persisted until the election. But by November 1984, the idea of gender voting appeared dead.

Gender voting resurfaced in 2000 in a different guise. "Being a woman appears to be helping Dole bring out a different kind of GOP constituency—younger people and women. . . . Soccer moms may have found their Republican primary candidate."[13] However, unlike 1984 or perhaps because of it, article after article raised the contradictions inherent in a woman running and running on women's issues. Dole was often referred to as "unsure how to raise the gender issue" and "ambivalent" about appealing to women voters.[14] Ultimately, citing the gender of the audience was a proxy for citing the "marvel of a woman running seriously for President."[15]

The coverage also attempted to link the novelty of a woman candidate to women's issues. Ferraro willingly took up the banner of women's issues, often citing the Equal Rights Amendment, as did the Mondale-Ferraro campaign. "Mondale's selection of a female running mate obviously boosted his credibility . . . on issues of equality, compassion, and social justice. [The] problem was that these were not the dominant issues on the voters' minds."[16] In the 2000 nominating season, even with Dole's candidacy, the campaign was not framed around "female" issues. Ironically, the absence of gender issues confused her coverage. Instead, Dole's coverage deliberately sought to challenge her tag lines from a gender perspective. In a statement reiterated over and over again, Dole claimed, "I am not running because I'm a woman; I'm running because I'm the most qualified."[17] Yet even that campaign standard, "I'm the most qualified," was challenged in terms of gender.

Elizabeth Auster argued in an opinion piece in the *Plain Dealer Reporter* that Dole's "main rationale for running seemed to be that she was a successful public figure who could make history by winning. That was not rationale enough. Because in the end, there was nothing remarkable about her candidacy except her sex."[18] George W. Bush noted that "Elizabeth and I agree on many of the important issues . . . including education reform, help for America's farmers, and the need for a strong national defense."[19] Ultimately, her policy positions were portrayed as "anti-women."[20]

Gender Commentary

The most pernicious coverage for both campaigns was the "lipstick watch." Almost 30 percent of Ferraro's coverage and over 40 percent of Dole's contained references to clothing, makeup, hair, and other distinctly feminine categorizations. In an interview, Geraldine Ferraro cited the ridiculousness of these categorizations. "When you're the only one wearing a bright-colored dress and wearing lipstick, it's pretty obvious who the woman candidate is."[21] Yet the press coverage mentioned these types of labels frequently.

After Ferraro's debate with George Bush, a reporter noted that "her manner was matched by her neutral brown suit."[22] Ferraro's "smudged mascara" was mentioned as a first for a presidential campaign.[23] In the years between the two campaigns, gender coverage still reigned. A *San Diego Union-Tribune* article began, "Ames, Iowa—Elizabeth Dole, clad in peach silk and perfect lipstick, glided smoothly through a throng."[24] Reporters queried Dole about walking an entire parade route in heels. Her spokesperson, Ari Fleischer complained, "Men don't get questions about their footwear!"[25]

The labels ranged from the obvious to the more derogatory. Newspaper articles feverishly repeated Ferraro's "bitchy" label offered by the vice president's spokesperson and his wife. "On National Public Radio . . . political analyst Stuart Rothenberg said Dole had to prove she was running for more than 'national hostess.'"[26] Even worse, one reporter claimed, after an interview, "'She looks great naked.' Would a reporter have said that about George W?"[27]

Media Bias

In 1984, the Mondale-Ferraro team lost to the incumbent president and vice president, whereas in 2000, Elizabeth Dole dropped out before the start of the primary season. Media coverage quickly turned to post-mortems and included coverage of the campaign as well as the coverage of gender. Reporters immediately considered whether the "female factor" contributed to the lack of success. Did Mondale lose because he chose a woman running mate? Was Dole having trouble on the campaign trail because she is a woman—"of course not, came the refrain. We're beyond that."[28] Yet, like a tooth about to fall out, reporters could not help picking at the point. Reporters questioned prerequisites for leadership— is it testosterone and not estrogen?[29] Are Americans ready for a woman president? Do conservatism and chauvinism prevent Americans from viewing women as authorities or potentially effective in power?[30]

The media coverage of its own behavior in 1984 focused primarily on the "first factor." Alex Jones claimed the coverage of Ferraro contained "uncharted waters" and that "a sex-blind standard" was not "possible because Representative Ferraro is a pioneer."[31] Ferraro's own press secretary claimed that "male reporters had a hard time dealing with Mrs. Ferraro on an informal basis. They didn't know how to start up conversations. A groundbreaking conversation for a male candidate is a lot easier. . . . There's a conversation starter, and it is sports."[32] However, by the end of the campaign many felt that "the raucousness of past campaigns" declined in response to a new sensitivity to charges of sexism.[33]

Twenty-seven percent of Ferraro's articles included gender coverage. Sixteen years later, during which time women were more prevalent on the campaign trail, gender coverage of Elizabeth Dole almost doubled Ferraro's (see Table 11.1). In 1984, only 4 percent of the articles on Ferraro cited a problem with the press coverage. The press accepted a learning curve on gender and even pronounced its behavior acceptable. However, by 2000, there was a fourfold increase in the number of articles citing media bias in Dole's coverage: 18 percent of the articles claimed coverage was an issue (see Table 11.1). What is interesting is that the percentage of women covering these historic campaigns remained about the same.

Senator Bob Dole noted in an editorial, "Much of the stingy coverage of Elizabeth Dole's campaign has been nitpicking and negative. Is it so because she is a woman, or could it be the mainstream media cannot abide the fact that she is a qualified Republican woman running for president?"[34] In September 1999, prior to Dole's exit from the race, Geneva Overholster of the *Washington Post* asked, "Why Is Dole Getting Short-Changed?"[35] Her examination of the coverage of the Republican pre-primary period found that both the *Washington Post* and Associated Press provided more coverage and thus more attention to the other candidates.[36] She writes, "Now I know Bush has swamped everybody else, in money, endorsements. . . . But how about Forbes and McCain, to pick two candidates? Why are they getting substantially more coverage than Dole?"[37] Joe Carroll wonders if "this is male sexism by the media, including this reporter. Deep down, do we really think a woman has a chance of becoming the next U.S. president?"[38] Wayne

Table 11.1 Gender Coverage[a] (in percent)

	Geraldine Ferraro[b]	Elizabeth Dole[c]
Articles with gender language	27	42
Articles citing media bias	4	18
Other coverage	69	40
Articles written by women	44	45
Articles citing audience gender	14	52
	N = 351	N = 452

Source: a. Lexis-Nexis Newspaper Database. Lexis-Nexis contains the full text of articles from thirty-three United States newspapers and twenty-two foreign outlets. b. Data from August 1984 (after the nomination) to November 30, 1984 (after the election). c. Data from August 1999 (prior to the Iowa caucus) to February 2000 (after the New Hampshire primary).

Woodlief noted that coverage of male candidates tends to be idea-based, whereas coverage of women tends to focus on personal stories.[39] Woodlief highlights the classic coverage problem for women candidates—they are portrayed as more intuitive than rational.

Ultimately, however, reporters used the circumstances of Dole's exit to temper their own chauvinism. Most reporters, political pundits, and even the candidate herself focused on Dole's inability to raise money and campaign shortcomings to explain her departure from the race. By September 1999, according to the Federal Election Commission, Bush's intake of money was fifty times larger than Dole's. The financial differential between the two candidates was certainly an influential factor, but for many reporters, the way candidates run their campaigns are often more significant. John McCain's favorable press coverage in January and February 2000 was often attributed to his accessibility, which contrasted to the highly scripted and monitored George W. Bush. "Political consultant Charles Cook added that Dole's response to reporters on issues often was, 'I'll have to look into that. I'm glad you raised that point'—very unspecific."[40] However, many of the articles on Dole explored her limitations. Reporters described her as "robotic," a "control freak," and "over-rehearsed."[41] "I agree entirely that there were too many stories on her red suit and her matching red pumps and red handbag," said Andrea Mitchell of NBC News. "But Dole also had problems within her own organization and her reluctance to take on issues."[42]

The Hurdle of Gender Coverage

The press plays a pivotal role in presidential campaigns as the link between citizen and candidate. As a result, the quality of the news coverage of candidates can shape citizens' pictures of the candidates and thus their willingness to vote for a candidate. The press discusses everything from candidate behavior to campaign management and links those behaviors to candidate viability. In Thomas Patterson's game scenario, the media associates and evaluates everything about a candidate with victory at the polls in mind.[43] Thus, gender is either a help, hindrance, or nonfactor for a candidate.

The selection of Geraldine Ferraro was an historic decision but was also good campaign strategy. Presidential candidates choose their vice presidential running mate to provide "the perceived need for geographic and ideological balance."[44] A good vice presidential choice will produce a positive response from the media. The vice presidential selection is the first major decision a presidential candidate makes after the primary cycle, and a poor choice can have a detrimental impact on the presidential campaign, as George Bush learned with the selection of Dan Quayle. Initially, Mondale received enthusiastic responses from the media for the selection of Ferraro. However, the notion that the selection of the first woman vice presidential candidate would harm the campaign never died. Nelson Polsby argued in 1985 that "Representative Ferraro appears to have contributed only slightly less to the Democratic ticket than vice-presidential candidates customarily do. She made a vigorous platform appearance and campaigned energetically. . . . Because the outcome of the election was not close, there could be no reason for the Mondale camp to regret having taken whatever electoral risks may have been associated with the innovative step of placing a woman on the ticket."[45] Gallup polls confirmed that more than 60 percent were either positive or neutral regarding a woman candidate.[46]

Given the somewhat positive view of the loss of the first presidential ticket to contain a woman, the gender issues and commentary Elizabeth Dole faced sixteen years hence were striking. She ran a poor campaign and did appear overrehearsed. She did have trouble filling key posts within her organization and distinguishing herself on the issues. Yet underlying all the problems, the gender issue was there. The increase of gender coverage for Dole after the Ferraro effort and the increased presence of women in the House and Senate suggests that the bias is rooted in societal conceptions of leadership that are played out within the media.

Vice presidential candidates can hurt a drive for the presidency but only offer limited help (e.g., Spiro Agnew and Dan Quayle). The two basic models of voting behavior (prospective and retrospective) suggest that voters' decisions usually center on the presidential candidate and not on the running mate. In contrast, Elizabeth Dole was obviously the focal point of her own campaign. As the focal point, Dole's candidacy forced an implicit discussion of the definition of leadership. Kim Fridkin Kahn argues that perceived stereotypes of the capabilities and liabilities of women continue to influence coverage. The stereotypes translate into these views of issues: male candidates handle foreign policy, trade, and defense issues better, whereas women are portrayed as better on health care, day care, poverty, and education.[47] Significantly, Kahn claims that "when the salient issues and traits of the campaign complement a woman candidate's stereotypical strengths, women will receive an advantage."[48] The coverage of Dole's campaign underscores that, unlike state, local, and even congressional positions, the presidency remains defined by the press in masculine terms in the absence of an overriding issue that advantages women. Thus, to achieve "Madam President," a candidate must either redefine leadership, redefine herself, or be helped by circumstances that trump current biases.

12

Is the United States Ready for a Woman President? Is the Pope Protestant?

Carole Kennedy

Roughly twenty women have declared themselves candidates for the U.S. presidency throughout its history. The first was Victoria Woodhull, who ran in 1872. Other notable candidates include Senator Margaret Chase Smith (R-1964) and Representative Shirley Chisholm (D-1972). In 1984, Geraldine Ferraro became the first and only woman vice presidential candidate on a major party ticket. Elizabeth Dole's tepid attempt to capture the Republican Party nomination for president in 1999 reintroduced the question to a whole new generation of Americans and inspired debate regarding the readiness of the American public to finally, seriously consider a woman president.

Supporters of the notion that the United States was really ready this time pointed to public opinion polls that showed a remarkable 92 percent of Americans indicated that they would be willing to vote for a qualified woman for the highest office in the land.[1] What tended to be downplayed in most of these popular analyses was the truly mixed picture that public opinion polling reveals about American attitudes toward women in general and the viability of a woman candidate for the presidency in particular. In addition, although Dole faced criticism that she had no prior elective experience, there was scant attention paid to the dearth of women in other executive positions of power in the United States. A total of nineteen women have served as governors of states, and as of 2002 there were currently five elected women state executives.[2] There are more women in the U.S. Senate now than there have ever been, and yet women represented a mere 13 percent of that august body in 2002. Finally, almost all popular analyses of U.S. readiness to elect a woman president neglect to take into account scholarly research

131

that has identified more subtle attitudinal barriers to a woman president, as well as persistent structural features of American society that hamper the possibilities for women to assume real political power.[3]

In this chapter, I examine contemporary public opinion polling data to construct a fuller and richer picture of the contemporary electorate and its attitudes toward women in general and women running for president in particular. Then I discuss various empirical studies regarding the persisting gender stereotypes that may hinder women's successful pursuit of executive office. Finally, I review the failed Dole presidential bid in 1999 to provide further support to the idea that we have a long way to go indeed before the United States is truly ready for a Madam President.

Public Opinion

Many popular and scholarly works on the topic suggest that public opinion polling reveals a steady climb in the number of Americans willing to vote for a woman for president.[4] As far back as 1937, the Gallup poll repeatedly asked Americans the following question: "If your party nominated a woman for president, would you vote for her if she were qualified for the job?" Whereas only 33 percent of respondents in 1937 answered in the affirmative, that proportion has increased fairly steadily over the years. The most recent Gallup poll that included this question (1999) reveals that fully 92 percent of Americans are willing to vote for a qualified woman for president. Let us take this statistic at its face value and consider its implications.

Seven percent of Americans polled in 1999 have indicated that they would not vote for a qualified woman for president (1 percent report having no opinion). Losing 7 percent of the presidential vote presents something of a problem for an otherwise qualified presidential candidate. Historically, the popular vote in presidential elections has varied among the two major party candidates from a very large difference of 24 percent in the 1972 election to the infinitesimal 0.2 percent in the 1960 and 1976 elections (see Table 12.1). If any given woman candidate starts out with a seven-point deficit in the popular vote, she will be hard-pressed to overcome that deficit in a close presidential election. That is especially important in the coming decade because the electorate is very closely split along partisan and ideological lines.[5] Although critics will no doubt find assessment pessimistic—seeing the glass as 7 percent empty instead of 92 percent full—the fact that six out of the past thirteen presidential elections were decided by a margin below 7 percent suggests that the figure is far from insignificant.

Table 12.1 Percentage of the Popular Vote for Major Party Candidates for the Presidency, 1952–2000

Year	Democratic Candidate	Republican Candidate	Difference
1952	44.6	55.4	10.8
1956	42.2	57.8	15.6
1960	50.1	49.9	0.2
1964	61.3	38.7	22.6
1968	43.0	43.4	0.4
1972	38.0	62.0	24.0
1976	50.0	48.0	0.2
1980	41.0	51.0	10.0
1984	41.0	59.0	18.0
1988	46.0	54.0	8.0
1992	44.0	37.0	7.0
1996	50.0	41.0	9.0
2000[a]	48.4	47.9	0.5

Source: Nelson Polsby and Aaron Wildavsky. *Presidential Elections: Strategies and Structures of American Politics.* 10th ed. New York: Chatham House, 2000.
Note: a. Associated Press. December 19, 2000, "Voter Turnout Was 2.2% Higher Than It Was in 1996, Figures Show."

The Gallup poll question is but one of several attempts by pollsters and political scientists to effectively measure the amount of discrimination likely to be encountered when a woman candidate actually confronts the U.S. electorate. Other polls paint a much gloomier picture. In a February 23, 2001, press release, the White House Project—a nonprofit, nonpartisan organization dedicated to electing a woman president by 2008—reported the findings from its Internet poll, in which 26,000 women and 20,000 men responded to a question assessing their likelihood of voting for a female president.[6] Fifty-nine percent of respondents indicated that they were very willing to vote for a woman president, another 26 percent indicated that they were somewhat willing to vote for a woman president, and 15 percent of respondents stated that they would not be willing to vote for a woman.[7] Within the same press release, the president of the White House Project, Marie C. Wilson, stated: "The message of our survey is clear: Americans, regardless of their party or gender, are ready and willing to vote for a woman president." This analysis of the poll results are not surprising, given the agenda of the pollsters. However, as Table 12.1 shows, a fifteen-point deficit would have cost a woman candidate the presidency in nine out of the past thirteen presidential elections.

Survey evidence is also mixed depending upon the question wording. A survey of several such assessments of public opinion over the past twenty-five years reveals an even greater concern. Although most Americans report that they personally would be willing to vote for a

woman president, other polls show that a majority of Americans still believe that the country is not ready to elect a woman president. I refer to
this phenomenon as the "third person effect."[8] This discrepancy also
points out the difficulty of accurately gauging public opinion on issues
in which there is a "socially desirable response" that might lead individuals to provide the socially acceptable response rather than their true
predilections.[9] An illustrative example of how the socially desirable response phenomenon can affect elections was revealed in the 1982 California gubernatorial race. Exit polls suggested that Democratic candidate Tom Bradley (an African American) had beaten his Republican
opponent, George Deukmejian. Yet, when the ballots were finally
counted, Deukmejian emerged victorious by a slim margin of 53,515
votes, out of nearly 7.5 million votes cast. A Field poll conducted on
election day found that 4 percent of those polled indicated they had supported Deukmejian because they did not wish to vote for a black person.[10] Scholarly assessments of the 1982 election disagree as to whether
racial prejudice played a decisive role in the outcome.[11] However, the
discrepancy between exit polls conducted on the day of the election and
the final outcome suggest that many who reported having voted for Tom
Bradley did not.

As Table 12.2 reveals, there is a discrepancy in results, depending
upon how the question regarding voting for a woman president is
phrased. The traditional Gallup poll measure has shown an increasing
number of respondents over time who indicate that they would be willing to vote for a qualified woman of their party for president. Although
73 percent of respondents said they would be willing to do so in 1975,
fully 92 percent responded in the affirmative in 1999. However, a side-
by-side comparison of these responses to differently worded questions
on the same subject illustrates the third-person effect. In 1984, for example, while the Gallup poll showed that 78 percent of respondents indicated that they would vote for a woman for president, an NBC News
Poll conducted by Harris and Associates found that only 17 percent of
respondents believed that the voters of this country were ready to elect
a woman president. A similar discrepancy was evident in 1999, when
the Gallup poll showed that 92 percent of respondents would vote for a
woman for president, whereas a CBS News Poll conducted by Harris
and Associates found that only 48 percent of respondents believed that
the United States was ready to elect a woman president.

Table 12.3 compares the Gallup poll question to the General Social
Survey (GSS), another barometer of political attitudes toward women in
politics that has been included in annual Gallup polls over time. The
only direct comparison by year occurred in 1975, when 23 percent of

Table 12.2 Polling Results for Gallup Poll Questions as Opposed to Other Opinion Poll Questions, 1975–1999

Gallup Poll Question				Other Opinion Poll Questions[a]		
If your party nominated a woman for president, would you vote for her if she were qualified for the job?				Do you think the voters of this country are ready to elect a woman president, or don't you think so?		
Year	Yes	No	No opinion	Yes	No	Not sure/No answer
1975	73%	23%	4%	N/A		
1982	N/A			41%	54%	5%
1983	80%	16%	4%	N/A		
1984	78%	17%	5%	17%	80%	3%
1987	82%	12%	6%	N/A		
1996	N/A			40%	53%	7%
1999	92%	7%	1%	48%	45%	7%

Note: a. The questions differed slightly by year.
1982 NBC News/AP Poll: "Do you think the American people would be willing to elect a woman as President of the United States within the next ten years?" N=1,597. Telephone poll, June 1982.
1984 NBC News Poll: "Do you think the voters of this country are ready to elect a woman President, or don't you think so?" N=1,600. Telephone poll based on responses by likely voters, June 1984.
1996 CBS News Poll: "Do you think America is ready to elect a woman president, or not?" N=1,077. Telephone poll, October 1996.
1999 CBS News Poll: "Do you think America is ready to elect a woman president, or not?" N=1,558. Telephone survey, December 1999.
N/A: no data were available on this question in this year.
Sources: Gallup Poll, Wilmington, DE: Scholarly Resources, 1999; Roper Center for Public Opinion Research, archived in Lexis-Nexis.

respondents to the Gallup poll said that they were not willing to vote for a woman for president, and 35 percent of respondents to the GSS poll indicated that "women should take care of running their homes and leave running the country up to men." Although a direct comparison in the 1990s is not possible, the 1996 GSS survey showed 16 percent of respondents agreeing that women should take care of running their homes and leave running the country up to men, whereas in 1999 the Gallup poll showed only 7 percent of respondents were willing to indicate that they would not vote for a qualified woman candidate of their party for president.

Finally, there are the findings from a 1991 survey commissioned by *Sports Illustrated* and conducted by Lieberman Research. Although at this point in U.S. political history, the most recent Gallup poll indicated that only 12 percent of Americans would not vote for a qualified woman of their own party for the presidency,[12] fully 29 percent of male respondents and 19 percent of female respondents reported that they would be

Table 12.3 Polling Results to Gallup Poll Questions as Opposed to General Social Survey Questions, 1975–1999

Gallup Poll Question				General Social Survey Question		
If your party nominated a woman for president, would you vote for her if she were qualified for the job?				Do you agree or disagree with this statement: Women should take care of running their homes and leave running the country up to men.		
Year	Yes	No	No opinion	Agree	Disagree	Not sure/No answer
1975	73%	23%	4%	35%	62%	3%
1983	80%	16%	4%	N/A		
1984	78%	17%	5%	N/A		
1986	N/A			23%	73%	4%
1987	82%	12%	6%	N/A		
1996	N/A			16%	80%	4%
1999	92%	7%	1%	N/A		

N/A: no data were available on this question in this year.

Sources: Gallup Poll, Wilmington, DE: Scholarly Resources, 1999; Mitchell, Susan, *American Attitudes: Who Thinks What About the Issues That Shape Our Lives,* Ithaca: New Strategist Publications, 1998; General Social Surveys, National Opinion Research Center, University of Chicago.

bothered by a woman president of the United States.[13] The only other situation that bothered respondents more was a woman fighting on the front lines (which bothered 35 percent of male respondents and 32 percent of female respondents). The conclusions that can be drawn from the variety of surveys and question wordings suggest that we must be cautious indeed about imputing reliability and validity to the Gallup poll numbers, when there is substantial evidence in other surveys that there is not nearly universal support for nor comfort among the American public for a woman president.

Gender Stereotypes

In addition to exploring the variety of public opinion measures that relate to the viability of a woman candidate for the presidency, it is helpful to examine persisting gender stereotypes that may impede the chances of success for a woman candidate for the presidency. Several scholarly studies have suggested that gender stereotyping of female candidates for political office is prevalent and can impede their success, especially for executive positions.[14] In general, as is discussed throughout this book, female candidates are stereotyped as *more* emotional, warm, and expressive and *less* tough, competent, and decisive than similarly situated male candidates. This attitude may prove to be a detriment to women seeking executive offices because there is a greater emphasis at the executive level (whether it be a state governor or the U.S. president) on instrumental rather than expressive traits.[15] Women candidates are also perceived to be better able to handle "women's issues" such as education and health care, whereas male candidates are perceived to be better able to handle foreign affairs and the economy.[16] This sexual division of competence has important consequences for women candidates seeking the presidency, because of the commander in chief responsibilities that attend to the role.

A poll commissioned by Deloitte and Touche and conducted by Roper Starch Worldwide revealed that American voters have prejudicial notions regarding the ability of a woman candidate to be tough.[17] Their study showed that voters rank the following characteristics as most important in a president: (1) ability to lead in a crisis, (2) ability to make tough decisions, (3) trustworthiness, and (4) honesty. Fifty-one percent of respondents reported that a man would do a better job than a woman with regard to the ability to lead in a crisis. Thirty-eight percent of respondents reported that a man would be better able than a woman to make tough decisions. Women were favored by the electorate over men on trustworthiness and honesty.

Women candidates are often stereotyped as less competent than their male counterparts[18] and this tendency is often reinforced by media coverage of women candidates that focus on their competence (or lack thereof) rather than their issue positions.[19] Geraldine Ferraro was asked by reporters covering the 1984 presidential campaign about her hairstyle and her recipes for baking pies. Political commentary on Elizabeth Dole's bid in 1999 was such that her statements on the Kosovo situation were being overshadowed by her new haircut.[20] Is it any wonder that women candidates are viewed as less credible than their male counterparts, given the biases apparent in press coverage and the lingering stereotypes that inform that coverage?

In a 1999 survey conducted by Fannie Mae Personal Finances Survey, respondents were asked to consider some common gender stereotypes and assess how much credence those stereotypes had in contemporary society (see Table 12.4). The responses indicate a recognition of some of the structural barriers that are impeding the progress of women in politics in general and the likelihood of a woman president in particular. Note that a majority of respondents still subscribe to the notion that women are the primary caregivers for children as well as being primarily responsible for family social obligations. These responses show that not much has changed since Arlie Hochschild penned the well-known book, *The Second Shift: Working Parents and the Revolution at Home,* in

Table 12.4 Excerpts from the Fannie Mae Personal Finances Survey, August 23, 1999

"I'm going to read you a list of stereotypical behaviors of men and women, and I would like you to tell me whether you think the stereotype is still in place, whether it is starting to change, or whether it has been broken in the past five years. . . ."

	In place	Changing	Not sure	Broken
Whether or not they work outside of the home, women primarily are responsible for household chores such as cooking, shopping, and cleaning.	40%	41%	17%	2%
Men are the principal breadwinners in the family.	21%	45%	32%	2%
Men primarily are responsible for making "big ticket" purchases, such as cars and expensive appliances.	25%	40%	32%	3%
Whether or not they work outside of the home, women are the primary caregivers for children.	51%	33%	12%	4%
Men are responsible for family finances.	26%	44%	26%	4%
Women are responsible for family social obligations, such as buying gifts and sending cards, as well as making social plans.	66%	24%	7%	3%

Source: Peter D. Hart Research Associates, N=1015 women and 289 men. Results are weighted to be representative of the national adult population.

1989. Hochschild documented the fact that women tend to continue to maintain responsibility for child rearing and family obligations, even when they work as many hours per week, or more, than their male spouses. This double standard is especially evident in the media coverage of Massachusetts governor, Jane Swift.[21] Governor Swift faced a barrage of criticism from both the left and the right for her decision to assume the governorship while continuing to work from home after the birth of her twins.[22]

The Double Bind Versus the Backlash

Kathleen Hall Jamieson has contributed a succinct categorization of persistent gender stereotyping of women pursuing leadership positions in American society (see Chapter 9 for a similar discussion). Her book, *Beyond the Double Bind: Women and Leadership,* describes a double bind as

> a rhetorical construct that posits two and only two alternatives, one or both penalizing the person being offered them. In the history of humans, such choices have been constructed to deny women access to power and, where individuals manage to slip past their constraints, to undermine

their exercise of whatever power they achieve. The strategy defines something "fundamental" to women as incompatible with something the woman seeks—be it education, the ballot, or access to the workplace.[23]

Jamieson describes five double binds that result from centuries of beliefs surrounding theology, biology, and law and the ways in which these beliefs and values have been constructed to the detriment of women's ambition to rise above them. In doing so, she offers an important tool for assessing barriers faced by women, including those in public life.

- Women can exercise their wombs or their brains but not both.
- Women who speak out are immodest and will be shamed, whereas women who are silent will be ignored or dismissed.
- Women are subordinate, whether they claim to be different from men or the same.
- Women who are considered feminine will be judged incompetent, and women who are competent will be judged unfeminine.
- As men age, they gain wisdom and power; as women age, they wrinkle and become superfluous.

Jamieson also takes great pains to illustrate that women are making sure and steady progress against these double binds and to distinguish her analysis from that of Susan Faludi in *Backlash: The Undeclared War Against American Women* (1991). Faludi, Jamieson claims, offers a much more pessimistic view of the progress of women in the face of persistent inequality and stretches the truth in order to do so.[24] Faludi painstakingly documented the political and social resistance to the gains made by feminists in the 1960s and 1970s by politicians, reporters, and other arbiters of popular and political culture in the 1980s. She recognized and gave a name to the series of events that began with the (re)birth of the Christian Right, the Republican Party's repudiation of the Equal Rights Amendment and abortion rights, and the rush to judge the "feminist experiment" a failure. In identifying these events in the 1980s as a "backlash," Faludi was accused of excessive pessimism, a failure to double-check her "facts," and a failure to recognize areas in which there had been progress.[25]

In her gentle excoriation of Faludi (which had been preceded and subsequently joined by many feminists and antifeminists over the years), Jamieson suggests that subscribing to a theory in which progress toward equality is inevitably met by a backlash from the male power structure constructs women as victims: "Backlash invites women and their allies to give up."[26] I would like to suggest a sixth double bind that is instructive for disentangling the debate between Faludi and Jamieson and also illuminates one of the pitfalls of analyzing women in American politics.

- Women who recognize sexism and patriarchy are victims, and women who deny the existence of sexism and patriarchy are victorious.[27]

Clearly, the reality lies somewhere in between this sixth double bind. Scholars and activists must be willing to question the persistent structural and institutional biases against women, just as Faludi and Jamieson do in their well-documented and well-reasoned analyses of history and contemporary politics. We must accept the variety of ways in which contemporary women can do battle with centuries-old superstitions and traditions. But we should not and cannot condemn theorists or practitioners who identify persistent sexist and patriarchal structures as contributing to the perpetuation of women's status as victims per se. The act of naming structural and institutional biases that inhibit the integration of women into positions of power may not necessarily equate to embracing women's status as "victims." Critics of this so-called victim feminism often fall into the second category of the double bind: insisting that there are no structural and institutional biases that cannot be overcome by individual women. Hence, any woman who fails to succeed in her pursuit of personal or political power is individually deficient, rather than constrained by institutional and societal norms and expectations. In particular, analysts of women in American politics cannot blithely ignore the resurgence of the Christian Right and its "submissive womanhood" project, along with the impact that this movement has on the prospects for women achieving political power. For example, a recent poll conducted by Princeton Research Associates on behalf of the Center for Gender Equality found that 36 percent of women respondents agreed with the statement, "Wives should submit graciously to their husbands' leadership."[28] How can one reconcile such a belief with an acceptance that a woman could possibly lead this country, if she must inevitably be led by her husband? Where does this leave Governor Swift? Where did this leave Elizabeth Dole?

A Critical Analysis of
Elizabeth Dole's 2000 Campaign

Events surrounding Elizabeth Dole's lackluster campaign for the presidency in 1999 can be interpreted as suggesting the United States is not ready for a woman president. Various compelling explanations have been given for the brevity of her foray into the presidential race (she announced in March and was through in October), including her lack of elective office experience, her lack of a compelling raison d'être other than her sex, and even the possibility that she was really just angling for the vice presidential slot. Yet a brief analysis of those months provides evidence that Elizabeth Dole was also caught in the double bind and attracted some backlash as well.

In March 1999, Elizabeth Dole announced the formation of an exploratory committee for a race for the presidency a mere three days after George W. Bush did the same.[29] It was only a matter of days before double bind number 4 was presented to the public. In the April 5 issue of the conservative publication *National Review,* a parody of her announcement was presented in the form of a fictional letter from Elizabeth Dole to Al Gore and read as follows:

> Hey Lover! Well, I made the big announcement—I wore the red—well, not red exactly, darker, my "Blood Drive" suit—and a white blouse which I accessorized simply. Had peach gels in all the lights. Did great! I had a nice segment on This Week with Cokie (Has she had work done? Her eyes look great! Of course, her neck is her neck—what can you do? You have kids, you spend all that time on NPR with those sad-sack lesbians, you forget how to take care of yourself. Still, I'd kill for her eyes.)

And it deteriorated fairly rapidly from there. The *New York Times* reported that a New Hampshire Republican supporter reacted to her candidacy by saying, "I don't believe a woman ought be in that particular place of leadership—the *Bible* teaches us that a woman should not have authority over men."[30] In other words, a woman's possession of a uterus precludes her possession of the wits to lead, or double bind number 1.

Political observer Bob Fertik predicted in January 1999 that Elizabeth Dole would be just as likely to convert her popularity into money, organization, and votes in much the same way that George W. Bush would: by inheriting fund-raising and organizational apparatus from their more politically experienced relatives.[31] Unfortunately for Elizabeth Dole, her politically experienced spouse turned out to be less than supportive, when in an interview in May with the *New York Times,* he mentioned that he wanted to contribute money to the campaign of Senator John McCain, his wife's rival for the Republican Party nomination.[32] In addition, Bob Dole made other comments that were disparaging about his wife's competence for the job.[33] This was at a time when Elizabeth Dole was running second in public opinion polls only to George W. Bush and outpolling Al Gore by several points. But Elizabeth

Dole slogged on, articulating centrist positions on abortion and gun control and traditionally hawkish views of foreign policy.

In June, political scientist John J. Pitney, Jr., compared Dole to "Jimmy Carter with helmet hair" and recalled that one of her former aides had told *Fortune* magazine, "She's progressive at the core."[34] Not so, said the left-wing *Nation* in an article entitled, "Why Not Elizabeth Dole," which castigated Dole for being "no champion of women's issues [and] assertively anti-abortion except in cases of rape, incest or the endangered life of the mother."[35] In July, the *National Review* ran an article suggesting that Dole would be an excellent vice presidential candidate—for Al Gore![36] The July issue of *Progressive* saw things differently, reporting, "On many issues she's right in line with the Christian Coalition."[37] Consistent with research on the subject, many observers believed that simply by virtue of her sex, Elizabeth Dole must be a liberal. However, she was criticized by liberals who actually paid attention to some of her issue positions. Certainly, her campaign has to own up to some of the blame for failing to project a consistent image, but the flak that she received from the right and the left and especially the tone of coverage on the right suggests that women seeking leadership positions face challenges to their credibility by virtue of their sex.

And the money just never seemed to materialize for Elizabeth Dole, lending credence to the catch-22, "You need money to be credible, but you have to be credible to obtain money."[38] In a *Fortune* magazine article entitled "Money, Money, Everywhere," only two of the top 139 national political fund-raisers were supporting Dole's candidacy.[39] Even worse was a report in the same article that two members of her finance committee had actually contributed money to George W. Bush.

In October, Elizabeth Dole withdrew from the race, citing a lack of money. "It's kind of a catch-22," she said of the money driving the presidential election.[40] Dole had raised $5 million, compared to George W. Bush's $56 million. Dole endorsed George W. Bush in January 2000, with an "eye on the vice-presidency," but was long gone from the scene and conspicuously absent from the short lists for cabinet positions drawn up by Richard Cheney and George W. Bush later in the year.[41]

Conclusion

In spite of the hype that hailed Elizabeth Dole as "the first credible woman candidate for president in history"[42] and public opinion polls that showed that she was the third most popular person in the United States in 1998 (behind Bill and Hillary Clinton),[43] Dole was unable to translate these qualities into the money necessary to continue her campaign. Analysts may disagree about the root causes of that failure, but an examination of media coverage of her campaign suggests that she battled with double binds and backlash that may have contributed to the lack of monetary support she was able to attract. Specifically, she was trivialized on account of her sex by the conservative press and attacked on feminist issues by the liberal press. The existence of public opinion polls showing that voters will not discriminate against a woman candidate did little to bolster her prospects for a successful bid for the presidency.

As scholars continue to seek an understanding of the challenges facing women in their attempts at achieving political power in the United States, there will continue to be disagreements about the relative merits of identifying and examining institutional and structural barriers to that progress. Hopefully, the sixth double bind presented herein will prove a useful heuristic device to inform that debate.

13

Gender, Race, and the Oval Office

Ann Gordon and Jerry Miller

Shirley Chisholm, the first African American woman elected to Congress, set her sights on the White House in 1972. At the Democratic National Convention, Chisholm received 152 votes. Though George McGovern captured the nomination, Chisholm's candidacy was a significant achievement. Her campaign was constantly beset by the question of her viability. She recalls that everywhere she went on the campaign trail she was asked "But Mrs. Chisholm—are you a *serious* candidate?"[1] The question of viability is still central for a woman who runs for president. In a recent Gallup poll, 92 percent of Americans said they would vote for a woman president if she were their party's nominee and 95 percent said they would support a black candidate. These numbers have steadily risen over the years (see Table 13.1). However, as Dianne Bystrom reports in Chapter 8, other surveys have demonstrated a greater reluctance to vote for a woman president. Voters have significant concerns about a woman's ability to deal with the economy and law and order among other issues. Support continues to diminish if the hypothetical woman is pregnant or has young children.

Scholars have identified stereotypes as an important factor in the reluctance of many Americans to support a woman or minority candidate for elective office. Some scholars have argued that gender has become less salient for women in congressional campaigns, but the same cannot be said for women seeking governorships, a seat in the U.S. Senate, or the presidency.[2] Voters do differentiate between male and female candidates for a variety of offices who appear identically qualified.[3] Therefore, in this chapter we seek to determine how stereotypes held by voters influence their assessment about women and men who seek the presidency or vice presidency. We use an experimental design to explore differing

145

Table 13.1 Percentage Who Would Consider Voting for a Presidential Candidate with Certain Characteristics (by year)

	1958	1967	1978	1987	1999
Women	54	57	76	82	92
African American	37	53	77	79	95
Jewish	62	82	88	89	92
Catholic	70	90	91	—	94
Atheist	18	—	40	44	49
Gay/Lesbian	—	—	26	—	59

Source: Gallup Polling data, summarized at gallup.com/poll/releases/pr990329.asp.

perceptions of candidate viability. Although viability assessments do not necessarily translate into votes, being perceived as electable is an important step toward success.

Stereotypes

Stereotypes represent significant obstacles for a woman's candidacy for president. The development of stereotypical beliefs about race and gender are inextricably linked to cultural histories, fostered on an individual basis during childhood by influential adults, and perpetuated by the social roles assigned in popular media.[4] The cognitive process of stereotyping "begins with a perceptual differentiation between groups of persons."[5] Differentiation does not necessarily create a stereotype, but the association of certain attributes with those persons does, resulting in categorization through which the individual is seen only as a member of a social group.

Stereotypical notions of men and women are described by Sandra Bem's Sex Role Inventory (BSRI). The BSRI has been used extensively to identify the similarities and differences in human action beyond simple male and female behavior.[6] By identifying behaviors as masculine, feminine, undifferentiated (including both low masculine and feminine characteristics), or androgynous (including both high masculine and feminine characteristics), research has focused our attention on one of the most vital parts of the socialization process—what it means to be male and female. Feminine traits include being gentle, tender, understanding, warm, sensitive to the needs of others, compassionate, sincere, helpful, eager to soothe hurt feelings, and friendly. Masculine traits suggest that men act as leaders because they have leadership qualities; are dominant, aggressive, willing to take a stand, forceful, assertive, competitive, and independent; and have strong personalities. These are the kind of characteristics used to stereotype a group.

When stereotyping occurs, people are restricted to the social roles that are deemed consistent with certain characteristics. These stereotypical beliefs dictate acceptable actions by members of the defined groups and result in subtypes. Men can be athletes, businessmen, and macho, whereas women can be mothers *or* career women. The result of such stereotypes can be both helpful and hurtful for a woman's chances of electoral success. For example, Senator Patty Murray was described as a "mom in tennis shoes" when running for election in Washington. Although Senator Murray's mom-in-tennis-shoes status was not one she personally supported and one that drew its fair share of criticism from others, it did create a positive image. In the September 4, 1992, issue of the *Seattle Times*, Murray is quoted as saying, "There is a voice missing in the United States Senate. It is the voice of families and working people in our state."[7]

However, Massachusetts governor Jane Swift was criticized for running for the office of lieutenant governor while pregnant, suggesting that a new mother could not meet the demands of public office and that it would be impossible for her to care both for her infant child and the needs of the state. Murray and Swift were similar in that both had to address traditional stereotypical beliefs, but the more refined stereotypes held by voters based on the respective subtypes of these two female candidates resulted in vastly different treatments by the media and general public. For many, it was unacceptable for a woman to campaign for office while pregnant. The *Boston Herald* reported on November 13, 1998: "When Jane Swift was elected lieutenant governor last week, the first question many people asked was not 'What are her plans for governing?' but 'What are her plans for day care?'"[8] This stereotypical response is not uncommon when attempting to explain the successes of men and women running for political office. Susan Mezy concluded that women were asked about their familial responsibilities more often than their male counterparts.[9] Moreover, a woman's viability as a political candidate is hindered because she is forced to delay entry into the political arena until after marriage and children. These delays have obvious negative consequences when considering any female politician as a contender for the Oval Office.

Research on gender stereotypes has identified two distinct expectations voters hold for female candidates—their personal characteristics and their presumed competence in dealing with particular issues. The characteristics that define women include honesty and compassion, whereas men are perceived as tough and knowledgeable. Furthermore, voters expect that men are more competent when dealing with economic issues and foreign policy, whereas women's expertise is believed to be in the areas of social issues, such as education or health policy.[10] These expectations influence the way the press covers candidates and the way voters evaluate them.

Political issues and candidate image, although sometimes studied as separate entities, interact with one another in their overall influence on voters' perceptions of candidate viability. For example, Leonie Huddy and Nayda Terkilden found that masculine traits were associated with greater assumed issue competencies on a variety of issues.[11] Voters infer a candidate's ability to deal with certain issues based on stereotypical perceptions of the candidate's personality traits. Similarly, a recent survey revealed that stereotypes held about women led respondents to evaluate women as less qualified to serve as president, less able to lead during national crises, and less able to make difficult decisions.[12] These findings suggest that female candidates must not merely address political issues important to their constituents but must do so while overcoming the traditional stereotypes that a majority of Americans hold about them—51 percent of those polled by Deloitte and Touche answered that a man could to a better job serving as president.[13] This survey evidence is further bolstered by experimental data that demonstrate that gender stereotypes are an essential component in assessments of a woman candidate's viability.[14] Therefore, gender stereotypes may prove harmful when they run counter to expectations for presidential candidates.

The gendered stereotypical character judgments held by voters may conflict with those maintained about presidential leadership. Character traits often associated with the presidency include competence, leadership, integrity, and empathy.[15] Of these four characteristics, empathy is associated with feminine traits and leadership is associated with masculine traits. When the judgments about presidential traits conflict with those held about gender, voters may express their preference for masculine characteristics at higher levels of office.[16] Furthermore, the responsibilities associated with the presidency reveal a gender bias as well because voters revere "masculine" presidential duties, such as being commander in chief, more than "feminine" presidential duties, such as promoting civil rights.[17]

Although there are preferences for certain masculine traits, there is some evidence that the gender gap among voters may be beneficial for women running for political office. Women have been more likely to support a female candidate than men in congressional races, and the presence of a female candidate may increase women's psychological involvement in the electoral process.[18] Although women are by no means a unified block, the 1996 election resulted in a gender gap that was significant enough to provide the margin of victory for Bill Clinton.[19]

Racial Stereotypes

The nature and pervasiveness of racial stereotypes have received a great deal of attention. Scholars have found that racial stereotypes are revealed when discussing political issues and evaluating candidate traits. Robert Entman found in one experiment that white subjects who thought blacks had a poor work ethic were also more likely to conclude that a hypothetical welfare mother would have more children to get a bigger welfare check.[20] Other issues that have become associated with racial stereotypes include criminal activity and affirmative action.[21] In addition, blacks are characterized as too liberal.[22] General stereotypes include the belief by a sizable number of white voters that most blacks are "lazy . . . not determined to succeed . . . aggressive, and . . . lacking in discipline."[23] Although these beliefs are not held by a majority of whites, the persistence of these stereotypes is likely to have an impact on candidate assessments, though the evidence is mixed.

For example, one study examined the 1996 congressional elections, in which three minority incumbents lost their special districts because of Supreme Court decisions declaring the majority-minority practice of identifying congressional districts unconstitutional. Despite the redistricting, Sanford Bishop and Cynthia McKinney of Georgia and Corrine Brown of Florida all won their reelection campaigns in the newly drawn districts but not without enduring a controversial campaign that included divisive rhetoric from both the civil rights community and the general public at large. Stephen Voss and David Lublin studied these campaigns to identify the extent of bias against black candidates.[24] Voss and Lublin conclude that in these cases, no evidence supports white discrimination against black candidates. Voss and Lublin go on to argue that the 1996 outcome may be the result of a Republican realignment in the white South that resulted in a stronger African American representation in the Democratic primaries.[25] Therefore, race was overshadowed by party affiliation in this particular study.

Although much of the discussion of racial conflict has focused attention on relations between whites and blacks, Latino populations may be subject to more overt racism.[26] Certain stereotypical assumptions persist that could hinder a Latino candidate's political viability as well: "the popular perception is that all Hispanics speak Spanish. Yet studies have shown that not all Latinos in the United States are Spanish-dominant. In fact, increasingly, a significant number among the second and later generations are English-dominant, and there are some, although relatively few, who do not speak Spanish at all."[27] Stereotypical groupings identify people only by their social group and a monolithic one at that. This perception is flawed because Latinos do

not all share the same religious, cultural, social, national, or historical backgrounds.

Rodolfo de la Garza, Angelo Falcon, and Chris Garcia draw attention to the rhetoric surrounding the values of Latinos. They found that
Mexican Americans and Anglos exhibit the same levels of support for
American values, such as individualism. In addition, Mexican Americans
showed higher levels of patriotism than Anglos. Nevertheless, with data
from a 1990 National Opinion Research Center survey, de la Garza, Falcon, and Garcia found that Hispanics were ranked last or next to last on
all six survey items comparing Jews, blacks, Asians, Hispanics, southern
whites, and whites on issues such as welfare and patriotism.[28]

Methods

To investigate the willingness of voters to support women, black, and
Latino candidates, for president or vice president, we used an experimental design. The subjects, 878 undergraduate students at Ohio University, were asked to read a newspaper article that discussed a member of Congress. The member of Congress was portrayed as a likely
candidate for the White House in 2004. The experiment varied with regard to whether the representative was male (John) or female (Julia);
white, African American, or Latino; and being discussed in terms of a
candidacy for the presidency or vice presidency of the United States.
The representative was described as a four-term member of Congress
who was concerned about issues such as taxes, education, health care,
international affairs, and the environment among others.

Subjects were randomly assigned to one of twelve groups (see
Table 13.2). The newspaper articles were identical in every way, save
for the experimental manipulations. After reading the article, participants were asked to answer a questionnaire in which they evaluated the
viability of the candidate, competence to handle a range of issues, personal qualities, and the likelihood of voting for the candidate. All subjects were debriefed at the conclusion of the study.

Analysis

All the candidates received similar evaluations on their competence to
deal with most issues, regardless of race or gender (see Table 13.3).
They were seen as equally able to handle the economy and jobs, education, health care, Social Security, and the environment. Among the domestic issues, only civil rights was the exception, with whites seen as

Table 13.2 Experimental Conditions

1. Male	White	President
2. Male	Black	President
3. Male	Latino	President
4. Female	White	President
5. Female	Black	President
6. Female	Latina	President
7. Male	White	VP
8. Male	Black	VP
9. Male	Latino	VP
10. Female	White	VP
11. Female	Black	VP
12. Female	Latina	VP

Table 13.3 Differences in Candidate Evaluations by Gender and Race of Candidate

	Women (all ethnic groups)	Latino	Black	White	All Candidates
Issue positions					
Economy	4.14	4.16	4.20	4.12	4.16
Environment	4.01	3.90	3.95	3.97	3.94
Foreign affairs	3.38	3.43	3.45	3.40	3.43
Social security	4.09	4.11	4.21	4.11	4.14
Military	3.11[a]	3.20	3.35	3.23	3.26
Education	4.60	4.53	4.60	4.50	4.55
Health care	4.78	4.83	4.82	4.72	4.79
Civil rights	4.25	4.21	4.44[b]	3.04[c]	4.20
Terrorism	3.26	3.29	3.40	3.22	3.30
Jobs	4.37	4.38	4.41	4.31	4.37
Personality traits					
Qualified	5.40	5.25[d]	5.44	5.39	5.36
Honest	5.26[e]	5.11	5.27[f]	5.04	5.14
Believable	5.11[g]	4.98	5.17	4.95	5.03
Sincere	5.23[h]	5.11	5.26[i]	4.95[j]	5.11
Strong	5.11[k]	4.87[l]	5.19[m]	4.95	5.00
Moral	5.40[n]	5.26	5.40[o]	5.18	5.28
Caring	5.53[p]	5.43	5.47	5.29	5.40
Decisive	5.15	4.98	5.18	5.07	5.08
Hardworking	5.73[q]	5.54	5.64	5.53	5.57

Note: Each value marked with a superscript is significantly different from the other values in the row, as tested by ANOVA. Entries are means, with a higher score representing a more positive evaluation. F-ratios are as follows: [a]$F(1,838) = 16.25$, $p < .01$; [b]$F(1,845) = 17.64$, $p < .01$; [c]$F(1,845) = 19.49$, $p < .001$; [d]$F(1,841) = 4.02$, $p < .05$; [e]$F(1,840) = 8.73$, $p < .01$; [f]$F(1,840) = 4.65$, $p < .05$; [g]$F(1,842) = 4.22$, $p < .05$; [h]$F(1,844) = 8.51$, $p < .01$; [i]$F(1,844) = 6.17$, $p < .05$; [j]$F(1,844) = 6.2$, $p < .05$; [k]$F(1,840) = 5.12$, $p < .05$; [l]$F(1,840) = 4.03$, $p < .05$; [m]$F(1,840) = 8.15$, $p < .01$; [n]$F(1,843) = 7.51$, $p < .01$; [o]$F(1,843) = 4.33$, $p < .05$; [p]$F(1,841) = 10.96$, $p < .01$; [q]$F(1,845) = 13.52$, $p < .01$

the least competent and blacks seen as the most competent. In addition, there were no statistically significant differences on international affairs in general or terrorism. However, subjects had a difficult time imagining a woman as commander in chief of the military.

As one female who describes herself as an independent and a moderate observed, "Especially in the wake of Sept. 11, the nation wants a male leader. Not many see the commander in chief as a woman" (Subject 9763). There were many more differences observed on personality traits attributed to the candidates. Consistent with gender stereotypes, women were seen as more honest, believable, sincere, and moral. They were also rated as stronger and more hardworking than their male counterparts. The African American candidates were evaluated as more honest, sincere, and moral as well, whereas whites ranked lowest on sincerity. Finally, Latino candidates were seen as weaker and less qualified than the other candidates.

Feeling thermometers were used to gauge overall reaction to the candidates. Subjects were asked to rate the candidates on a scale of one to 100, with one representing cold feelings, 100 representing warm feelings, and fifty being neither warm nor cold. Latino candidates were rated an average of three degrees cooler on the feeling thermometer, even when results were controlled for party and ideology (see Table 13.4). All candidates were rated an average of six degrees cooler on the feeling thermometer by Republicans, which was expected since the candidates in the stimulus were all Democrats. Likewise, conservatives gave the candidates a cooler rating as well. Although women and blacks received a bit warmer rating, these differences were not statistically significant.

Finally, the candidates were rated on their viability as contenders for the White House in 2004. As Table 13.5 indicates, despite being ranked similarly on the issues, there were distinct differences in evaluations of viability. The white male candidate was seen as viable by 84 percent of Democrats and 88.9 percent of Republicans.

Table 13.4 Candidate Feeling Thermometers

Candidate	B	Standard Error
Woman	1.72	1.25
Latino	−3.44[a]	1.52
Black	.322	1.54
Party	−6.38[a]	1.56
Ideology	−2.87[a]	.55
Constant	75.74[a]	2.16

Note: Entries are unstandardized regression coefficients and standard errors;
a. $p < .05$, n= 878.

Table 13.5 Projected Candidate Viability for President by Candidate Gender, Race, and Subject's Party Identification

	Subject's Party	
Candidate	Democrats	Republicans
White Male	84.0	88.9
Black Male	84.0	59.4
Latino Male	61.5	49.5
White Female	68.2	45.2
Black Female	40.0	47.6
Latina Female	40.7	25.9

Note: Percentages are subjects rating the candidate as "very" or "somewhat" viable (n= 878).

As one subject who describes himself as slightly conservative noted, "We're still a country that thinks white males are the only ones who can lead the country. . . . Sad, but true" (Subject 1215).

The African American male candidate received the same viability score as the white male candidate at 84 percent among Democrats, but that number dropped to 59.4 percent for Republicans. Many subjects cited Colin Powell in the answers: "Tradition is very hard to break. An exception [would be an] African American man. . . . Colin Powell could pull it off due to strong leadership and military ties" (Subject 9712). In contrast, African American women were seen as viable by 40 percent of Democrats and 47.6 percent of Republicans. Among Democrats, the next most viable candidate after black and white males was a white woman, with 68.2 percent ranking her as viable. Her rankings fell to 45.2 percent among Republicans.

Latino males did well among Democrats, with 61.5 percent rating them viable, though that is a distinctly lower score than either black or white males received. Latinas were rated as less viable than their male counterparts, with only 40.7 percent of Democrats believing that Julia Garcia would make a viable candidate for president. Her ratings were even lower among Republicans, with only 25.6 percent giving her a chance at the Oval Office. One female Democrat explained her rating by saying, "I think that there aren't too many Hispanics in government," though she added hopefully, "I think it will come in the future" (Subject 6512). Similarly, another female Democrat who describes herself as liberal said, "Unfortunately, there are still racial stigmas. African Americans are more visible politically. I think Latino women have a lot more liberating to do!" (Subject 6517). A male Republican blamed the media's portrayal of Latinos for their lower viability and pointed to "Cheech and Chong movies" and *Scarface* as examples (Subject 6505).

Several subjects mentioned the issue of citizenship and immigration. There was concern that the candidate might not be a "natural born U.S. citizen" (Subject 10861) or might have a "foreign accent . . . looks" (Subject 9775).

Subjects were more open to the idea of a woman or candidate of color as vice president. As a woman who describes herself as a conservative Republican observed, "Americans seem more willing to take more 'risks' with the Vice Presidency than for the Presidency" (Subject 1151). Similarly, a liberal female Democrat said, "I think before we have a woman President, we need a female V.P. to warm the public up to the idea of giving women so much power" (Subject 7556). Another subject, a conservative Republican, noted: "Presidential candidates usually look for a person to 'balance the ticket' so the viability [for a woman or minority] increases" (Subject 1121). Others explained that the number two position was not as critical and therefore was more accessible to women: "The U.S. would be willing to see a woman in less of a leadership role. . . . Americans do not view the Vice Presidency as large of a responsibility as the Presidency" (Subject 7554).

Discussion

Perceptions of candidate viability are influenced by political issues, personality traits, party, and, of course, race and gender. The question of whether a woman can be commander in chief persists. When Geraldine Ferraro was a guest on *Meet the Press* during the 1984 campaign, Marvin Kalb asked her, "Are you strong enough to push the button?"[29] Previous research found that women were ranked as less competent on a variety of issues, including military leadership, which is clearly problematic if one wants to be commander in chief. However, the present study reveals a hopeful sign about perceived issue competence in that no differences were noted in the perceived abilities of the male and female candidates being considered as contenders for the White House. This optimism should be qualified, however, because of the overwhelming evidence provided in the present volume that continues to demonstrate a bias against women running for the highest office in the land. In addition, the subjects were college students, who are generally more open to ideas of racial and gender equality. Finally, one cannot remove the study from the environment in which it was conducted. In the wake of the terrorist attacks on September 11, 2001, the issue of military may have been more salient on the minds of the subjects, potentially rendering other issues less important. At a time when the military becomes more important, such as during wartime, women may be at a disadvantage. At other times, when the public's attention is focused on domestic issues, women may be at an advantage. Still, the role of commander in chief is likely to remain of central importance in the evaluation of presidential candidates.

Another issue that proved significant was civil rights. Blacks were seen as more competent when addressing civil rights. Interestingly, although Latinos were viewed as slightly more competent than whites when addressing civil rights issues, they were not perceived to be as competent as blacks. Therefore, subjects in this study viewed civil rights as a black issue.

Equally important to perceived issue competence are voters' perceptions of candidate personality traits. In the present experiment, Julia was at an advantage because she was perceived as more honest, moral, and sincere. However, had Julia been Latina, she would have been seen as less qualified and weaker than the other candidates. The cumulative effects of gender and racial stereotypes are clearly visible in the assessment of overall candidate viability.

Both Democrats and Republicans ranked John as the most viable as a white male, but Democrats considered him to be just as viable as an African American candidate. Although Republicans viewed John as less viable as an African American candidate, they still saw him as more viable than any of the other candidates. When considering Julia's candidacy, she was seen as most viable as a white candidate among Democrats.

Because stereotypes are entrenched, it may be difficult to counteract their effects. As Mark Snyder contends, "Having adopted stereotyped ways of thinking about another person, people tend to notice and remember the ways in which that person seems to fit the stereotype, while resisting evidence that contradicts the stereotype."[30] However, Tali Mendelberg has demonstrated that Americans are committed to egalitarian ideals and that this commitment helps overcome racial prejudice. Thus, exposing racial and gender stereotypes helps to combat them.[31]

14

Profile:
Geraldine Ferraro, Media Coverage of History in the Making

Robert P. Watson and Ann Gordon

COURTESY OF THE GERALDINE FERRARO COLLECTION AT MARYMOUNT MANHATTAN COLLEGE

Born on August 26, 1935, in
   Newburgh, New York
B.A. in English from Marymount
   College in 1956
Law degree from Fordham
   University in 1960
Served in the 96th–98th
   Congresses (1979–1985)
Democratic Party vice presidential
   nominee in 1984

"Gerry," as she is known by family and friends, appears to have developed her trademark determination and resilience in childhood. The Ferraros experienced tragedy in the loss of two young children and the death of Gerry's father from a heart attack when she was only eight years old. Subsequently, the family businesses failed, and her widowed mother moved Gerry and her surviving brother to a low-income neighborhood in the South Bronx.

After graduating from college, Ferraro taught grade school while attending law school at night at Fordham University, graduating in 1960. That same year, she married John Zaccaro, a realtor and businessman. In 1974, she became the assistant district attorney for Queens, which helped launch her political career when, in 1978, she was elected to the U.S. House of Representatives from New York's 9th District. Her rise to prominence began immediately, when she was elected to serve as secretary of the Democratic Caucus in 1980 and again in 1982 and also gained a seat on the Steering and Policy Committee and Budget Committee. In 1984, she chaired the Democratic Platform Committee, becoming the first woman to do so.

The Vice Presidential Campaign

In 1984, as the Democratic Party's vice presidential nominee, Ferraro made history as the first woman on a major party's presidential ticket, but her selection also surprised the country. Although Ferraro was a noted and powerful member of Congress, she did not have national name recognition. The incumbent, Ronald Reagan, looked hard to beat, but he was not popular with many women. The selection of Ferraro was thought by Mondale and the Democratic Party to take advantage of the "gender gap," whereby women have been more likely to support Democrats and women.

During the campaign, Ferraro encountered both opposition and fascination as a woman running for the vice presidency. Her husband's tax returns and business were probed for irregularities and used to attack her. But she earned the admiration of many women's groups and was impressive in her debate with the Republican vice president, George Bush. Although Mondale and Ferraro managed to win 41 percent of the popular vote, they carried only Mondale's home state of Minnesota and the District of Columbia in the Republican landslide victory.

Surprisingly, women were more likely to vote for Reagan-Bush than Mondale-Ferraro (55 percent voted Republican), although they were less inclined to vote Republican than men (64 percent voted Republican). The gender gap was a mixed bag in the 1984 presidential election, with a gap in presidential voting of roughly 7–9 percent, regardless of the fact that most women voted Republican. Also, around the country, many Democrats and a few women were elected because they carried the majority of the women's vote. Still, Ferraro received unfair criticism. As she responded, "It is a sorry fact in this country that the defeat of one woman is often read as a judgment on all women."[1]

In some ways, her candidacy showed that the media, voters, and opposing party treated a female candidate differently than a male candidate. Ferraro's family became more of an issue, she was asked questions about her relationship with her father (Reagan and Bush were not asked these questions), and her support of abortion rights was made an issue by opponents of abortion to an extent not witnessed by male candidates who supported abortion rights. There were also issues that became apparent during her trailblazing campaign, like the lack of female agents in the Secret Service. It was a *first,* and no one knew exactly what was going to happen during the campaign. As Ferraro has stated, "The real test of my candidacy will come when the next woman runs for national office. Only then will we know if she, too, is going to be judged by a standard different from that used for her male opponents."[2] It is to be hoped that the next woman to campaign as part of a presidential ticket will find less attention paid to the style of her campaign and more attention paid to the issues of the campaign.

In her own words, Ferraro's historic campaign "meant that the sign on the door of the White House that said 'Men Only' was taken down."[3] Ferraro did not think that a woman would be elected soon after her vice presidential campaign, but she was optimistic that another woman would be on either the Democratic or Republican ticket in subsequent elections. Accordingly, she has expressed concern that it has not happened within the two decades of her bid.[4] She feels that the majority of people are beyond thinking only of a candidate's sex when casting a vote, although some still oppose electing women and others want to elect women to public office. To Ferraro, the biggest obstacle to women winning elected office is incumbency, given incumbent advantage at the polls and the fact that most incumbents are men.[5] Although she has devoted herself to championing women and has become an icon for many women, Ferraro has tempered her views regarding the prospect of women achieving political equality. For instance, she does not believe she will live to see women compose 50 percent of the U.S. Senate, lamenting, "never, never."[6]

Life After the Historic Campaign

Since her history-making campaign of 1984, Geraldine Ferraro has remained active and visible. In 1988, she served as a fellow at Harvard University's John F. Kennedy School of Government and was later appointed by President Bill Clinton to head the U.S. delegation to the United Nations Human Rights Convention in Switzerland. Ferraro also serves as copresident of G and L Strategies, a consulting firm, and provides media commentary on politics.

Ferraro ran unsuccessfully for the U.S. Senate in 1992 and 1998, the same year that she was diagnosed with multiple myeloma, an incurable form of blood cancer. Facing the disease as one might expect of her, she has shown great courage and determination. Known for being a very private individual, she chose to keep quiet about her health condition for over two years before announcing it publicly and testifying before Congress on myeloma in an effort to raise public awareness and support for research on the disease.

In 1994, she was inducted into the National Women's Hall of Fame in Seneca Falls, New York. Of the honor of being the first—and so far the only—woman on a presidential ticket of a major party: "Being the first was terrific, but being the only one? Not so terrific."[7] Ferraro rightfully remains a role model for women around the nation.

PART 4
GOVERNING

15

Presidential Leadership: Governance from a Woman's Perspective

Lori Cox Han

The date is January 20, 2005, and another presidential inauguration has arrived. Across the nation, Americans gather in front of their television sets to witness the ritual and tradition of seeing the newly elected president place left hand on the Bible, right hand in the air, and with the help of the chief justice of the U.S. Supreme Court, take the oath of office. But today, Americans will do more than just witness the start of yet another presidential administration, with the requisite inaugural address, parade, and endless parties and celebrations throughout the nation's capitol. Americans will also experience an important and historic first in this nation's politics. The final political glass ceiling has been broken— a woman has been elected president of the United States! And while the public and political pundits alike grapple with the soon-to-be-familiar term *Madam President,* it is clear that nothing about the office will ever be the same.

Or will it? What role does being a woman play in presidential leadership? Does the job of president, both defined and constrained by enumerated, implied, and inherent powers within Article II of the U.S. Constitution, change based on the sex of the occupant of the Oval Office? Would scholarship on the subject of presidential power and leadership, crafted and refined over the past several decades by political scientists, historians, and journalists, be suddenly rendered useless in its ability to explain the office because the new president is a woman? Although these questions may seem somewhat oversimplified, they are nonetheless timely and important. The likelihood of the above scenario, although optimistic, is not completely out of the realm of possibility, as women continue to make gains in the number of elected offices and other positions held within government at all levels. And although electing a woman president by the end of the first decade of the twenty-first century may still be a long shot, perhaps a more viable option would be the election of the first-ever woman vice president. Even so, the issues of presidential leadership and governance for a woman, particularly one who either inhabits the Oval Office or is a heartbeat away from the presidency, are essential to understand as the United States comes closer to the possibility.

The challenges that the first woman president may encounter in the White House are examined in this chapter. Relying on literature devoted to the U.S. presidency, particularly presidential leadership and the powers and limitations of the office, it is possible to predict if gender will present any unique problems for governing. In this discussion, I must assume that many of the challenges the first woman president will face to get elected have already been met during the presidential campaign. Therefore, it is instructive to point out that any new president, upon surviving the electoral process, inherits a new set of challenges upon entering office, and that presidential greatness, as it is defined by the public and scholars alike, is more often the exception than the rule.

Governance, Leadership, and the Presidency

The terms *governance* and *leadership* have separate and distinct definitions yet are inextricably intertwined, especially within the context of the U.S. presidency. Governance is "the process of implementing modern state power, of putting the program of those who govern into place."[1] Governance within a democracy implies a relationship between a political leader and citizens and between the leader and other government officials holding positions of power. Leadership has a variety of definitions, but in general terms, it is a process that involves influence, occurs in groups, and includes attention to goals.[2] The definition of leadership can also include "individual traits, leader behavior, patterns of interacting, role relationships, relations with followers, and follower perceptions." The job of the president, then, obviously encompasses both governance and leadership— occurring through "formal aspects of government and in a multitude of ways surrounding formal governing."[3]

Based mostly on the scholarship of political scientists, the definition of presidential leadership that emerged in 1960 was Richard Neustadt's view that modern presidential power equates the ability to bargain and persuade.[4] Since then, other important works have redefined, modified, and expanded the notion of presidential leadership to encompass various views of presidents and the presidency, including the president as a transformational leader as well as the state of the post-modern presidency.[5] Other important topics shaping the definition of presidential leadership have included changes in the political environment,[6] the institutionalization of leadership within the executive branch,[7] policymaking and the president's relationship with Congress,[8] and the public presidency and changes in White House communication strategies.[9]

Presidential candidates must exhibit both the knowledge and skills necessary for the job and should appear to be strong, assertive, and dominant (important presidential skills in times of crisis).[10] But once in office, presidents must remember that their job, by constitutional design, is one of both shared and limited powers. A strong paradox exists in presidential power in that Americans expect great things from their presidents, but "the resources at the disposal of the president are limited and the system in which a president operates can easily frustrate efforts at presidential leadership."[11] As such, presidents must maximize their opportunities to gain influence and achieve success with their policy agendas, in dealing with Congress, and certainly in the eyes of the American public in determining job approval.

Three essential factors help to determine the extent of successful presidential leadership: vision (the ability to articulate a clear vision and purpose that inspires the American people about the direction of both government policies and the nation as a whole), skill (the ability to take advantage of opportunity and circumstance through a good sense of timing, policy skills, and political savvy), and political timing (an overall sense of power and when to use it appropriately given the circumstances and political environment).[12] Other factors must also be considered if presidents are to maximize their leadership potential, including effectiveness as a public communicator, organizational capacity (staffing and leadership style within the White House), cognitive style (intellectual curiosity coupled with either attention to detail or abstract thinking skills), and emotional intelligence.[13]

Would the necessity of these leadership qualities differ for a woman president? By constructing three general (albeit not all inclusive) categories of important traits for successful presidential leadership—political experience (viability as a candidate, knowledge of government policies), political skill (the ability to work with Congress and other political actors, effective leadership of the party, and influence over the national agenda), and political communication (mastery of the bully pulpit, successful news management)—how a woman would fare in this job and the impact of gender on the presidency can be examined.

Political Experience:
Women as Viable Candidates

Aside from the constitutional requirements for the office of the presidency—being at least thirty-five years old, a fourteen-year U.S. resident, and a natural-born citizen—no other formal criteria exist for presidential candidates. However, several informal qualifications have limited the pool of potential candidates, including religion, race, and gender. Nearly all presidential and vice presidential candidates have been Protestant, white, and male. John F. Kennedy, a Catholic, remains the only non-Protestant to hold the office of the presidency. Geraldine Ferraro's nomination as the Democratic vice presidential candidate in 1984 and the first woman to run on a major party ticket, followed by Joseph Lieberman's nomination as the first Jewish vice presidential candidate in 2000, were two notable exceptions to the rule. The intense public interest in a possible presidential run by General Colin Powell in 1996, as well as Elizabeth Dole's brief foray into the 2000 Republican primaries, suggest that some progress has been made in how the American public views potential candidates for president and vice president.[14]

It is important to note that many of the issues surrounding presidential leadership and whether the candidate will succeed at the job are first addressed during the presidential campaign. The character, personality, and style of presidential candidates have become a mainstay in the evaluation process during both the primaries and the general election. The health and age of the candidate, as well as family ties and personal relationships (particularly marital status and fidelity) are also important characteristics in the public's mind.[15] Although party affiliation and policy preferences are still important factors among voters, the decline of partisan loyalty and the desire for party nominees to appeal to moderate, middle-of-the-road voters during the general election has placed more emphasis on the candidate as an individual. Certainly during the television age of politics and as political news reporting has become more cynical, sensationalized, and hypercritical, scrutinizing the character or style of a presidential candidate through the lens of the news media is common practice throughout the campaign.[16]

Given these qualifications, where do Americans find their presidential and vice presidential candidates? An "on-deck" circle exists of "at most forty individuals in any given presidential election year: governors, prominent U.S. senators, a few members of the House of Representatives, and a handful of recent governors or vice presidents who have successfully kept themselves in the news media."[17] During the invisible primary, which now lasts one year or longer prior to the first presidential primaries, the importance of name recognition among political elites and the reaction of the news media, as well as access to money and the ability to successfully raise funds, cannot be overstated. Also important is the time available to campaign and raise funds, which can give an important advantage to a candidate not currently holding office or perhaps a governor from a small state (Bill Clinton of Arkansas) or a state with a part-time legislature and constitutionally weak position of governor (George W. Bush of Texas).

In recent years, holding the office of the vice presidency or being a governor of a large state has elevated the public status of several presidential hopefuls. The Washington insider versus outsider phenomenon has also emerged; four of the last five presidents (Jimmy Carter, Ronald Reagan, Clinton, and George W. Bush) were previous state governors, and Kennedy was the last president elected directly from Congress, in 1960. Although many factors have contributed to this trend, the most prominent is the public fallout from the imperial presidencies of Lyndon Johnson and Richard Nixon. Vietnam, Watergate, and the increasing credibility gap between the public, the press, and government officials during the 1960s and 1970s drastically changed the political environment for presidential candidates. The image of "master politician" (political experience and substantive policy accomplishments), once necessary to run for the White House has given way to the image of the "Washington outsider," which requires strong speaking skills, an emphasis on anti-Washington rhetoric, and broad public appeal outside the beltway.[18] The outsider strategy proved successful for Governors Carter, Reagan, Clinton, and Bush; however, to varying degrees each faced difficulty in governing skills, particularly a lack of experience in the international arena and the initial inability to play the game within Washington.

How do women politicians fit into these categories for selecting presidential candidates? The potential pool of women candidates has never been larger than following the 2000 elections. In 2001, women held seventy-two, or 13.5 percent, of the 535 seats in the 107th U.S. Congress (thirteen of the 100 seats in the Senate and fifty-nine of the 435 seats in the House of Representatives, both all-time records). At the state level, women held eighty-nine of the 323 statewide elective executive offices across the country (27.6 percent). Also, 1,663 (22.4 percent) of the 7,424 state legislators in the United States were women. The number of women serving in state legislatures has increased more than fivefold since 1969 when 301, or 4 percent, of all state legislators were women.[19]

However, there has traditionally been a dearth of women governors, both past and present, which suggests at first glance that women candidates may not benefit from the insider versus outsider phenomenon in the race for the presidency. Prior to the five women governors serving in 2001, only fourteen women had previously served as a state's top executive, beginning as early as 1925 with Democrat Nellie Tayloe Ross of Wyoming, who replaced her husband after he died in office (two other women replaced their husbands upon their death or impeachment). Ella Grasso, a Democrat from Connecticut who served from 1975 to 1980, was the first woman elected as governor in her own right. Republicans would not elect their first woman governor until 1986, with the election of Kay A. Orr of Nebraska. And although the governor's office of large states is one of the most likely stepping-stones to the White House, only one of the five-largest electoral states (California, New York, Texas, Florida, Pennsylvania) has ever elected a woman as governor—Democrat Ann Richards of Texas, elected in 1990.[20]

Taking a closer look at gender stereotyping suggests that the lack of women governors as potential presidential candidates may not be such a bad thing from the perspective of a women's viability during the campaign. Research in recent years has shown stereotypes to exist about both male and female candidates. Women, who are considered more compassionate, are seen as more competent in the traditional "female" policy areas of health care, the environment, education, poverty, and civil rights. Men, who are considered more aggressive, show stronger competencies in the traditionally "male" policy areas of military and defense matters, foreign policy, and economic and trade issues.[21] These same traditionally "male" issues are highlighted during U.S. Senate campaigns, whereas traditionally "female" issues are emphasized in gubernatorial races.[22] Therefore, women governors seeking the White House may very well be hurt by their lack of policymaking experience with traditionally "male" issues, like foreign policy and military matters, and women members of Congress may actually benefit more by the insider label from political experience at the national level. All governors running for president must overcome the perceived lack of experience in the international arena (Clinton and Bush are recent examples). Therefore, women presidential candidates coming from Congress, especially those members serving on committees dealing with economic, military, or international issues or perhaps having a cabinet-level presidential appointment, may have an easier time answering the inevitable question about their political experience and knowledge of relevant national and international issues.

Given the necessary traits it takes to run for president in the current political environment, as well as the skills necessary to be a successful leader in the White House, it is instructive to consider how women have fared as candidates in recent years for either Congress or statewide offices, since so little evidence exists to determine a female candidate's long-term viability as a presidential contender. Although no one would deny that women have made gains since the early 1990s in holding more elected positions at both the state and federal levels, traditional barriers still exist for women seeking elected or appointed government positions. These barriers, which either deter women from running for office or keep them from winning if they do run, include stereotypes (political participation is not compatible with the traditional female role in society), career choice and preparation (traditional female professions, such as teaching and nursing, are incompatible with political aspirations), family demands (the public perception that women with children cannot handle the responsibility of both family and elected position), sex discrimination (lack of party support for women candidates), and the political system (money, campaign finance laws, party organization, winner-take-all electoral systems, and incumbency).[23] Future women presidential candidates will undoubtedly face many of the same barriers.

Political Skill:
Leadership and the National Agenda

Even prior to election and inauguration, a potential president must create a strong image of leadership in the minds of U.S. voters. Appearing presidential, both during the campaign and once in office, is an essential ingredient for political success. However, how leadership is conceptualized has served as an important barrier for women in politics, particularly for those seeking elected office. Leadership has historically been defined on male, not female, terms. Whether in politics, business, or military circles within the United States, strong leadership is defined as an attempt to exert one's will over a particular situation, a societal view that "has been conditioned by the interpretation of American history as written." This, in turn, affects how the public will view other aspiring leaders, particularly women.[24] Also not helpful to women seeking the presidency is the notion of "presidential machismo," which is the image desired by many Americans to have their president exhibit tough and aggressive behavior on the international stage. Even though the unilateral actions of a president to wage war or carry out other military actions may run "counter to aspects of democratic theory of governance," public opinion polls routinely show that Americans admire this type of behavior by presidents, forming "the basis of a cult that often elevates presidents, primarily those regarded as strong and who waged successful wars, to the status of heroes."[25]

The political process in the United States is viewed as the realloca-
tion of resources within society, with the winners exerting their power
and influence over the losers within the political arena. This view better
represents the male view of leadership, since men are traditionally
expected to be competitive, strong, tough, decisive, and in control.
Women, however, are expected to exhibit traits that are cooperative,
supportive, and understanding and to show a willingness to serve others. Characteristics of women in leadership positions also include using
consensus decisionmaking, viewing power as something to be shared,
encouraging productive approaches to conflict, building supportive
working environments, and promoting diversity in the workplace. Gender can play an important role in defining leadership, and socialization
and chosen career paths can help explain the differences in the leadership styles of women as opposed to men.[26]

Studies that have looked at gendered differences in leadership show
that in some areas, particularly politics and business, women often bring
"a more open, democratic, and 'people-centered' approach to their leadership positions." However, it has also been suggested that a more inclusive and participatory approach to leadership is not exclusive to
women and that since women have yet to reach parity with men in leadership positions, not enough evidence yet exists to categorize leadership
styles based on gender alone.[27] Nonetheless, of the examples from other
countries, women national leaders have exhibited diverse leadership
styles—some more traditionally "male," like that of former British
prime minister Margaret Thatcher, and some more traditionally "female," like that of former Philippine president Corazon Aquino.[28]

However, if any of these stereotypes about women leaders are to be
believed and accepted, then a woman president may actually have an advantage in working within the federal system of shared powers. According to David Gergen, an experienced political adviser to Presidents
Nixon, Gerald Ford, Reagan, and Clinton, "a president should see himself as the center of a web" and develop cooperative working relationships with six distinct groups: Congress, the press, the public, foreign
powers, domestic interest groups, and domestic elites. All these groups
share the expectation of being included within the decisionmaking
process in the White House. However, several recent presidents, most
notably Nixon, Carter, and Clinton, did not include these groups in the
shared responsibility of governing and, in some respects, paid a heavy
price in the area of legislative achievements. As Gergen points out, it is
"difficult enough to govern in today's climate, but they managed to make
it almost impossible by doubling the resistance to their agendas."[29]

Like it or not, a president must work with Congress to achieve legislative success. The framers of the Constitution saw cooperation among

the branches, particularly between the legislature and executive, as a means to create a viable national government and to protect it from tyranny. Constitutionally speaking, presidents have limited powers over the actions of Congress. Political parties, especially which party happens to be in power, can also affect the relationship between Congress and the president, although unified government does not always guarantee legislative cooperation. More important, the relationship between the two branches can be determined by "how each judges the legitimacy and competency of the other."[30] Presidential leadership of Congress can occur, and experience from serving in Congress can make a difference in understanding the ins and outs of policymaking. Lyndon Johnson demonstrated this by the legislative success that he enjoyed, which was due in part to his many years on Capitol Hill and experience as Senate majority leader.[31] Again, if we assume that women leaders tend to exhibit leadership styles that focus on cooperation, and given the earlier prediction that a woman presidential candidate coming from the Congress would have an electoral advantage, a woman president would be no more constrained in this area than her male counterpart and might enjoy an advantage.

Women do tend to bring different priorities into the policymaking arena than their male counterparts, and women are also more likely to work across party lines to achieve their goals. The female members of the U.S. Senate have exhibited a clear example of this leadership style in recent years. Although their party affiliations and ideological perspectives differ, the women in the Senate have been known to make their collective voices heard on bipartisan issues affecting women, such as the Homemaker Individual Retirement Account (cosponsored by Democrat Barbara Mikulski of Maryland and Republican Kay Bailey Hutchison of Texas) and a resolution in support of mammograms for women in their forties (cosponsored by Mikulski and Republican Olympia Snowe of Maine).[32] But because women legislators have tended to be slightly more liberal in their policy approach, should it be assumed that a woman president would be more liberal as well?[33]

Not necessarily, given the fact that the president serves as his or her party's de facto national leader. The role of political parties has diminished in recent decades, but the president is nonetheless the most visible spokesperson for the party and its legislative program. Therefore, a president's agenda can be shaped or even limited by the party he or she represents, with Democrats pursuing a more moderate-to-liberal agenda than Republicans.[34] Partisan alignment, then, is probably a better predictor of political ideology than gender. A counterargument can also be made about the role of parties in presidential politics, since some recent presidents have moved away from their responsibilities as party leaders by exhibiting a more independent brand of governing. This trend is also consistent with the emergence of candidate-centered politics, which suggests a more middle-of-the-road, moderate ideology for a presidential candidate to get elected. Therefore, if presidents are elected based on the idea of candidate-centered politics, then a woman president from either party would probably be more centrist in her approach to the legislative agenda and would not focus solely on "women's issues."

Political Communication: Constructing a Presidential Image

A president's communication strategy—public activities, speechwriting, and presidential and press relations—is an important base of power for presidents during the television age.[35] The rise of the rhetorical presidency and use of the presidential bully pulpit date back to Theodore Roosevelt, who advanced the president's role as the national leader of public opinion and used his rhetorical skills to increase the power of the presidency through popular support. Later presidents, though not all, would follow Roosevelt's strategy of relying on the bully pulpit in an attempt to lead democratically as the spokesperson for the American public. Use of the bully pulpit has become especially important since the start of the television age, where a president's overall success or failure as a leader can be determined by his rhetorical skills and public influence.[36]

Since the 1950s, three presidents stand out as successful in their use of the bully pulpit—Kennedy, Reagan, and Clinton. All were known for their frequent use of inspiring and eloquent speeches about public policy and their visions for the country. Other presidents during the twentieth century either abdicated the bully pulpit or used it ineffectively, which diminished presidential power during their terms and curtailed their leadership potential by allowing other political actors to shape the public debate. As it has evolved during the past century, a president's skillful use of the bully pulpit is necessary to promote his philosophy for governing as well as the overall moral and political vision of the administration. It can also determine the effectiveness of presidential governance and whether a president can accomplish his policy and broader ideological objectives through rhetorical skills.[37]

Can a woman president master the bully pulpit? Communication and linguist scholars have pointed to differences in how men and women communicate. In general, men view communication as negotiations in which they must maintain power, an "individual in a hierarchical social order in which he [is] either one-up or one-down." Women view communication as an opportunity for confirmation, support, and consensus, "an individual in a network of connections."[38] This difference has benefited women politicians in recent years. Television as a medium demands intimacy and the ability to express the private self, a skill that most presidents, with the exception of Reagan and Clinton, have had difficulty perfecting. Male politicians discuss goals, whereas women politicians reveal themselves through an intimate, conversational, and narrative style of speech. Presidents now govern extensively through the mass media, and "because the mass media are fixated on differences between the private and public self of public figures, a comfort with expressing instead of camouflaging self . . . is useful for a politician. The utility benefits females."[39]

The news media are also an important political actor for the president to consider, since the press can keep the president apprised of major concerns of the public, enable presidents to convey their messages to the public and political elites, and allow the president to remain in full public view on the political stage.[40] The president makes news simply by virtue of being the "ideological symbol of American democracy and nationhood" to both the press and the public. The president's relationship with the press is a combination of both strengths and weaknesses. Since the president is under constant scrutiny by the press, presidential leadership can be undermined both by a failure of the administration to effectively manage the news and by newsgathering norms within the journalism industry and the skepticism of the press.[41]

Women politicians have traditionally been viewed by the press as an anomaly —a unique occurrence that deserves attention because it is outside the norm.[42] Trivialization of women in the news media has also continued, through portrayals on television and in the movies that can lead to "symbolic annihilation" of women in general,[43] as well as the stereotyping that occurs in news coverage of women candidates and politicians.[44] In many campaigns, news media coverage has added to the negative stereotyping of women candidates, thus hurting their efforts to win an elected office, since the news media pay more attention to style over substance when covering female candidates. Since many voters may doubt the policy qualifications of women candidates, news coverage that downplays issues and highlights personal traits develops less favorable images for female candidates.[45]

The focus on style versus substance was certainly apparent in Ferraro's vice presidential candidacy in 1984, with numerous stories about her appearance (her hairstyle and wardrobe), her public interactions with running mate Walter Mondale (should they hug in public or merely shake hands?), her husband's business dealings, and the infamous debate about her ability to bake blueberry muffins. However, although the novelty of Ferraro's campaign as the first woman on a major party ticket was evident in news coverage, a closer analysis of newspaper coverage showed that style dominated over substance in coverage of both Ferraro and her opponent, Vice President George Bush.[46] That is not to say that the first woman president will not be treated as a novelty by the press, which is known for its extensive coverage of "firsts," especially in "soft" news stories that will inevitably focus on her hairstyle and sense of fashion (traditional coverage for first ladies), as well as her husband (or lack thereof) and his role as "first spouse." But eventually, "hard" news will prevail and return to the front pages of the *New York Times* and *Washington Post,* which play an important role in informing Americans about their government and politics. Perhaps an effective news management style, which is essential to all presidents during the television age, will go a long way for the first woman president in shaping her public image through political accomplishment and not gender.

Conclusion

In their discussion on women as national leaders, Michael Genovese and Seth Thompson point out that while the effects may be subtle, the role of gender cannot be overlooked.

> Anyone who rises to the top of a political system will have developed a set of strategies and a repertoire of behaviors for dealing with both challenges and opportunities. For the successful woman, the strategies she has developed and her style will inevitably be shaped and influenced by her society's definitions and expectations of gender. She will have learned, consciously or not, how to cope effectively with, and even turn to her advantage, the fact that she is a woman in a "man's world."[47]

There is little doubt that the first woman president will face significant challenges, especially in the accomplishment of reaching the White House. It may be difficult to predict how the nation will react to this historic first—although we know that she will be a woman, we cannot predict what style of leadership she will employ. It is known, however, that the presidency is an office, by constitutional design, of shared powers and limitations on presidential leadership. The style of leadership and governing may be fluid from administration to administration, and some presidents have overcome the constitutional barriers to achieve success, but the institutional features of the office remain static.

For a woman who has achieved the ultimate political prize of winning her party's nomination and the presidency, several gender questions will have already been addressed. Therefore, from an institutional standpoint, a woman president will face similar challenges as her male predecessors upon taking office. To achieve success in the current political environment, presidents must master the bully pulpit and employ an effective strategy of going public, develop an effective working relationship with Congress, and provide strong leadership at the international level. If even strong leaders are limited in their potential for greatness because of the potential for divided government or an uncooperative Congress, as well as the unpredictability of economic factors and international events, then issues of gender for a woman president, once elected, may be secondary. Or they may actually work to her advantage. If leadership, personality, and character can make a difference in the potential for presidential success, then perhaps the first successful woman president will embody certain characteristics and skills, gender-specific or not, that are similar to those of her more successful male predecessors. Women leaders must be judged as individuals, not merely as women. In the final analysis, it is important to remember that many men have also failed at the job of president, whereas only a handful have been considered successful or strong leaders. Some presidents are destined for greatness and some for obscurity, regardless of whether they are addressed as "mister" or "madam" president.

16

A Female Leader
for the Free World:
The First Woman President
and U.S. Foreign Policy

Tom Lansford

The vagueness of the Constitution has allowed the president to take a large amount of control in formulating and implementing the nation's foreign policy. Each president has the latitude to craft policy that reflects both personal and political preferences. Nonetheless, structural factors, including congressional control of fiscal matters and the legislature's oversight functions, the role and influence of the foreign policy elite, and the continuing effect of longstanding traditions in U.S. foreign policy have combined to produce remarkable consistency in the nation's diplomacy. It will be an important factor following the election of the first woman president, since she will be under enormous pressure from both the political left and right. Liberals will seek policies to reorient U.S. diplomacy toward a more feminist approach by incorporating issues that were often labeled as "women's concerns" in the past. Concurrently, conservatives will attempt to compel the president to be more hawkish or "masculine" than her male counterparts (in the mode of Margaret Thatcher).

In this chapter, I discuss the role of the president in foreign policy formulation and the challenges likely to be faced by the first female president. The work also examines the twin, though contradictory, trends in U.S. foreign policy of isolationism and moralism and their impact on the future president's policy options. Finally, the range of women's issues that have heretofore been marginalized in U.S. diplomacy will be reviewed in the context of their relationship with the nation's foreign policy.

The President's Role in Foreign Policy

The president is the central figure in the development of foreign policy.[1] Under Article II of the U.S. Constitution, the president is granted both explicit and implicit powers to conduct the nation's diplomacy, including the express power to appoint ambassadors and make treaties (with Senate approval). Also, in their role as chief executive, presidents have the authority to appoint individuals to posts within the agencies involved in foreign affairs, including the State Department, Commerce Department, and Defense Department. In addition, in the twentieth century, presidents have increasingly used executive agreements as a means to bypass the need for congressional approval of bilateral or multilateral accords.[2] Furthermore, the president's role as commander in chief places the military power of the nation at the disposal of the chief executive. For instance, the president may order military action for up to sixty days without congressional approval. The president may also use the considerable deployment capabilities of the military to pressure foreign governments.

Potentially the greatest foreign policy power of the president is the ability to influence public opinion. The chief executive may use the "bully pulpit" inherent in the office of the presidency to rally public support for specific initiatives or for broad policies. The president has an unmatched capability to communicate with the American people.[3] The president also serves as the bridge between the people and political elites or interest groups and as the means to reconcile domestic and foreign policy.

This role as a bridge between the people and groups is especially significant since, as Mark Logan contends, "elites play a surprisingly significant role in democracies, especially in the foreign policy realm, where the mass public consciously or unconsciously cedes influence to experts and self-appointed experts."[4] Furthermore, Gabriel Almond asserts that most average Americans are historically "indifferent" to foreign policy but often react in "anger" to global intrusions on the domestic front. This ignorance in turn leads to "dangerous overreactions" on the part of the populace.[5] As a result, the president is often expected or even forced to serve as the mediator between the people and international events.

One result of this relationship between the people and the president is that the chief executive can usually count on initial support, or at least a degree of latitude, in foreign policy, especially during periods of international crisis. Brigitte Lebens Nacos describes this tendency in the following manner: "according to conventional wisdom and scholarly inquiry Americans tend to line up supportively behind their presidents in times of international crises in a surge of patriotism" that causes a "sudden jump in presidents' public approval."[6] This patriotic reflex of rallying around the flag may often be short-lived if the president does not utilize the rhetorical powers of the office and work to maintain domestic support. In addition, even when the president and administration work to maintain approval for policies, the tide of public opinion can turn, as it did despite Lyndon B. Johnson's efforts with regard to Vietnam and Ronald Reagan's efforts to maintain aid for the Nicaraguan contras.

Domestic Constraints on Foreign Policy

The pivotal role and considerable powers of the chief executive will grant the first woman president significant freedom in developing policy. Her main constraints will be domestic, not international. Robert Putnam best summarized the connections between foreign and domestic policy as a "two-level" game:

> The politics of many international negotiations can usefully be conceived as a two-level game. At the national level, domestic groups pursue their interests by pressuring the government to adopt favorable policies, and politicians seek power by constructing coalitions among those groups. At the international level, national governments seek to maximize their own ability to satisfy domestic pressures, while minimizing the adverse consequences of foreign developments. Neither of the two games can be ignored by central decision makers, so long as their countries remain interdependent, yet sovereign.[7]

The first woman president will not formulate policy in a vacuum. She will be constrained in her policy options by domestic groups that can bring significant political pressures and resources to the promotion of their interests. Like her predecessors, she will have to balance the potential costs of security policies and programs in regard to national economies and social spending.[8] Consequently, actions or initiatives that may appear irrational at the international level will occur because policies that are rational at the international level may be "impolitic" at the domestic level and thus may not be taken.[9]

The main domestic constraints on policy exist at both the formal and informal levels. Often the most visible impediment to a president's foreign policy is Congress. The oversight function of Congress manifests itself in five ways: (1) the Senate must ratify all treaties by a two-thirds majority; (2) the Senate must confirm the president's senior-level appointees to the State Department and other agencies involved in foreign affairs; (3) Congress as a whole may pass legislation that either expands or restricts U.S. diplomacy; (4) Congress also controls the budget authority necessary to fund various initiatives, including military operations; and (5) Congress may conduct hearings into the conduct of agencies or operations in order to influence public opinion or legislation.

The necessity of securing the required two-thirds majority approval for treaties has led to the demise of numerous foreign policy initiatives in U.S. history. The Senate rejection of the Treaty of Versailles in 1920 effectively derailed Woodrow Wilson's post–World War I peace initiative and dealt the president one of the most famous, or infamous, foreign policy reversals in U.S. history.[10] More recently in 1999, President Bill Clinton suffered a similar foreign policy defeat when the Senate rejected the Comprehensive Test Ban Treaty (CTBT) after he failed to lobby moderate Republicans on behalf of the agreement or to expend political capital in any public relations campaign to garner grassroots support.[11] Secretary of State Madeleine Albright even acknowledged that the administration's efforts had been too little, too late.[12] The lesson from both examples is the necessity for the president to work closely with senators from both parties and to use the bully pulpit to rally public support in order to ensure ratification by the Senate.

The importance of congressional support has increased since the end of the Cold War. During the period of bipolar rivalry, there was a remarkable consensus on foreign policy, and presidents enjoyed considerable leeway in their pursuit of policy. In fact, there was such a disconnect between presidential successes in foreign versus domestic policy that Aaron Wildavsky put forth his famous "two-presidency" thesis, which held that the foreign policy president could dominate the external affairs of the nation, but the domestic president found himself in a constant battle for control of internal policies.[13] However, in the post–Cold War era, Congress has become much more assertive in foreign policy. Examples of this trend include the Senate rejection of the CTBT or the 1994 congressional rejection of "fast track" trade authority that prevents Congress from amending international commercial agreements (from 1974 until 1994, presidents had been granted fast track trade authority).

On the informal level, the foreign policy elites that tend to dominate both the foreign service and the interest groups most involved in policy formulation remain male-dominated. Nancy E. McGlen and Meredith Reid Sarkees characterize the situation thus:

> In the United States, and in most other countries, women have generally been excluded from the institutions that make and implement foreign policy and conduct war. This near ostracism from the centers of power and the agencies responsible for foreign affairs has meant that

women have rarely been present when the most critical decisions a nation faces have been made, especially the decision to go to war. However, women have been, and still are, deeply affected by such foreign endeavors.[14]

This exclusion is significant since this pattern extends to both the political or economic elites, whose influence is informal, and the bureaucratic elites, whose influence can directly affect policy formation and implementation.[15] Here an individual president can have enormous influence through appointment power. For instance, President Bill Clinton appointed Madeleine Albright to be the first female secretary of state and arranged for seven of the top ten positions within the State Department to be held by women. In addition, Clinton created the Interagency Council on Women, which was chaired by Albright, to coordinate efforts to implement the Platform for Action that was adopted at the 1995 United Nations Fourth World Conference on Women in Beijing.

In addition, a variety of interest groups have emerged that advocate on behalf of women's issues in foreign policy and for an increased role for women in the governmental bureaucracies that conduct the nation's diplomacy. For instance, in 1981, the Women's Foreign Policy Group (WFPG) was established as an educational organization whose primary goals centered on the "promotion of the leadership of women in international affairs professions."[16] In addition, within the broad field of international relations theory, a growing subfield of feminist or gender international relations theory has gained increased attention as feminist scholars seek to draw greater public and governmental attention to gender issues and to deconstruct the traditional security-centric focus of foreign policy analysis.[17] One potential result of these new methods of inquiry and expanded awareness is increased attention paid to foreign policy issues that were previously marginalized. Nevertheless, one of the most significant informal constraints on the first woman president's foreign policy will continue to be the established trends and foundations of U.S. diplomacy.

The Foundations of U.S. Foreign Policy

The centrality of the president to policy formulation has often resulted in dramatic swings in U.S. diplomacy. In fact, the history of U.S. foreign policy is marked by a series of inconsistencies. These inherent incongruities are tied to the contradictory patterns that underlie the nation's interaction with foreign powers: isolationism and internationalism. Isolationism has been a recurrent feature in U.S. foreign policy throughout the nation's history. George Washington's parting admonishment to "avoid permanent alliances" was translated into codes of action early on through the formulation of policies such as the Monroe Doctrine. Washington's premise that permanent military or political alliances were harmful to the nation, when combined with the Monroe Doctrine, curtailed endeavors to promote U.S. influence outside the hemisphere.[18]

The appeal of isolationism to Americans has always been twofold. First, there is a long-standing and culturally important creed of U.S. "exceptionalism." Joseph Lepgold and Timothy McKeown contend that exceptionalism is rooted in the belief that "Americans depreciate power politics and old-fashioned diplomacy, mistrust powerful standing armies and entangling peacetime commitments, make moralistic judgments about other people's domestic systems, and believe that liberal values transfer readily to foreign affairs."[19] Second, there is also a widely held perception that involvement in the global arena diverts resources away from problems or policies in the United States.

Although the popular conception of exceptionalism reinforces the isolationist tendencies in the United States, it is also the basis for U.S. internationalism. Staunch internationalist presidents such as Theodore Roosevelt, Woodrow Wilson, or Franklin D. Roosevelt believed that U.S. exceptionalism carried with it an implicit duty to try and spread the nation's core principles around the globe. They pursued policies that endeavored to promote democracy and free market capitalism.[20] U.S. internationalism is bound with the notion of "democratic universalism," and it reflects the political ethnocentrism at the core of most Americans' view of the world: "everyone ought to be like us."[21]

The first woman president will also face a more imminent foreign policy legacy upon entering office—that of her immediate predecessor. The impact of an inherited agenda can significantly constrain policy options. It is true that candidates seeking the presidency often endeavor to portray themselves as a "favorite son," or daughter in this case, by presenting their candidacy as the logical successor to the policies of an incumbent or popular past chief executive.[22] Nevertheless, once in office, the foreign policy priorities of her predecessor can prevent the development of new or divergent initiatives. If she is elected from the party currently not in control of the White House, she will have considerably more freedom to formulate policy that meets her personal and political inclinations.

The challenge for the first woman president will be to carefully craft policy that acknowledges both the isolationist and internationalist traditions in U.S. foreign policy. Through the use of the bully pulpit, she will be able to garner public support for selected policies. Concurrently, she will need to work closely with Congress to ensure Senate approval of treaties and agreements and to secure congressional support and funding for policies. In other words, she will have to be able to adroitly manage the domestic component of the two-level game in order to be successful in the international arena.

The International Dimension

In many aspects, the United States trails behind other nations in the political empowerment of women. The percentage of women in Congress hovers at around 12–13 percent, the first two female justices of the Supreme Court are on the current high court, and secretary of state is the highest national office held by a woman. In comparison, as is discussed in further detail elsewhere in this book, a number of nations have had woman heads of state or chief executives.

When the first woman is elected president of the United States, it will mark a significant turning point for the nation. However, in U.S. interaction with its closest allies, the event will not dramatically alter the course of diplomacy. Women leaders, although not seen in numbers that reflect their proportion of the population, have served as the prime ministers for a number of the nation's closest allies, including the United Kingdom, France, Turkey, and India. In fact, among the western European nations, woman leaders are not uncommon and have left lasting impacts on their respective nations' foreign policies. Margaret Thatcher's leadership of the United Kingdom during the Falkland Islands War and her staunch support of the Reagan doctrine during the 1980s were two examples of the ability of women to master power politics. Conversely, Mary Robinson's contribution to international relations came after she left office in Ireland and became a driving force in the promotion of human rights in the post–Cold War world.

Perception and Misperception
in International Relations

The divergent approaches to global relations of Thatcher and Robinson are demonstrative of the fact that the record of female leaders is just as varied as their male counterparts and demonstrates the impracticality of using gender to differentiate between leadership styles. This point is significant because of the lingering perception that women may not be as aggressive or assertive as men and, therefore, that women leaders would be overwhelmed in dealings with foreign male leaders and would be unable to engage in power politics. J. Ann Tickner offers the following summary:

> Diplomatic practices and the art of war are the business of princes, princesses belong on pedestals in private spaces, guardians of a morality that is unsuitable and even dangerous in the world of realpolitik. . . . As Donald Regan, President Ronald Reagan's National Security Advisor, proclaimed in 1985, "Women are not going to understand missile throw-weights or what is happening in Afghanistan . . . most women would rather read the human interest stuff."[23]

Writing in 1998, Francis Fukuyama echoed this sentiment and suggested that males were by nature more violent than females and consequently more likely to go to war.[24] Writing in response, Jane S. Jaquette adroitly points out that

> Several decades of research shows that women do differ from men regarding war. Women are markedly less interested in and knowledgeable about it. Women prefer lower military expenditures in times of peace and negotiations instead of force. But this does not mean that women are unaggressive; they can sometimes be more aggressive than men. When women are allowed to carry arms, they are often fierce fighters, as was true of many Central and South American guerrillas. Once war commences, there is little evidence that women withhold support from the male-dominated states.[25]

History is replete with examples of woman leaders who engaged in aggressive foreign polices and were more than a match for their male counterparts. In the twentieth century, Golda Meir, Indira Gandhi, or Margaret Thatcher are demonstrative of the ability of women to engage in power politics and lead their nations in time of international insecurity and strife. In the history of U.S. foreign policy, during the Clinton administration, Albright was considered to be the most "hawkish" member of the cabinet on the more prominent security issues, including the containment of Iraq, military action in the Balkans (in both Bosnia and Kosovo), and the enlargement of the North Atlantic Treaty Organization (NATO).

Nonetheless, the first woman president will have to balance her policies so that initiatives that emphasize peaceful resolution of conflicts will not be perceived as weakness or an unwillingness to undertake strong action. Concurrently, she must be careful not to overreact to international threats to U.S. interests to "prove" her toughness. However, many presidents come into office with prior foreign policy credentials that grant them considerable latitude in policy formulation. For instance, Richard Nixon's reputation as a staunch anticommunist and his previous diplomatic experience meant that there was little negative domestic or international criticism of his reestablishment of diplomatic and trade ties with the People's Republic of China in 1972. Presidents do not need extensive foreign policy experience to be perceived as strong leaders in international relations, as Ronald Reagan demonstrated. Reagan came into office with no real diplomatic experience but was able to "reinvigorate" the nation's foreign policy and overcome perceptions of malaise and the demise of U.S. primacy.[26]

A Woman's Foreign Policy Agenda

The terrorist attacks on September 11, 2001, against the United States and the subsequent anthrax incidents reaffirmed the centrality of traditional security concerns in the nation's foreign affairs. It also highlighted the importance of existing security relationships with nations in western Europe and the relevance of renewed relationships with states such as Pakistan, India, and Russia. Nonetheless, the nation's first female chief executive, be she Republican or Democrat, liberal or conservative, will be under significant overt and tacit pressure to incorporate women's issues to a greater degree in her formulation of foreign policy. One of the greatest challenges faced by the first woman president will be the task of carefully integrating a variety of priorities in such a fashion as not to alienate either Congress or the public but still promote women's issues. Feminist activists and scholars have called for a recalculation of the nation's foreign policy to more adequately address the status of women in three major international areas: human rights, security, and economic interactions.[27]

Although the United States has been among the world's foremost proponents of human rights, its foreign policy record has often fallen victim to concerns over expediency and "realism's cost-benefit reasoning."[28] In turn, this tendency has led the United States to support and maintain relations with even those nations that have dismal human rights records.[29] In the arena of women's rights, the United States has a particularly bleak history. The United States is not among the 160 nations that have ratified the United Nations Convention on the Elimination of All Forms of Discrimination Against Women, although the accord was promulgated in 1979.

International women's rights advocates specifically target three areas in which U.S. support would be beneficial: (1) increased integration of human rights regulations into national law to protect women in the home and in family life by ending "state policies towards the family

. . . [that] reinforce the subordination and traditional roles of women,"[30] (2) incentives for expanded political participation and representation in government at all levels, and (3) efforts to improve access to health care, including reexamination of discriminatory policies in regard to women's sexual and reproductive rights.[31] Former secretary of state Albright listed such gender abuses faced by women: "coerced abortions and sterilizations, children sold into prostitution, ritual mutilations, dowry murders, and domestic violence."[32]

Beyond human rights concerns, there is growing international pressure for the United States to reexamine its security policy to more adequately address the concerns of women. Such a recalculation of security would require the first woman president to accept a less state-centric view of global affairs, wherein international norms and rules transcend national sovereignty.[33] The feminist critique of traditional notions of security is based on the premise that "women's systemic insecurity is . . . an internal as well as external dimension of state systems."[34] Nation-states are most often the primary perpetrators of military aggression and human rights abuses against both their own populations and external groups.

In addition, since the end of the Cold War, the majority of armed conflicts in the world have been substate conflicts. Most of these conflicts are based on religion or ethnicity and have produced a disproportionate share of women casualties. Studies have shown that 80 percent of external refugees and internally displaced persons are women and children.[35] Ethnic strife in the Balkans and Africa demonstrated the inability of some states to effectively manage substate conflict and provide security for their citizenry (especially women). Indeed, some states could not survive such warfare and disintegrated. Therefore, the optimum means to elevate the security of women worldwide is to lower the state barriers to international efforts to promote peace and stability by expanding the influence of international bodies such as the United Nations. Such regional or international organizations also provide the optimum means to counter nonmilitary threats to security, such as environmental degradation, drug trafficking, and immigration.

The final challenge will be in the arena of international economics. The disproportionate number of poor women in the world have led to the feminization of poverty. By the late 1980s, women comprised more than 60 percent of the world's poor, and poverty was increasing 50 percent faster among women than among men.[36] This trend has a range of consequences that have lasting effects on international relations. In addition, many assert that the feminization of poverty should be considered a legitimate foreign policy concern. Because women are increasingly economic actors and heads of households as well as mothers, their poverty slows economic growth. Moreover in poor countries, their disadvantage feeds a destructive spiral of poverty, population growth, and environmental degradation. In a world of blurring borders, women's poverty creates enclaves of want in the midst of wealth and puts pressures on the developed world, whether by fueling humanitarian crises or by unleashing—for the first time—waves of females who migrate without spouses to seek work in richer countries.[37]

Albright echoed this theme when she contended that "in addition to bearing and nurturing the children women do most of the non–child related work."[38] The United States has traditionally supported a variety of international aid programs designed to alleviate women's poverty. For instance, in 1997, the U.S. Agency for International Development (USAID) initiated a program for management and operational training for 5,000 women dairy farmers and the women managers of former collective farms in eastern Europe.[39] The United States has also found that the use of microcredit—small loans issued for short durations—has been very successful in promoting entrepreneurship among women in developing nations.[40] The nation's first woman president will face the task of improving existing programs and formulating even more effective policies to counter the feminization of poverty. Most important, the president will also have to lobby Congress and the American people to support such initiatives.

Conclusion

The first woman president will face a variety of challenges in the realm of foreign policy. Many of these hurdles are those faced by any incoming president. Other challenges will be tied to gender issues. One of the main constants in foreign policy that she will face is the necessity for strong leadership to secure domestic approval. As Richard N. Haass has pointed out, "The absence of a consistent and coherent foreign policy agenda inevitably creates a vacuum that other political forces are more than willing to fill. Chief among those forces is Congress."[41] Battles between Congress and the presidency over foreign policy demonstrate the need for the president to successfully manage two-level games in such a manner as to win in both the domestic and international arenas.

Madam President will have to effectively maintain relations with Congress to ensure senatorial approval of treaties and to secure congressional approval and funding of her policies. Concurrently, the president will also have to use the formal and informal powers of her office to engage the public and develop support for both specific policies and the broad framework of her priorities. Greatest among these powers is that of persuasion. The bully pulpit provides the president with the basis to shape public perceptions and to inform the American people about foreign affairs. The president will need to make extensive use of her persuasive powers to manage the nation's foreign policy.

The nation's first woman president will have to accept the presence of misperceptions in international relations about gender and about her ability to conduct U.S. diplomacy. However, the presence of assertive and effective female leaders in the global arena has provided examples of action and policy. They have demonstrated the great capacity for management and success by woman leaders. Furthermore, the president will not assume office in a policy vacuum. She may come into office with an inherited agenda or with considerable foreign experience. Nonetheless, the president will have the formidable task of navigating between the twin foundations of U.S. foreign policy, isolationism and moralism. She might also want—or feel compelled by her constituency—to integrate the expanding range of women's issues into the nation's foreign policy. Of course, any pressure to do so might create another double standard for women, and efforts to address the relative lack of women's rights and issues in the nation's foreign policy might come with potential drawbacks. Finally, in order to achieve foreign policy success, the nation's first woman president will have to maintain her role as the bridge between domestic and international actors and her leadership of the policy process.

17

Confronting the Myths: The First Woman President and National Security

John Davis

During his presidency, Thomas Jefferson warned that women partici-pating in political life was "an experiment which the public is not pre-pared for, nor am I."[1] On the question of national security, some might feel it is appropriate to ask the same question again or even wonder whether the first woman president is prepared for the arduous task of confronting the realities associated with national security. More signif-icantly, however, one might ask whether the national security bureau-cracy is ready for Madam President.

In this chapter, I am concerned with how the first woman president will confront three issues: "foreign challenge blues," management of the national security bureaucracy, and the use of force. In particular, I address a series of "myths" associated with each of the aforementioned issues; namely, that during the tenure of the first female occupant of the White House, U.S. national security interests will decline or that somehow, in part because of her gender, the country will experience more crises.

National Security and Women: In Search of a Role

Prior to the terrorist attacks on the United States on September 11, 2001, the subject of national security had been losing much of its pre-eminence. The dilemma associated with this problem concerns the ever-increasing confusion between national security and foreign policy. In-deed, some argue the two concepts are inseparable.[2] Foreign policy involves the promotion of the national interests of the United States and the maintenance of foreign relations with countries around the globe in an attempt to create conditions favorable to U.S. interests. The chief instrument in the conduct of foreign policy involves the employment of traditional diplomacy, whereby countries use ambassadors and other envoys to communicate with each other. In contrast, national security differs from foreign policy in two important respects: there is a greater emphasis on security, and national security concentrates on potential and actual adversaries, with particular focus on the use of force.[3]

In the ever-changing landscape of international affairs, the subject of national security has become tempestuous. As this quote indicates, national security remains an amorphous and problematic concept:

> No formal definition of national security as a field has been generally accepted; none may be possible. In general, it is the study of national security problems faced by nations, or policies and programs by which these problems are addressed, and also of the government processes through which the policies and programs are decided upon and carried out.[4]

In general, national security requires the confidence among national security administrators and actors that the United States maintain the military capacity and effective decisionmaking apparatus to preclude the nation's enemies from employing force as a means to disrupt or destroy the far-flung security arrangements and interests of the United States.

Discourse on the subject of national security and the role of women has received scant consideration. The seminal debate on the role of women and national security occurred during the Reagan administration. In a special event at the National Defense University in Washington, D.C., in June 1983, the administration held the National Security Forum for Women. The forum had two objectives: promoting the sharing of information among women in the field of national security and increasing the number, role, and leadership of women in national security. Assistant Secretary of Defense Lawrence Korb best described the efforts of the administration

> To get women more involved in this particular area, which Secretary [Caspar] Weinberger remarked two years ago, at our first Forum, for too long women had been excluded from this area. We're trying to get them involved. There are many reasons for that. Many more than I can go into. But I think the way to break it is to make a conscious effort to get women into positions of high visibility in the defense or the national security areas.[5]

Beyond what was a three-year endeavor of the Reagan administration, one would be hard-pressed to find a more high-profile effort from the

U.S. government. To date, regional conferences remain the central source of discourse concerning women and national security. In a recent example, on June 22–24, 2001, in Atlanta, the Carter Center held a major forum called the Conference of Women for Responsible National Security. The forum addressed the following three issues: (1) Will the missile defense system really protect the United States from nuclear attack? (2) Are American tax dollars being spent wisely in the name of national security? (3) How can we have peace and security and ensure socioeconomic justice for all our people?

As these issues suggest, the forum epitomizes the peace-oriented platform that has symbolized the role of women in national security. In spite of the increasing number of conferences and other venues, each suffers from minimal national exposure and real accomplishments.

"Foreign Challenge Blues"

Since the end of World War II, foreign governments have tested the resolve of U.S. presidents. These events usually occurred during the early stages of a presidency and have come in any number of forms: during superpower summits, probes from rogue states, and crises that test presidential responses.

Following their superpower summit in Vienna, Nikita Khrushchev left with the impression that President John F. Kennedy was inexperienced and vulnerable. Based on this supposition, the Soviet leader installed offensive nuclear missiles in Cuba, touching off "thirteen days" of nuclear brinkmanship. From the outbreak of the crisis, President Kennedy exhibited dynamic leadership, eventually forcing the Soviets to remove the missiles and ending one of the most intense periods of the Cold War.

Crises result as a matter of circumstance or by a planned foreign initiative. Two cases during the administration of George W. Bush are instructive: the crisis over the Chinese island of Hunan in which an American EP-3 Surveillance Aircraft and crew became captives of the Chinese government and the al-Qaeda suicide attacks on the United States. In the first incident, Bush worked assiduously to prevent a wider crisis while quietly employing diplomacy to force the return of U.S. military personnel and the downed spy aircraft. On the subject of the terrorist attacks, the administration has drawn praise for the management of the crisis and development of a grand strategy to confront future terrorist attacks.

Viewed collectively, these and other tests yield the following insights: (1) the tests by themselves did not determine the overall success or failure of presidents, (2) failure in one venue does not by itself indicate failure in another, and (3) in national security, there is often a learning curve before presidents become comfortable with the issues, their staff, and their management style. During the learning period, mistakes are made, directions misinterpreted, and goals frustrated. In the end, presidents recover and administrations survive, and they use the experiences for future crises.

Historically, every post–World War II U.S. president has found himself in this position to varying extents and managed to a degree to recover. Of interest then is the function of the first female president and how she might confront foreign challenges designed to test her presidential leadership. The distinguishing debate that accompanies tests of presidential resolve concerns two issues: Is the first female president up to the challenge? How would she respond to a crisis?

Defending U.S. National Interests

Female presidential candidates have endeavored to address this issue during presidential campaigns. For example, according to a survey conducted by the White House Project, "voters worry women lack the experience and ability to conduct foreign policy and promote U.S. defense and strategic concerns."[6] It is for this reason that presidential candidates issue major speeches designed to deflect attention away from this issue, or in the case of Elizabeth Dole, meet the challenge head on. In an address to the College of Charleston in September 1999, the presidential candidate stated:

> In the Dole administration, [the Clinton] era of wishful thinking, vacillation, and equivocation will end. I will lead the United States firmly and resolutely. I will advance and defend our national security interests. The United States will rebuild and restore its military. . . . We will develop and implement national and theater missile defense systems. You can be assured that our country's military and other security assets will be fully protected. . . . We must do everything in our power to combat the growing scourge of terrorism. Let me assure you, ladies and gentlemen, in a Dole administration, . . . we will deal with them from a position of strength and resolve.[7]

This speech exhibited the strength and articulation found in most major foreign policy addresses, but as impressive as Dole's speech was, ironically enough, women were dissatisfied with it. On this point, Judy Mann observed the "public still believes a man will do a better job in the most crucial areas of the presidency, ranging from the ability to lead and make tough decisions, to securing law and order and conducting foreign policy."[8] Even more troubling for Dole and female presidential candidates, in an audience of women, many were upset that the subject of her address was foreign policy rather than domestic policy, leaving many to question whether she could lead the so-called invisible army of Americans disenchanted with beltway politics.[9]

This evidence—along with research on gender discrimination and public opinion—suggests that, in the eyes of others, the first female president may not be up to the challenge of managing U.S. national interests. One assumes that, in running for the office, each candidate recognizes that she or he brings something unique to the table. The nation selects its president, at least in part, for her or his "philosophy and . . . judgment and conscientious conviction of what is right."[10]

The president must believe and assert her or his own priorities and "must always strive to preserve the power and prestige of the office, the availability of options, and the long-range interests of the nation."[11] As leader of the nation, the first female president will falter on occasion, as do all presidents. The ability to minimize those errors—in the face of public skepticism—will be a barometer of the success or failure of Madam President in the protection of national security interests.

A Female President's Response to a Crisis

One particular crisis worth considering is a scenario in the Middle East. Cultural differences suggest the first female president will have all kinds of difficulties mediating the Palestinian-Israeli dispute. The prevailing opinion posits that a woman attempting to offer a major diplomatic initiative in this region would face challenges to her authority and credibility from the parties to the dispute.

This observation discounts two variables: the fact that a female president will operate under the same national security process as previous presidents and the notion that she may impart a different perspective to the issue of Middle East peace than other U.S. leaders. On the first issue, the first female president will have the luxury of a process that favors ingenuity and staunchly supports activity. This diplomatic activity provides momentum and authority to an otherwise dormant bureaucracy, culminating in one of three approaches: (1) organizing a series of conferences designed to jump-start the peace process, (2) dispatching the secretary of state or a presidential envoy in an exercise of shuttle diplomacy, and (3) conducting personal diplomacy. In each case, the national security machinery plays a substantial part in the process.

With the national security machinery in place, Madam President might pursue similar approaches to those used by her male predecessors in Middle East peace and other national security problems. However, there is the possibility that the first female president will offer a different form of leadership and approach to the process. In terms of leadership, many previous women leaders demonstrated the tendency to be consensus builders. Entering a region where men completely dominate the culture, such an approach might be necessary to break down barriers. Additionally, according to former secretary of state Madeleine Albright, women are more apt to pay attention to "context and parameters," ensuring that both parties and their views are heard.[12]

It has been suggested that women by nature are peace-oriented. However, studies indicate that "women insiders"—those that operate in senior positions at the national level—are gravitating toward male norms and behavior. In a study by Nancy McGlen and Meredith Reid Sarkees, the authors conclude that "the consistent 8–9 percent gender gap has made women as a whole more peaceful than men in their approach to foreign policy since the 1950s." But on the basis of their survey of women's views within the Departments of State and Defense, the authors concluded that the gender gap was much less evident in the case of insiders. They suggest that "traditional women preferred peace, but empowered women were prepared to play the same game as men."[13]

The study indicates that empowered women are likely to adopt similar attitudes and approaches to the issue of national security as men. If so, should we conclude that, when required, Madam President might summon the parties to the dispute and issue tough statements to both with the desire of directing the participants toward an agreement? On the other side of the spectrum, it is unclear (no relevant study exists) what to make of a woman supportive of traditional "women's issues" when dealing with national security. Until the first female president actually engages the Middle East quagmire, one is left to ponder her role.

The Use of Force

In the lexicon of national security, the use of force remains the standard instrument in the protection of U.S. national interests. Following the dissipation of the Cold War, postwar expectations were raised regarding the use of force: the prevailing belief argued that conflict would decline.[14] Two developments indicated that this reality never came to pass. The first development concerned the rapid proliferation of ethnic and religious conflicts, which collectively increased the use of force. On the second point, Robert W. Tucker and David C. Hendrickson contend that in the absence of a rival to check its adventurism and in pursuit of its national purpose, the United States has given military force a new and expanded role in statecraft.[15]

In this climate, two issues emerge for the first female president: What are the predispositions of women on the use of force and the utility of this option in the protection of U.S. national security? In addressing these issues, it is important to note the difficulty in answering the question, owing to the great variety of views and behaviors of women leaders. Considering the issue of women and the efficacy of force, Leonie Huddy and Nayda Terkildsen studied gender stereotypes of women candidates and concluded that women are more likely than not to adopt male characteristics, particularly those regarding the military and the use of force when seeking national office.[16] This modern perspective aside, the notion of gender transformation on matters of national security is not new. Rhodri Jeffreys-Jones points out that Margaret Chase Smith was the first woman in the United States to confront this challenge.

> In order to enter the male world, some women have appeared to sacrifice the attributes of gender, becoming just like the "normative" men, who were tough and aggressive and who habitually resorted to war. The idea of the "transformational" woman who surrenders her gender characteristics and often eschews feminist goals has gained currency even among informed observers.[17]

If that were not enough, on the road to power women had to work twice as hard and, as a byproduct of the challenges they faced, endeavored to be equally as tough once in office.[18] For many proponents of force, this information represented a welcome reality. This point is particularly significant when a foreign country attacks U.S. interests. One thing is certain regarding Madam President's reaction and subsequent strategy: the first challenge will be an indicator of what will follow. In other words, the mishandling of one crisis may produce future tests of presidential credibility, even to a degree surpassing what a male president might face.

Since the end of World War II, some female leaders have embraced the idea of using force. The evolution of the efficacy and employment of force by women as an instrument of national policy developed during the early phase of the Cold War. Much of this convergence on the use of force can be traced to several significant women, among them Cold War hawk Eleanor Lansing Dulles, sister of Alan and John Dulles, who held the post of special assistant to the German Bureau. Another was Clare Booth Luce, named ambassador to Rome in 1953, during a period when the Central Intelligence Agency (CIA) was heavily involved in the internal affairs of the Italian government. These two individuals notwithstanding, one cannot dismiss the role of U.N. ambassador Jeanne Kirkpatrick and her advocacy of force during the Reagan administration.

Former secretary of state Madeleine Albright, the highest-ranking woman ever to serve in the U.S. government, was known for her threat to employ force.[19] Stating that she would do everything in her power to ensure that a female president is elected soon, Albright rebuts the polling data that "women are not sufficiently tough, experienced or knowledgeable to conduct foreign policy and tackle defense issues."[20] A public advocate of force in the Balkans, Albright complained, "what is the point of having a military, if you are unwilling to use it?" In a related statement, Albright argued that the United States was the "indispensable nation" and was duty-bound to promote democracy abroad, even if military force was necessary.[21]

To assess the first female president's decision on force, Jeffreys-Jones conducted a comparative analysis to compensate for the absence of women leaders in the United States. By studying other women leaders, scholars are able to anticipate how the first female president would behave.[22] Jeffreys-Jones concluded that the notion of the "iron lady" was mythical and that women leaders of foreign countries have generally had peaceful dispositions. But the study is problematic for a number of reasons. First, it is next to impossible to equate the use of force for world leaders from history with the first female president of the United States. Second, the national security process is such that several institutions (Defense Department, CIA, State Department, Congress, etc.) will participate in the process, shaping the president's actions and decisions. Third, the myriad of threats to U.S. interests and role of the nation as world leader place extensive pressure on U.S. presidents.

The national security bureaucracy will play an important function in the application of force and decisions surrounding the issue. "The posture and power of various agencies within the national security establishment, the interplay of personalities within the presidential office, the reassertion of congressional power in the policy process, the politicization of national security issues, and the changed domestic and international political environment" all shape the responses by U.S. presidents.[23] Yet, as President Lyndon Johnson acknowledged, policy recommendations emerge from a score of bureaucratic sources, "but there is only one that has been chosen by the American people to decide" among those choices.[24]

Managing the National Security Bureaucracy

Management of the national security bureaucracy continues to evolve. It is asserted here that the first woman president will confront a series of issues that will force her to dramatically alter the ebb and flow of the bureaucracy. She will likely face issues from the bureaucracy that her male predecessors have not faced. The concern is with the relationship of presidential style in the implementation and pursuit of national security objectives and how external variables force presidents to reconsider the way policy directives are implemented.

On the matter of style, a former aide to President Kennedy, Theodore Sorenson, opined that the president "must believe in his own objectives" and should always be on guard to "preserve the power and prestige of his office, the availability of his options, and long-range interests of the office."[25] This advice is important in considering two determinants—the bureaucracy and crises—in the management of the national security process.

Understanding the bureaucracy represents a critical step in the management of national security. At one time or another, post–World War II presidents have had to confront a bureaucracy out of step with their policies and form alliances to frustrate opposition strategies or policies. As Joseph Goulden maintains:

> A shadow "opposition government" exists within the bureaucracy, staff, attorneys and assistant division chiefs and deputy administrators, a Civil-Service old-boys'-club, ever ready to whisper information embarrassing to an administration with which it disagrees. Politics, mischief, altruism—the motive really isn't important. Every administration lives with the knowledge it can be clobbered by a brick thrown from its own backyard.[26]

One way to guard against this problem is to appoint a trusted team of presidential advisers familiar with and skilled at bureaucratic politics. If this strategy fails, presidents have two additional alternatives. As was the case during the Clinton administration, presidents may reduce the appointment of deputy and other middle-level managers, thereby decreasing the opportunity and number of individuals available to thwart presidential policy initiatives.[27] Second, as a measure to circumvent the bureaucracy, U.S. presidents have tended to become dependent on a close "inner circle" of advisers.

On the larger, more arduous dilemma of confronting crises and their ability to disrupt the normal orchestration of the national security objectives, presidents Clinton and George W. Bush provide instructive examples on how the executive operates when confronted with unforeseen external variables. In both cases, each president employed presidential power to restore order to the bureaucracy and to allay concerns about U.S. security interests. With U.S. economic supremacy receiving some challenge from Japan and the European Community, President Clinton created the National Economic Council (NEC). The goal of the NEC was the creation of an "Economic Security Council, similar in status to the National Security Council, with responsibility for coordinating America's international economic policy."[28] This instrument played a major role in what became an important area of Clinton's legacy—the remaking of U.S. foreign economic policy.

On October 8, 2001, nearly one month after the devastating al-Qaeda terrorist attacks, President Bush established the Homeland Security Council (HSC). The purpose of the HSC was to coordinate the "executive branch's efforts to detect, prepare for, protect against, respond to, and recover from terrorist attacks within the United States."[29] In response to bureaucratic infighting and the failure of some forty executive departments to cooperate and share intelligence, the White House again took the extraordinary measure of employing an executive council as means to coordinate the work of the bureaucracy against future terrorist threats to the United States. During a press conference on October 29, 2001, President Bush endeavored to set the record straight on his decision to circumvent the traditional national security process, saying, "Our task is to do everything we can to protect the American people from any threat whatsoever. The American people are beginning to understand that we are fighting a two-front war against terrorism."[30]

After such significant departures from the traditional management of national security affairs, the question remains as to whether a female president would act similarly. Two points would seem to support the conclusion that she would continue to use special councils and new, innovative responses to problems: an ever-changing security environment and the absence of rules within the international system. During the Cold War, the Soviet Union represented the chief source of international instability. To counterbalance this threat, beginning with Harry Truman and ending with George Bush, U.S. presidents relied on the National Security Council as the principal national security mechanism to frustrate Soviet adventurism.

In the post–Cold War world, international security is no longer one-dimensional. As the communist ideological threat ended, the security environment became diffuse, and multidimensional threats—consisting of subnational and religious conflicts, failed states, humanitarian contingencies, terrorism, and the proliferation of weapons of mass destruction—became issues commanding the stage. These burgeoning threats will most likely continue to force future presidents—and Madam President—to transform and reinvent the structural instruments used to manage increasingly multidimensional threats to U.S. security. The first female president will be presented with some of the same issues and with threats heretofore unseen. The national security bureaucracy was empowered in part by the presence of a powerful, known entity—the Soviet Union—and a single, massive strategy—containment. Even though those days are gone, the bureaucracy will continue to play a role in national security policy, and a female president will, like her predecessors, have to deal with it. The extent to which the national security bureaucracy works with her—and the extent to which her sex is an issue—are hard to predict (see Table 17.1).

Conclusion

Several speculative conclusions might be offered regarding the questions posed in this chapter. Initially, it appears that the first female president will face national security challenges similar to previous presidents having nothing to do with her sex, including such pressing issues as managing the national security bureaucracy, confronting the use of force, and preparing for heretofore unseen foreign policy challenges. Second, because she is likely to be an empowered woman, Madam President might be expected to adopt male norms, as have other women in leadership positions, in responding to national security threats. Third, she will, like other presidents, be dependent on the bureaucracy, senior aides, and a host of other institutional forces in the making of national security policy.

Finally, and perhaps most significantly, on the issues of foreign challenge blues, management of the national bureaucracy, and the use of force, the research indicates that Madam President will confront many

Table 17.1 The Transformation of National Security

Former Focus	Current Focus
National defense	International security
Unilateral action	Coalition diplomacy
Threat-based policy	Objective-based policy
Control	Adaptation
Capabilities	Intentions
Domestic politics as a variable	International politics as a variable
Force application	Statecraft and negotiation
War preparation	Peace preservation
Win by outproducing the enemy	Win by outwitting the foe

Source: Douglas Stuart, *Organizing for National Security.* Carlisle, PA: Strategic Studies Institute, U.S. Army War College, 2000, p. 149.

of the same dilemmas—foreign leaders eager to test her leadership, bureaucratic elements out of step with her policy preferences, bureaucrats willing to delay and defeat policy initiatives, and the unwillingness to employ instruments of national power—as her male predecessors. In resolving these issues, she will likely make mistakes and enjoy successes, just as have her male predecessors. However, she might be afforded even less room for error and less leeway in terms of a learning curve, not only from the public and press, but perhaps also from the national security bureaucracy. Above all, her own strength of character and leadership qualities will come into play in protecting U.S. national security.

18

Profile: Elizabeth Dole, Executive Leadership

Robert P. Watson and Ann Gordon

COURTESY OF ELIZABETH DOLE

Born July 29, 1936, in Salisbury, North Carolina
B.A. with honors from Duke University in 1958; M.A. from Harvard University in 1960; and J.D. from Harvard University in 1965
Secretary of Transportation (1983–1987); Secretary of Labor (1989–1990)
President, American Red Cross (1991–1999)
Presidential candidate, 1999

Elizabeth Dole has the distinction of being the first presidential candidate's spouse—Bob Dole sought the presidency in 1992 and 1996—to campaign for the same office herself. She also mounted the most prominent bid by a woman for the presidency yet undertaken.

Elizabeth Hanford grew up in Salisbury, North Carolina, where she distinguished herself in her educational pursuits. After completing two college degrees, she enrolled in Harvard Law School, where she was one of the few women in her class. In 1974, she married Bob Dole, who was then the chair of the Republican National Committee. Both were thirty-nine years old, and he was divorced. Two years after their wedding, her husband was placed on the Republican ticket as Gerald Ford's vice presidential running mate.

Even though Dole was a registered Democrat and received her break in politics in the administration of Lyndon B. Johnson—where she worked in consumer affairs and in the Department of Health, Education, and Welfare—she changed parties, becoming an independent in an effort to retain her career after President Richard Nixon won election in 1968. In the Nixon White House she served as White House liaison and was appointed in 1974 to head the Federal Trade Commission. Dole would spend the remainder of her long political career as a Republican, working for every subsequent Republican administration, until her own bid for the Oval Office in 1999.

Her impressive résumé of public service—which included serving as President Ronald Reagan's special assistant and secretary of transportation as well as President George H. W. Bush's secretary of labor—propelled Dole's name to the short list of possible vice presidential candidates during several election cycles. Dole had also gained nationwide exposure, attracted a large and diverse following, and was seen as an able administrator, all traits necessary for her own eventual presidential bid. As secretary of transportation, Dole managed to balance such competing goals as promoting Reagan's aggressive deregulation efforts and ensuring automobile safety through, for example, seatbelt and airbag regulations and the installation of a third brake light, which was even nicknamed the "Dole light." She would continue to balance sensitive administrative and political assignments as George Bush's secretary of labor, where she participated in privatizing Conrail and arbitrating strikes in the coal industry.

In January 1999, Elizabeth Dole resigned from the presidency of the Red Cross to pursue the U.S. presidency. In the early stages of the race, she was running a competitive second place to front-runner George W. Bush. Throughout her campaign, analysts and pundits were forced to consider the possibility of a woman president. The public also witnessed the discomfort and hesitancy surrounding a woman candidate by the media and political establishment. To some, she was a curiosity, and to others she was simultaneously labeled as too conservative *and* too liberal, and she endured gender-based questions male candidates would find unthinkable. Critics alleged Dole was a control freak and a perfectionist, overly cautious, and scripted to the point of inaction. Her fans saw a principled, competent, and experienced leader who possessed a knack for consensus building.

In spite of her extensive résumé and political connections, Dole experienced difficulties in raising adequate funds to mount a winning campaign. Forbes and Bush enjoyed huge fund-raisin advantages over Dole. Some saw her inability to raise adequate funding as a gender-based obstacle facing all women candidates for high office. In response to the matter, Dole stated, "It's more important to raise issues than to raise campaign funds."[1] Although shortages of cash limited the Dole campaign, some critics asserted that it was not her gender that caused the problem but her tendency to rarely field questions from reporters or answer tough questions on the stump and her inability to define a reason for her candidacy other than her gender. Yet Dole established herself as a genuine listener, noted for asking supporters, "What's on your mind?"

In an unfair blow to Elizabeth Dole's campaign for the highest office, some critics labeled her efforts little more than the symbolic gesture of a woman pursuing the presidency. However, Dole's campaign was not only groundbreaking but viable. In her words: "Much has been made of the symbolism of my candidacy . . . but, along with the symbolism, there was also substance. . . . "I think what we've done is pave the way for the person who will be the first woman president."[2]

PART 5

CONCLUSION

19

Madam President: Sooner or Later?

Karen O'Connor

On December 6, 2001, several female members of the House Congressional Women's Caucus gathered in the Cannon House Office Building to voice their indignation over the results of a study by the White House Project. That report, "Who's Talking: An Analysis of Sunday Morning Talk Shows," analyzed the sex of male and female guests on Sunday morning political programs. Not surprisingly, White House Project researchers found that not only were women rarely seen on Sunday morning shows, but once on, they were rarely asked back for a return performance. In stark contrast, a large proportion of the men appearing on the shows were invited back.[1]

As several of the chapters in this volume underscore, many studies have found that women as candidates or politicians often face unequal treatment from the mass media, the vehicle from which most Americans get their news.[2] The premise of the White House Project report was that appearances on Sunday morning talk shows give the guests on those programs immediate credibility and national recognition as experts. This imprimatur as an "expert" translates into additional appearances for men and hence greater name recognition and greater electoral potential. The women in Congress, in spite of their best efforts, do not enjoy this status.[3]

The need to be viewed as an expert, as well as electable, is especially critical when we speak of potential women candidates for all offices, but particularly that of U.S. president. Although some women, such as women's rights pioneers Victoria Woodhull and Myra Bradwell, sought the nation's highest office even before women got the right to vote, no woman has yet to win a major party's nod as its presidential candidate. Although Geraldine Ferraro won the Democratic Party's nomination to be Walter Mondale's running mate in 1984, she never faced the grueling primary process that Elizabeth Dole experienced when she sought the Republican Party's nomination for presidency in 1999. As others point out in this volume, it was impossible for Dole to overcome media bias and its resultant effect on the viability of her candidacy as she attempted to raise enough money to run a campaign against the front runner, George W. Bush, and John McCain, a media darling.[4]

Throughout this volume, several themes emerge as to why no woman has yet to be nominated by a major party, let alone elected president of the United States. Almost all the chapters underscore the importance of positive, substantive media coverage for women aiming for any elective office. In other chapters, several authors note the paucity of women in the pipeline—that is, in lower elected positions that could ultimately produce a greater pool of women presidential candidates. As Erika Falk and Kathleen Hall Jamieson point out in Chapter 4 of this book, in 2000, there were very few women serving in positions that historically have produced presidents. The relative rareness of women governors (and senators) makes it difficult to envision a pool of strong women candidates. After all, not all male governors or senators have presidential ambitions, nor should we expect all women to have them. Given long-term cultural and social biases that militate against women running for elective office in the United States, it may take longer for a woman to be elected in her own right than some would expect.

To some extent, it is difficult to understand how the United States, a nation that prides itself on its progressiveness, has yet to see a woman emerge as a strong candidate for the presidency. This puzzle becomes even more intractable when one looks to the progress of women in other nations. Two of the United States' closest allies—Great Britain and Canada—have had women prime ministers. Women have found it easier to get elected president in nations as diverse as Finland, Guyana, Indonesia, and Panama than in the United States. Thus, in this concluding chapter I examine the experiences of women in other nations to see what lessons might be learned for women in the U.S. context. Next, I explore what it is about the U.S. political system—one in which the majority of voters are often women—that even necessitates the need for a volume such as this one. And, finally, I discuss some strategies to help pave the way for women candidates and speculate about the possible implications of September 11, 2001, on the chances of a woman being elected president in her own right in the near future.

Premiers, Prime Ministers, and Presidents

In 1960, Ceylon's parliamentarian, Sirimavo Bandaranaike, was sworn in as that nation's prime minister following the death of her husband. She would serve in that position until 1965 and later from 1970 until 1977, during which time Ceylon returned to its former name, Sri Lanka. In 1994, she again became prime minister. In that same year, her daughter, Chandrika Kumaratunga, became president of Sri Lanka. They ruled this parliamentary democracy as president and prime minister until 2000, when Bandaranaike died. Another kind of mother-and-daughter team developed in Bangladesh. There, a mother and daughter each served as prime minister sequentially. Khaleda Zia followed her husband as prime minister from 1991 to 1996; her daughter succeeded her and served from 1996 to 2001. In 2001, Zia again became her nation's prime minister.

Earlier, in 1974, Isabel Perón became the first woman president in the world when, as vice president, she succeeded her husband, dictator Juan Perón, upon his death. In many ways, these women's collective paths to power are ones that underscore many of our impressions of women leaders. At least initially, both in the United States and abroad, women often came to head nations, states, or serve in Congress, as one political scientist noted, "Over His Dead Body."[5] And, in some nations, such as Bangladesh, India, Pakistan, and Sri Lanka, being a daughter or a wife clearly sets women candidates for higher office apart from many women who seek office with no familial ties.[6]

As Table 1.1 revealed, thirty-seven nations have had a woman in the office of premier, president, or prime minister. These nations represent the large and small, the powerful and not powerful, and a range of power-sharing arrangements. Eight nations—Bangladesh, Bermuda, Haiti, Ireland, New Zealand, Netherlands Antilles, the Philippines, and Sri Lanka—have had more than one woman serve as premier, president, or prime minister. Two women—in Guyana and Sri Lanka—served both as prime minister and president of their respective countries.

Of the nearly fifty women who have served as a premier, prime minister, or president, thirteen have followed in their husbands' or fathers' footsteps, if not, in fact, over their dead bodies. Women such as Perón, and Janet Jagan of Guyana, came to power to fill the void when their spouses died in office. Others, including Violeta Chamorro of Nicaragua and Corazon Aquino of the Philippines, were mobilized to seek office after their husbands—both of whom were political dissidents—were assassinated by opposing political forces. Still others, such as Mireya Moscoso, saw their husbands driven from office. Moscoso fled to Miami from Panama with her husband and lived with him in exile for years. Returning to Panama, she ran for the presidency and was elected in 1999. Other women, including Benazir Bhutto, the former prime minister of Pakistan, and Gloria Macapagal-Arroyo, elected president of the Philippines in 2001, learned about politics from their fathers, who also headed their respective governments at one time. It is impossible to measure the effect of strong political pedigree on the political successes of these women. Undoubtedly, their associations with their husbands, mothers, or fathers prepared them for the positions they ultimately attained. But although we often attribute the large number of women leaders outside the United States to the importance of their family connections, it is important to note that the majority of women world leaders (61 percent) rose to power without the benefit of a long line of familial ties to national politics.

Factors Affecting Women Who Want to Run

As many authors in this volume note, several factors may contribute to the failure of any U.S. woman to become president over eight decades since winning the vote. These include but are not limited to cultural stereotypes, sex discrimination, and the political system.

Cultural Stereotypes

A commercial for the new, woman-oriented Oxygen network opens with a pink baby hat on the floor. As a befuddled nurse retrieves the cap and puts it back on the newborn, she looks up to see several more pink hats being thrown into the air out of the bassinets. A lone baby fist rises courageously upward. It is not Helen Reddy's "I am Woman," but the message is clear. Look out for a new generation of stronger and bolder women. Another not so obvious message of this commercial underscores the fact that from the minute girls are born, they are assigned to certain roles because of their sex. It is pink for girls and blue for boys. Just as babies are categorized from birth, young girls continue to be categorized and subjected to a host of cultural stereotypes, even when raised in progressive families. Although in many homes it is no longer acceptable to raise girls to be nurses and boys to be doctors, young girls are routinely separated from boys in a variety of situations, whether it is in a line to walk to the cafeteria or to pick teams in a physical education class. And a host of studies continue to show that young girls still often face a chilly classroom climate where their contributions go unnoticed and unrewarded.[7] Instead, young girls who exhibit the characteristics that we often associate with future political leaders—daring, inquisitiveness, and assertiveness—are often penalized for what some perceive as their unfeminine behaviors.[8]

Thus, from an early age, many women are taught to comply with feminine ideals and are often punished for violating cultural stereotypes. Since all of us are bombarded with these expectations—teachers, students, journalists, voters, candidates, potential candidates, campaign contributors, and so on—it is not surprising to understand that it will be hard to elect a woman as president in the current sociopolitical climate.

As others in this book note, although more and more people continue to report to pollsters that they are willing to vote for a woman for president, those polls ask respondents if they would vote for a "qualified" woman for president if she were their party's nominee. In 1996, for example, 92 percent of U.S. women and 88 percent of the men reported that they would vote for a woman president under those circumstances.[9] But perceptions of what constitutes "qualified" vary according to the lens by which each voter accesses each candidate. Thus, it may be much harder for women to jump over a man's threshold of what constitutes a "qualified" candidate, especially since Gallup polls and others reveal that 42 percent of those queried think that a man would make a better president.[10]

Maryland lieutenant governor Kathleen Kennedy Townsend is a case in point. Several of her male Kennedy cousins have been considered as serious congressional candidates without much experience, yet rarely were their claims to seek office questioned. In fact, the Kennedy family is the closest thing we have in the United States to a political dynasty of the kinds that exist in Sri Lanka, Bangladesh, or even Pakistan. Still, as Townsend initially sought to run for governor of Maryland in 2002, many questioned her "executive experience." Both the *Washington Post* and the *Baltimore Sun* editorial pages made her experience an issue. At the same time, leading male Democratic and Republican contestants for the office—all of whom have far less executive or leadership experience than Townsend—were touted as alternatives to her.[11] If her seven years as lieutenant governor do not qualify her to become the governor of Maryland, as some pundits initially opined, and if men were held to the same standards, then many statehouses would go leaderless. The point is, no matter how well qualified women are for some jobs, some men and even some women will not rate them well qualified enough to merit their vote for president or governor.

Given these prevailing and pervasive cultural stereotypes, one begins to see how difficult it will be to elect a woman as president. If men (and women) will vote only for a "qualified" woman for president, if the threshold for what makes a woman qualified is higher than for a man (among some voters), and if about 10 percent of the electorate will not vote for a qualified woman for president, then the near future does not bode well for potential women presidential candidates. Given the closeness of recent presidential elections, any candidate starting out with a 10 percent deficit does so at a tremendous disadvantage.

Sex Discrimination

The cultural stereotypes that permeate our political system formerly resulted in or at least were reflected in sex discrimination. Early on, women were not allowed to vote, at least in part based on legal principles that made a married man the head of his household. As such, the husband was the sole qualified voter in the family unit. Once women won the franchise, few even voted because they had not been socialized to do so. It was not until 1980 that women began to outvote men in presidential elections.[12]

Moreover, most states prohibited women from serving as jurors, a duty of citizenship often closely associated with the vote. Indeed, many states for many years relied almost exclusively on voter lists to draw potential jurors. It was not until 1979 that the Supreme Court ruled that states could not automatically ban women from serving as jurors because they were women.[13] Women's rights activists had long argued that women could not be considered to be men's political equals if they are not obliged to participate in all facets of democracy equally. For every "benefit" of citizenship, such as voting, one should gladly consent to performing a "duty," such as jury service. This kind of sex discrimination simply served to perpetuate women's second-class status within the polity.

Discrimination in and by the political parties. Political parties, which historically have been at the core of the U.S. political system, in spite of the wishes of the Framers to the contrary, long have discriminated overtly and covertly against women. Only a handful of women have served as the chair of either the Democratic or Republican national or state party committees. In late 2001, when national Republican committeeman James Gilmore, the governor of Virginia, resigned his post, his cochair, Ann Wagner, was rarely mentioned as a possible replacement. Thus, it was not all that surprising that she was overlooked and a male was appointed. Despite the fact that it is women who historically have done the nuts and bolts work so central to winning elections, on the national and state level the parties largely continue to be run by men.[14]

Political scientists continue to find that both major parties are more welcoming to women candidates, although many women officeholders continue to believe that the parties still discriminate against them.[15] The 2002 congressional elections leave room for some optimism. Both the Democratic congressional and Senate campaign committees are chaired by women—Representative Nita Lowey (D-NY) and Senator Patty Murray (D-WA), respectively. But even significant decreases in sexism in the major parties are unlikely to help prospective women candidates for the presidency very much. By law, political parties must stay out of the primary process and cannot endorse or help particular candidates seeking a party nod. Thus, women candidates must look to the media and political contributors to support their campaigns, places where tremendous amounts of discrimination continue to exist.

Discrimination in and by the media. Throughout this book, the role of the media in presidential campaigns has been finely detailed. It has been well documented that, in large part, the media continues to be dominated by men, who in turn view the political world through a male lens. Women, too, often perpetuate stereotypes about women or fail to advance the cause or perspectives of women. Several studies conducted by the White House Project have documented the nature and degree of that discrimination. Its most recent report, "Who's Talking: An Analysis of Sunday Morning Talk Shows," reflects the extent to which bias continues to exist. Women represented just less than 11 percent of those who appeared on five major talk shows (with presidential candidates being excluded from the analysis). These numbers plummeted after September 11. In the wake of that national tragedy, women made up only 6.8 percent of the guests. The week before the study was announced, no women were invited guests on these programs. Lieutenant General Claudia Kennedy (the retired former assistant deputy chair of the Staff on Intelligence), who came out near the top of a White House Project poll of potential women candidates for president, lives in the Washington, D.C., area where the Sunday programs originate but was not even asked to appear at a time when these shows were focusing on U.S. intelligence.[16] Just as troubling is the fact that nineteen male senators were invited back as guests on *This Week* and twenty-one male senators were invited back as guests on *Meet the Press,* but not a single woman senator was asked for a return appearance.

Equally distressing as the nature of this kind of stifling of women's voices is the fact that the media in general has reacted poorly to the report. Both *USA Today* and the *Washington Post* reported on the study in the "Style" section rather than in the "News" section; the issue received little coverage in other news outlets. The *Post* story, noticeably subtitled "Public Affairs Shows Reflect Shortage of Women in Power," began: "Most of the officials, lawmakers, experts, and pontificators who parade their opinions on Sunday morning television have something in common. They don't wear panty hose."[17]

Clearly, the editors of these respective papers believed that this report better belonged in the "fluff" section of their papers, as Howard Kurtz's treatment of the subject in the *Post* reflects. Even his subtitle reveals how much he "just didn't get it." The White House Project report showed how there *were* women who could be asked; they simply *were not*. Instead, Kurtz takes the blame off the media and "spins" the story as one about how the dearth of women logically leads to their exclusion from the airwaves.

Just as distressing were the reactions of the offenders. "I don't consider it a problem," one female producer commented.[18] "To a man—and woman—anchors and producers of all the Sunday programs dismissed the group's [White House Project's] complaints. . . . We cover the news we find," said NBC's *Meet the Press* host Tim Russert.[19] As long as the kind of attitudes reflected above by the media continue, it is difficult to see how a woman candidate for president could expect to be taken as seriously, let alone even close to equitably, as her male opponent.

Discrimination by political contributors. Fund-raisers for Elizabeth Dole during her bid for the Republican Party nomination for president were shocked to learn how hard it was to raise money for a candidate who was doing as well as Dole was doing in the polls, although her media coverage did not reflect that status. One Dole operative expressed her frustration, "I couldn't believe it was so hard to get people to contribute $500 to attend a political dinner for Dole. If I was working for Bush, I could get people to contribute $1,000 to eat with Barney, his dog."[20] Potential donors cannot help but be affected by the subtle and not so subtle prevailing stereotypes about women that manifest themselves in the media's treatment of women candidates at most levels.

The case of Lieutenant General Claudia Kennedy, who was profiled as a potential president or running mate prior to the 2000 campaign season, is illustrative.[21] As the first woman three-star general in the U.S. Army, Claudia Kennedy received a considerable amount of press attention. Over and over again, she could be found on lists of potential presidential candidates or, at the very least, a possible vice presidential nominee. When she left the Army in 1999, she settled in northern Virginia and began exploring the possibility of a run against John Warner, the incumbent four-term senator from Virginia. Other women had succeeded in such feats, although Debbie Stabenow (D-MI), who was able to knock off one-term senator Spencer Abraham in Michigan, was a popular representative with a long history in Michigan politics. Claudia Kennedy's initial foray into Virginia politics, although encouraged by women's groups, was greeted with little enthusiasm by the Democratic establishment in Virginia. Perhaps more important, potential big donors failed to embrace her candidacy. Kennedy did not have a record on the issues that could appeal to them and had not made the kinds of political and big money connections during her distinguished career in the armed services that one needs to launch a successful statewide race. Recognizing that she would have to raise at least $12 million to become a viable candidate, shortly after September 11, Kennedy decided not to run. Given her problems with fund-raising before September 11, she immediately recognized her task would now be impossible.

The Political System

Many of the women noted in Table 1.1 rose to their positions of political power in parliamentary democracies. In those systems, parties that either win a majority of seats in a legislature or that are able to forge a working majority are able to select the prime minister. Thus, when the Conservative Party took control of the British Parliament in 1979, Margaret Thatcher carefully cultivated other members of Parliament to support her bid to lead the government. When Representative Nancy Pelosi (D-CA) became the first woman elected to a formal leadership position in the U.S. Congress, she and her supporters did much of the same political wrangling to ensure her election as the House Democratic Whip. That position is second only to that of the minority leader on the Democratic side of the aisle. Her election may be the harbinger of positive things to come for women in the House of Representatives, but it will not have any immediate effect on the U.S. political system that makes it more difficult for women to seek the presidency than a prime ministership. In fact, women have been elected in their own right as president in very few nations. And in countries such as Ireland, which has had two women presidents, that position is far less powerful than that of prime minister.

Because of the nature of the U.S. federal system and how the party system has evolved, candidates for the nomination of the major parties must seek delegate votes at the state level. There, arcane state laws often govern the selection process. In some states, delegates are picked in caucuses of party faithful; in others, delegates are selected by primary election by the party faithful; some states do not even require that voters be registered with a particular party to vote in that party's presidential delegate election.

This multiplicity of systems and the "front-loading" of the process, which makes it important to win early caucus and primary elections, make money and a strong campaign staff all the more crucial. To date, no woman has been able to garner the kind of national enthusiasm and support that is necessary to negotiate the primary process. Neither have many male candidates. In 2000, both Al Gore and George W. Bush fairly easily crushed their competitors long before the last primary was held. There are few women with the visibility and connections within the business community and with other large donors to make a strong run. And few, with the exception of Hillary Clinton or Kathleen Kennedy Townsend (both often profiled as potential presidential candidates), have the family ties of an Al Gore or George W. Bush and the ability to raise funds nationwide as campaigns become more and more expensive each election cycle.[22]

Possible Remedies

The cultural, sociological, and political realities that militate against women becoming president in the near future are formidable. As discussed here and elsewhere in the book, the White House Project was founded in the late 1990s to "foster the entry of women into positions of leadership, including the U.S. presidency."[23] Under the leadership of Marie Wilson, the White House Project has devised a host of strategies in pursuing that goal, as it attempts to elevate the development as well as discussion of potential women leaders. For example, recognizing that little girls have few role models in top offices, the project worked with Mattel to launch a "Madam President" Barbie. Although this collaboration had its critics, the project correctly assumed that young girls might think more about aspiring to the presidency if they could imaginatively play with an attractive woman doll who came replete with an inaugural gown, business suit, and a presidential platform.

In a different tactic, the White House Project launched a nationwide ballot to suggest and advance potential female running mates for the two major party political candidates. Although none of its top four vote-getters (Elizabeth Dole, Dianne Feinstein, Claudia Kennedy, and Christine Todd Whitman) were tapped, Feinstein is still in the Senate, Whitman now heads the Environmental Protection Agency in the Bush administration, Dole has moved to North Carolina to run for the Senate, and Kennedy considered a run for the Senate in Virginia and has not ruled out a run at a later date. Thus, all four continue to provide powerful role models for young girls as well as for potential candidates for any office.

Groups such as the White House Project must keep up the pressure on the media to recognize unequal treatment of women and to encourage possible women candidates for the presidency as they help publicize possible candidates.

It may be a useful tactic for groups such as the White House Project to recognize the powerful role of political dynasties, for better or worse. They have helped women come to power in other nations and may be a gateway to the White House for women in the United States.

Many of the world's first women presidents or prime ministers followed in the footsteps of their husbands or fathers. But others soon followed, although their paths to their respective nations' highest offices were quite diverse. In the United States, the first woman of late to launch a serious bid for her party's presidential nod was Elizabeth Dole. Few would or could seriously argue that Elizabeth Dole—although a remarkably able politician—would have been on the list of serious presidential contenders without the visibility that her husband, Senator Robert Dole, had given her over the years through his unsuccessful vice presidential and then presidential bids. She undoubtedly came to the notice of Ronald Reagan, who appointed her to his cabinet, through her ties to her husband. In fact, some believe that her bid for the 2000 nod was irreparably harmed when her husband told a reporter that he planned to give money to Senator John McCain, who was also seeking the Republican nod but running below Dole in the polls. Dole, who emerged as a serious candidate for Senate in her home state of North Carolina in 2002, may finally be finding her way out of her husband's shadow. Should Dole's bid be successful, she would be a much more viable candidate for the presidency but for two things: it is unlikely that George Bush will not be the 2004 Republican candidate and her age. By 2008, Dole will be over seventy years old, and in all likelihood will be viewed as too old to be considered a serious candidate for the office.

Interestingly, Senator Hillary Clinton (D-NY), also vaulted onto the public radar in a wifely role—first as a governor's wife and then as first lady. And Clinton already has been elected in her own right and represents an electorally rich state. She also is younger and is a member of a political party that will be looking for presidential and vice presidential candidates in 2004 as well as 2008. Although Clinton is far more controversial than Dole, given extant political circumstances, she may have a shot to be more like her hero, Eleanor Roosevelt, than she ever thought—by spending a possible sixteen years in the White House, one way or another.

Other women on the horizon also have the patina that goes with a family with a long political tradition. Kathleen Kennedy Townsend, should she become the governor of Maryland, is well situated to build on her family fortunes and make a serious bid for the presidency. Similarly, Senator Mary Landrieu (D-LA) comes from a family steeped in Louisiana and southern politics, also making her one to watch.

This is not to say that other women without benefit of well-known families cannot make a credible run at the nomination for president. In 2002, there were at least seventeen open governorships. Given how many current and recent presidents have come from governor's mansions, it is critical to get women to run and win in these states to begin to increase the presidential eligibility pool. Most helpful would be the election of more women in electorally rich states. The White House Project and EMILY's List both are actively encouraging more women to run at the state level to garner executive experience apparently valued by the U.S. electorate. EMILY's List is actively encouraging its members to contribute to the candidacies of pro-choice Democratic women; the White House Project is attempting to train both Republican and Democratic women candidates for governor about how to deal more effectively with the media.

It may well be, as pointed out elsewhere in this volume, that the most likely way Americans will see our first female president will be by a woman being added to the ticket as a vice presidential running mate, as was the case in the historic selection of Geraldine Ferraro. That momentous act is not forgotten by those old enough to remember it. A future Republican candidate for the presidency, especially one from the South, would be well advised to look long and hard at Massachusetts acting governor Jane Swift. Townsend, too, could easily be tapped by a Democrat nominee.

In the wake of September 11, however, it may be that governors, untested in foreign affairs, may not be quite as attractive running mates. Women are already often viewed as stronger on domestic affairs. Should a presidential candidate want to find a running mate with foreign relations experience, he need only look to the Senate, where Susan Collins (R-ME) and Mary Landrieu (D-LA) serve on the Senate Armed Services Committee. They, of course, are only some of the women who would make outstanding running mates and then be in the position, if elected, later to run in their own right for the nation's highest office.

Appendix:
The White House Project

Marie C. Wilson

Mission and Background

The White House Project (WHP), a national nonpartisan organization, is dedicated to enhancing public perceptions of women's capacity to lead and fostering the entry of women into positions of leadership, including the U.S. presidency. The organization's programs are designed to build a more representative democracy and to generate increased opportunities for women to fully participate in governing the United States and to lead in all spheres of society.

Founded in 1998, the organization's groundbreaking initiatives aim to shift the political and cultural climate so that it becomes commonplace in the eyes of the public and the media for women to be governors, chief executive officers, and president. The White House Project's strategies encompass research, national media campaigns, initiatives to encourage civic engagement, and measures to influence popular culture.

Activities

"Conversations with Women Leaders" Series

Produced in partnership with the *New York Times*, this series features far-reaching, candid discussions with high-profile women leaders that explore the challenges and opportunities facing women in political leadership. Featured guests include former secretary of state Madeleine Albright, Environmental Protection Agency (EPA) head and former New Jersey governor Christine Todd Whitman, astronaut and author Mae Jemison, and Brown University president Ruth Simmons. The series is designed to heighten the visibility of women leaders, educate the public, and encourage dialogue about women's leadership.

Women's Leadership Summit
The White House Project's Women's Leadership Summit has featured over 100 distinguished participants from an array of fields who work together to create a new blueprint to move women's leadership forward in the twenty-first century. Participants create a cross-sector infrastructure, network, and identify strategies to change the climate for women's leadership. Participants include Heidi Miller, vice chair of March, Inc., and Cathie Black, president of Hearst Magazines.

"Welcome to the White House, Ms. President!"
This innovative curriculum teaches children ages five to eleven about the presidency and women's leadership. The curriculum has been distributed through Kids Voting USA and Girls, Inc., featured on *Nick News* with Linda Ellerbee, and published in *New Moon Magazine,* an international magazine for girls. The curriculum is available through the WHP website.

"Ms. President" Girl Scout Patch
In a historic move, the WHP has partnered with the Girl Scouts to create the first "Ms. President" Girl Scout Patch. This new venture gives girls the opportunity to learn about women's leadership and civic and political leadership.

Scholastic National Essays Contest
The WHP and Scholastic have created a new White House Project Women's Leadership Award, which will be featured in Scholastic's Arts and Writing Award program. The award recognizes young artists and writers who submit an original work focusing on women's leadership.

National Petition for Progress
The petition calls on the major parties to recruit and support more women for future presidential and vice presidential slots. Anticipated to be signed by thousands, the petition is available through the WHP's website.

Sports Ballot Box
The WHP and the Women's Sports Foundation have teamed up to work with women's professional sports leagues to consider creating a women's

"Sports Ballot." This initiative will allow young girls to see and vote for an all-star roster of female athletes who have demonstrated leadership skills on and off the court or field.

Screenwriting Contest
Positive media images of women leaders help shift the political and cultural climate so that women in powerful roles become commonplace and accepted in today's society. Thus, to encourage more films with women leader protagonists, WHP, in conjunction with industry leaders, has launched a screenwriting contest.

Barriers and Opportunities Research: Profiles and Persuasion
WHP has commissioned a new, groundbreaking research project, which will examine how women running for executive office can communicate an effective and strong leadership profile that appeals to voters. As with previous research, the organization will disseminate the findings through national forums and a published report.

Women's Leadership Institute
WHP's institute will feature innovative programs to engage more women of all ages, backgrounds, and levels of experience in political leadership. The central goal is to assist women in becoming political leaders ready to serve and advance in public office.

Strategies for Equal Representation Forum
The United States ranks forty-fifth in the world regarding women's representation in national legislatures or parliaments. To identify and evaluate strategies used by other countries to increase women's representation, WHP will host national symposia. The events will feature activists and elected officials from around the world. WHP's partners in this project are the Annenberg School of Communication at the University of Pennsylvania and the Ford Foundation, with strategic guidance provided by Joan Scott of Princeton's Institute for Advanced Studies.

Media Outreach
Ongoing proactive and strategic communications efforts are central to educating key audiences about women's leadership. Toward that end, we work with reporters providing background and commentary. White

House Project president Marie Wilson has appeared on the *News Hour* with Jim Lehrer, *Good Morning America,* and CNN and has been quoted widely in newspapers across the country.

Education Fund Series

The WHP publishes Education Fund Series reports on issues pertaining to women's leadership. Examples of reports include *Style over Substance: Newspaper Coverage of Female Candidates: Spotlight on Elizabeth Dole* by Sean Aday and James Devitt and *Pipeline to the Future: Young Women and Political Leadership* by Lake Snell Perry and Associates.

Polls

Over 45,000 Internet users responded to a President's Day (2001) weekend survey on women's political leadership. Conducted jointly by America Online and the White House Project, the survey potentially represents the nation's largest survey of public attitudes about women and the presidency. Approximately 26,000 women and 20,000 men responded to the online survey, which asked when they think a woman will be elected president and which woman they would most like to see elected to the nation's highest office. They were also asked to assess their likelihood of voting for a female president.

Among the results:

- 85 percent indicated that they are willing to vote for a woman as president, with 59 percent saying they are "very willing" and another 26 percent choosing "somewhat willing." Only 15 percent stated that they would not be willing to vote for a woman.
- 15.5 percent think the United States will elect a female president by 2004, while 30.2 percent picked 2008, and 19 percent said they think this will happen by 2012.
- 38.5 percent chose Senator Hillary Clinton as the woman they would be most likely to vote for as president. Oprah Winfrey was the second-highest vote-getter at 25.3 percent, followed by U.S. EPA administrator Christine Todd Whitman at 20 percent, National Security Adviser Condoleezza Rice at 11 percent, and Senator Dianne Feinstein at 5 percent.

Contact Information: The White House Project, 110 Wall Street, 2nd Floor, New York, NÝ 10005, Phone: (212) 785-6001, Fax: (212) 785-6007, Website: www.thewhitehouseproject.org.

Notes

Chapter 1

1. See the Congress homepage for information on the number of women in Congress (www.congress.gov). See also Whitney et al., *Nine and Counting*. A good source on the state of women in politics is Costello and Stone, *The American Woman 2001*.

2. Watson, *The Presidents' Wives*.

3. The literature suggests that is difficult for women to win in a presidential system; most female leaders have gained office in a prime minister system. See Clift and Brazaitis, *Madam President*.

4. Seltzer, Newman, and Leighton, *Sex as a Political Variable*, p. 3.

5. Surprisingly little research has been completed on the topic of women and executive governance and even less on the prospect of the first woman president. For a good assessment of women and executive governance, see Genovese, *Women as National Leaders;* and Duerst-Lahti and Kelly, *Gender, Power, Leadership, and Governance*. For sources on the first woman president, see Clift and Brazaitis, *Madam President*. A special issue of the journal *White House Studies* edited by Ann Gordon focuses on the first woman president: see vol. 1, no. 3, 2001.

6. A rich literature base exists examining women's campaigns for *legislative* office. See Leeper, "The Impact of Prejudice on Female Candidates"; Newman, *Perception and Reality;* Rule, "Why Women Don't Run."

7. See the CAWP report, "Women in Elective Office." See www.rci.Rutgers.edu/~cawp/ to access CAWP's reports.

8. Weir, "The Feminist Face of State Executive Leadership."

9. Stambough and O'Regan, "Female Candidates for Executive Office."

10. An extensive body of literature exists on the challenges women in politics face. See, for example, Jamieson, *Beyond the Double Bind*; Kahn, *The Political Consequences of Being a Woman;* Mezy, "Does Sex Make a Difference?"; Rule, "Why Women Don't Run."

11. Ibid.

12. Nancy Pelosi is the first woman in a leadership position in Congress. For more information on Pelosi, see her website, either www.congress.gov or www.house.gov.

13. In addition to a gender gap on the issues, research has also explored the possibility of "shared issue concerns" among women benefiting female candidates with female voters. See, for example, Sapiro, "If U.S. Sen. Baker Were a Woman"; Sigelman and Sigelman, "Sexism."

14. See Kahn, *Political Consequences of Being a Woman*; Cook, Thomas, and Wilcox, *The Year of the Woman*.

15. Lucretia Mott and Elizabeth Cady Stanton were the leaders of this early movement. A good source for information on the Seneca Falls gathering is Gurko, *The Ladies of Seneca Falls*.

16. William Lloyd Garrison's leadership of this movement and relationship to the many women abolitionists is discussed in Mayer, *All on Fire*.

17. Women were the foot soldiers in the fight against slavery. Many took an even more assertive position against slavery than some of the men equated with the movement, and some of these leaders, such as Lucretia Mott and Elizabeth Cady Stanton, opposed the Fifteenth Amendment on grounds that it did not extend suffrage rights to women. See Gurko, *The Ladies of Seneca Falls*, and Mayer, *All on Fire*.

18. Women's groups varied considerably, both in their views on women's rights and on strategies to be used to achieve their goals. For a good discussion of this subject, see Braude, *Radical Spirits*, and Stalcup, *Women's Rights Movements*.

19. See Purvis, *Emmeline Pankhurst*, and Pankhurst, *My Own Story*.

20. Friedan, *The Feminine Mystique*.

21. See Gabriel, *Notorious Victoria*.

Chapter 2

1. Forman, *The Life and Selected Writings of Thomas Jefferson*.

2. See Skidmore, *Legacy to the World*, pp. 100–101.

3. Ibid., p. 65; see also Tyler, *Freedom's Ferment*, p. 425.

4. Withey, *Dearest Friend*, p. 39.

5. Fuller, *Woman in the Nineteenth Century*, p. 174.

6. Skidmore, *Legacy to the World*, p. 177.

7. Clift and Brazaitis, *Madam President*, p. 27.

8. Ibid.

9. Skidmore, *Legacy to the World*, p. 226.

10. Cited in Skidmore, *Legacy to the World*, p. 225.

11. 36 L.Ed. 2n 593 (1973).

12. Clift and Brazaitis, *Madam President*, p. 28.

13. Quoted in ibid., pp. 98–99.

14. Lebsock, "Women and American Politics," p. 37.

15. See, for example, Cooper, *The Warrior and the Priest*, p. 209.

16. Skidmore, "Theodore Roosevelt on Race and Gender," p. 37.

17. Miller, *Theodore Roosevelt*, p. 100.

18. Skidmore, "Theodore Roosevelt on Race and Gender," p. 38; on Roosevelt as police commissioner, see the definitive work by Jeffers, *Commissioner Roosevelt*.

19. Cooper, *The Warrior and the Priest*, p. 225.

20. Skidmore, *Legacy to the World*, p. 265.

21. Quoted in Clift and Brazaitis, *Madam President*, p. 29.

22. Melich, *The Republican War Against Women*, p. 197.

23. Quoted in ibid., p. 197.

24. Ibid., p. 199.

25. Ibid.

26. Ibid., p. 202.

27. Ibid., p. 203.

28. Ibid., p. 204.

29. Ibid., pp. 204–205.

Chapter 3

1. Costain, *Inviting Women's Rebellion*, p. 1; Evans, *Personal Politics.*
2. Costain, "Women's Claims," pp. 153–155; Costain, *Inviting Women's Rebellion*, pp. 79–80.
3. Costain, *Inviting Women's Rebellion*, p. 79.
4. Ibid., pp. 84–85.
5. Costain and Fraizer, "Media Portrayal," pp. 159–163.
6. Costain, "After Reagan."
7. Gamson, *Talking Politics;* McCombs and Shaw, "The Agenda Setting Function"; Page and Shapiro, "Educating and Manipulating."
8. Iyengar, Peters, and Kinger, "Experimental Demonstrations"; Rochon, *Culture Moves;* Zaller, "The Myth of Massive Media Impact Revived."
9. Rochon, *Culture Moves;* Melucci, *Challenging Codes.*
10. Costain and Fraizer, "Media Portrayal."
11. Costain, Braunstein, and Berggren, "Framing the Women's Movement," pp. 209–210.
12. "Mothers Replacing the Career Woman," *New York Times,* January 18, 1956, p. 13.
13. "YWCA Study," *New York Times,* April 24, 1957, 37.
14. Friedan, *The Feminine Mystique.*

Chapter 4

1. Seebach, "How Not to Elect Women to Office," p. 1B.
2. See the White House Project website for information on the poll, www.thewhitehouseproject.org.
3. Havel, *U.S. Presidential Candidates.*
4. Mandel, "The Political Woman."
5. Center for the American Woman and Politics (CAWP), "Women in the U.S. Senate, 1922–2002."
6. Ibid.
7. Roger A. Lee, "Five-Star Generals and Admirals of the United States," www.historyguy.com/5-star-military.htm (January 26, 2002).
8. See www.four-stars.com/america's_fourstars.htm. The list does not differentiate between those who wore four stars on active duty and those who achieved that rank in retirement or posthumously.
9. Mandel, "The Political Woman."
10. Ibid., p. 46.
11. Seltzer, Newman, and Leighton, *Sex as a Political Variable.*
12. Ibid.
13. Mandel, "The Political Woman," p. 46.
14. Ibid., p. 51.
15. Ibid., p. 46; Seltzer, Newman, and Leighton, *Sex as a Political Variable.*
16. Newman, *Perception and Reality.*
17. We looked at the largest circulating newspaper in Chase Smith's home state of Maine, the *Bangor Daily News;* the largest circulating newspaper in Rockefeller's home state, the *New York Daily News;* and the *New York Times.*
18. All variables were reliable at Krippendorff's Alpha of .7 or better.
19. News coverage of the 1964 presidential primary in New Hampshire as reported in the *Bangor Daily News, New York Times,* and *New York Daily News.*
20. Vaccaro, "Sen. Smith," p. 1.
21. Penley and M. Sullivan, "Ladies at Odds," p. 1.

22. Rowe, "What Counts Is Content of Vote," p. 10.
23. Jamail, "The Inquiring Fotographer," 1963, p. 53.
24. Jamail, "The Inquiring Fotographer," 1964, p. 35.
25. Jamail, "The Inquiring Fotographer," 1972, p. 45.

Chapter 5

1. Chisholm, *Unbought and Unbossed*.
2. Ibid., 73.
3. Hinkley, "Shirley Chisholm Riding Alone," p. 19.
4. Washington, *Outstanding Women Members of Congress*, p. 17.
5. Chisholm, *Unbought and Unbossed*, p. 97.
6. Chisholm, *The Good Fight*, pp. 30–34.
7. Shelby, "Chisholm Hits Old Trail in Library Fete," p. 1.
8. Chisholm, *The Good Fight*, p. 3.
9. Hinkley, "Shirley Chisholm Riding Alone," p. 19.
10. Chisholm, *The Good Fight*, p. 3.
11. Washington, *Outstanding Women Members of Congress*, p. 20.
12. "House Bill Lauds Efforts of 1st Black Woman in Congress, Shirley Chisholm," *Jet*, July 2, 2001, 22.

Chapter 6

1. They are, respectively, "Winning Women" in the RNC and the "Women's Vote Center" in the DNC.
2. Green, National Women's Political Caucus study; to access the report, see www.nwpc.org/news_weekly.cfm; Burrell, "Campaign Finance."
3. Party decline theorists are discussed in Herrnson, *Party Campaigning in the 1980s*.
4. Herrnson and Green, *Multiparty Politics in America*.
5. Jacobson, *The Politics of Congressional Elections*.
6. Polsby and Wildavsky, *Presidential Elections*.
7. Particularly noteworthy advocates of party involvement in presidential selection from 1980 onward include Mayer, *In Pursuit;* Cohen et al., "Beating Reform"; Polsby and Wildavsky, *Presidential Elections*.
8. Polsby and Wildavsky, *Presidential Elections*, p. 99.
9. Ibid., pp. 54, 101.
10. Ibid., p. 55.
11. Mayer, "Forecasting Presidential Nominations," pp. 54–67.
12. Ibid., p. 48.
13. See Polsby and Wildavsky, *Presidential Elections*.
14. Ibid., p. 97.
15. Beck and Hershey, *Party Politics in America*, p. 96.
16. Polsby and Wildavsky, *Presidential Elections*, p. 98.
17. Mayer, "Forecasting Presidential Nominations," pp. 65–66.
18. Ibid., p. 66.
19. Beck and Hershey, *Party Politics in America*, p. 96.
20. Polsby and Wildavsky, *Presidential Elections*, pp. 93–94.
21. Ibid., p. 93.
22. Ibid., p. 54.
23. Center for Responsive Politics, "Election Overview, 2000," www.opensecrets.org/parties.

24. Ibid.

25. Beck and Hershey, *Party Politics in America*, pp. 87–89.

26. Ibid.

27. Ibid., p. 96.

28. Ibid., p. 96; Polsby and Wildavsky, *Presidential Elections*, p. 44.

29. Polsby and Wildavsky, *Presidential Elections*, p. 58.

30. Beck and Hershey, *Party Politics in America*, p. 97.

31. Ibid., p. 97.

32. Ibid.

33. Busch, "New Features," p. 59.

34. Ibid., p. 62. Other recommendations of the task force were that states must forward to the RNC their primary date by July 1 of the year prior to the primaries and that all primaries and caucuses had to take place between the first Monday in February and third Tuesday in June.

35. Ibid., pp. 63–65.

36. Ibid., pp. 63–64.

37. Ibid., pp. 68–71.

38. Ibid., pp. 66–67.

39. Herrnson, *Campaigning in the 1980s*, p. 39.

40. Ibid., pp. 39–41.

41. Beck and Hershey, *Party Politics in America*, p. 97.

42. Ibid., pp. 96–97.

43. Ibid., p. 110.

44. Price, *Bringing Back the Parties*, p. 156; Beck and Hershey, *Party Politics in America*, p. 99.

45. Price, *Bringing Back the Parties*, pp. 160–171.

46. Hale, "The Democratic Leadership Council," pp. 250–262.

47. Ibid., p. 255.

48. Ibid.

49. T. Ferguson, "'Organized Capitalism,'" pp. 118–139.

50. Hale, "The Democratic Leadership Council," p. 254.

51. Ibid., p. 258.

52. Beck and Hershey, *Party Politics in America*, pp. 96–102.

53. Jennings, "Women in Party Politics," p. 223.

54. Information provided by the Information Division of the Republican National Committee on May 8, 2002.

55. Information provided by the RNC and DNC on May 8, 2002.

56. Baer, "The Political Interests of Women," p. 115; Baer notes that in 1996 women had ten of the state Democratic committee chairmanships (meaning that they were vice chairs in forty states) and Republican women held six party chairs.

57. Ibid., p. 109.

58. Ibid., p. 111.

59. Ibid., pp. 109, 111.

60. Ibid., p. 110.

61. Ibid., p. 115.

62. Ibid., p. 111; Freeman, "Whom You Know vs. Whom You Represent," pp. 215–244.

63. Some of this information was obtained through analyses available from the DNC Women's Vote Center, May 8, 2002.

64. Cott, "Across the Great Divide," p. 162.

65. Women's Leadership Forum, www.wlf-online.org.

66. Burrell, "Women's Political Leadership," p. 170.

67. National Federation of Democratic Women, www.nfdw.org.

68. Baer, "The Political Interests of Women," p. 111.
69. National Federation of Republican Women, www.nfrw.org.
70. Ibid.
71. Freeman, "Whom You Know vs. Whom You Represent," pp. 222–225.
72. Burrell, "Women's Political Leadership," pp. 170–171.
73. Nelson, "Women's PAC's in the Year of the Woman," pp. 185–187.
74. Susan B. Anthony List, www.sba-list.org.
75. B. Burrell, "Campaign Finance," pp. 30–37.
76. Democratic National Committee chair Terry McAuliffe cited in *Democratic News,* June 8, 2001.
77. Burrell, "Women's Political Leadership," p. 171.
78. Mueller, "The Empowerment of Women," pp. 16–36.
79. Baer, "The Political Interests of Women," p. 113.
80. Ibid.
81. Ibid., p. 112.
82. Ibid., p. 111.
83. From the "Capital Eye Newsletter," vol. 6, no. 4, Center for Responsive Politics, www.opensecrets.org.
84. Ibid.

Chapter 7

1. Barabak, "Dole Drops Bid for Presidency"; for further information, see also Schemo, "Curiosity in Dole Exceeds Support"; Ayres, "Nothing Wasted"; Polman, "A Woman in the White House."
2. Barabak, "Dole Drops Bid for Presidency."
3. Ibid.
4. Ibid.
5. Wolffe, "Dole Blames Cash Woes."
6. Scholars have examined the idea that money is a key factor for women at lower levels of public offices. For example, see Burrell, "Women's and Men's Campaigns"; Uhlaner and Schlozman, "Candidate Gender and Congressional Campaign Receipts"; Theilmann and Wilhite, *Discrimination and Congressional Campaign Contributions.*
7. "Early Money Is Like Yeast" was started in 1985 by Ellen Malcolm with the mission of making Democratic women more competitive at all levels of government.
8. "Women in the Senate and the House" started more recently than EMILY's List and seeks to assist Republican women running for office. Another organization, the National Federation of Republican Women, was formed to advance Republican women leaders.
9. This project was started in 1998 by a group of women activists led by Marie Wilson of the Ms. Foundation for Women. They urged the public to consider the question, "Why not a woman for president?" (That is the White House Project's slogan.) The project also "shifted the emphasis from 'whether' a woman should be on the ticket to 'which' woman, and from 'why a woman?' to 'why not a woman?'" See Costello and Stone, *The American Woman 2001.*
10. For further analysis regarding women running for office, see Sullivan, "Images of a Breakthrough Woman Candidate"; Thomas and Wilcox, *Women and Elective Office;* Carroll, *Women as Candidates in American Politics;* Freeman, *A Room at a Time.*
11. For example, Barbara Boxer is on the Senate Foreign Relations Committee.

12. The question posed was: "If you were voting for President of the United States, how would you feel about voting for . . . a woman? Would you prefer that, would it make you uncomfortable, or would it not make any difference at all?" Approximately 330 registered voters nationwide combined in a three-day rolling average for a daily total sample of approximately 1,000. The telephone public opinion poll was conducted from March 1 through November 5, 2001.

13. Costello and Stone, *The American Woman 2001*, p. 55.

14. Green et al., "Individual Congressional Campaign Contributors"; Fred, "Gender Politics"; Weber, "Sex, Money and Politics."

15. Dolan, "Voting for Women in the 'Year of the Woman.'" Dolan found that "Women voters are more likely to support women House candidates than are men and are also more likely to use gender-related issue positions in determining their vote choice when there is a woman candidate. In Senate elections, issues are much more important to determining vote choice than in House elections. Here women again exhibit distinctly different issue concerns than men and employ a greater number of gender-related issue concerns in their evaluations." Other experts indicate that getting women to vote for a woman candidate may not be so easy.

16. The fascination with the growth of women in the Senate can be seen in the publication of Whitney, *Nine and Counting*.

17. This theme is explored throughout this book.

18. For a discussion of women's participation in politics and the stereotypes they face, see Shapiro, *The Political Integration of Women*.

19. For a general discussion, see Farrar-Myers, "The Fundraiser-in-Chief."

20. Figure 7.2 includes the fifty-eight women who won election to the House in 2000. A fifty-ninth woman, Diana Watson (D-CA), was elected to the House via a special election in 2001 but is excluded from this analysis.

21. For purposes of the analysis herein, the winning candidate for the 2000 Missouri Senate election was the late Mel Carnahan. Carnahan died in an airplane crash about a week before the election, and his name remained on the ballot. When the deceased won the election, his widow, Jean, was appointed to fill his seat. Thus, even though Jean is serving the term, it was Mel who undertook the bulk of the fund-raising necessary for the campaign. For that reason, Jean Carnahan was not included with the other women senators for this analysis.

22. Because of limitations on readily available data and the small number of women in the Senate available for this analysis, Table 7.1 does not disaggregate individual contributors between small and large donors, nor does it break down sources of funds based on partisanship. The analysis for men in Table 7.1 is based on a number of male candidates equal to the number of women candidates, with each male selected in a manner designed to match up with each woman in terms of geographic proximity and being elected in the same year. For example, Mary Landrieu, elected to the Senate in 1996 from Louisiana, was matched up with Tim Hutchinson, elected in 1996 from Arkansas.

23. Because of certain limitations on what data were available, the analysis in Figures 7.4 and 7.5 examines the sources of funds for incumbent House members who were reelected in 2000.

24. Because of limitations in readily available data, two women (Cantwell and Clinton) and one man (Ensign) were excluded from the analysis in Table 7.1.

25. As noted above, twelve men were selected for this analysis in a way that matches them to the women senators in terms of geography and year elected. The men chosen were: Smith (NH), Hutchinson (AR), Wyden (OR), Breaux (LA), Specter (PA), Crapo (ID), Burns (MT), Santorum (PA), Ensign (NV), Bingamen (NM), Jeffords (VT), and DeWine (OH).

26. Hollywood producer David Foster was developing a script titled "Madame President" in the fall of 1999. See Dowd, "Why Can't a Woman."

27. Ibid., p. 15.

28. Whitney, *Nine and Counting,* p. 58.

Chapter 8

1. Trent and Friedenberg, *Political Campaign Communication,* p. 301.

2. Ibid., p. 115.

3. Ibid.

4. Gallup Organization, "Media Use and Evaluation," www.gallup.com/poll/indicators/indmedia.asp.

5. Delli Carpini and Keeter, *What Americans Should Know About Politics.*

6. Banwart and Bystrom, "Gender Influences on Gathering Political Information"; Kenski and Jamieson, "The 2000 Presidential Campaign and Differential."

7. See Kahn, "Does Being Male Help?" pp. 497–517; Kahn, "The Distorted Mirror," pp. 154–173; Kahn, "Does Gender Make a Difference?" pp. 162–195; Kahn and Goldenberg, "Women Candidates in the News," pp. 180–199.

8. Smith, "When All's Fair," pp. 71–81.

9. Devitt, *Framing Gender on the Campaign Trail.*

10. Bystrom, Robertson, and Banwart, "Framing the Fight," pp. 1999–2013.

11. Aday and Devitt, *Style over Substance;* Bystrom, "Media Content and Candidate Viability"; Heldman, Carroll, and Olson, "Gender Differences in Print Media."

12. Bystrom, "Media Content and Candidate Viability"; Heldman, Carroll, and Olson, "Gender Differences in Print Media."

13. Aday and Devitt, *Style over Substance.*

14. Heldman, Carroll, and Olson, "Gender Differences in Print Media."

15. Bystrom, "Media Content and Candidate Viability."

16. Yepsen, "Beat the Press," 2001.

17. Quoted in Witt, Paget, and Matthews, *Running as a Woman*, p. 207.

18. Quoted in ibid., p. 208.

19. Kaid, "Political Advertising."

20. "The Critical Role of Television in Political Campaigns."

21. See Geiger and Reeves, "The Effects of Visual Structure"; Joslyn, *Mass Media and Elections;* Kern, *30-Second Politics*; Patterson and McClure, *The Unseeing Eye;* West, *Air Wars.*

22. West, *Air Wars,* p. 1087.

23. Dolan, "Gender Differences," pp. 27–41.

24. Deloitte and Touche, "Women in Leadership Poll," January 3, 2000, www.us.deloitte.com.

25. Ibid., p. 2.

26. Ibid.

27. Ibid., p. 4.

28. Ibid., pp. 6–7.

29. Ibid., pp. 3, 7.

30. Rubin, "45,000 Cast Their Votes for a Woman President in New Survey," White House Project, February 23, 2001, www.thewhitehouseproject.org.

31. Deloitte and Touche, "Women in Leadership Poll," p. 1.

32. Rubin, "45,000 Cast Their Votes," p. 1.

33. See Bystrom, "Candidate Gender and the Presentation of Self."

34. Kaid and Davidson, "Elements of Videostyle."

35. See Bystrom, "Candidate Gender and the Presentation of Self"; Bystrom and Kaid, "Videostyle and Technology"; Bystrom, Kaid, and Miller, "The Evolution of Videostyle"; Bystrom and Miller, "Gendered Communication Styles"; Bystrom and Kaid, "Videostyles of Women and Men"; Bystrom and Kaid, "Are Women Candidates Transforming Campaign Communication?"

36. Bystrom, "Candidate Gender and the Presentation of Self."

37. Bystrom and Miller, "Gendered Communication Styles."

38. Bystrom and Kaid, "Are Women Candidates Transforming Campaign Communication?"

39. Ibid.

40. Ibid.

41. Iyengar et al., "Running as a Woman."

42. Ibid., p. 96.

43. Ibid., p. 98.

44. Banwart and Carlin, "The Effects of Negative Political Advertising."

45. Witt, Paget, and Matthews, *Running as a Woman,* p. 214.

46. Kaid, "Political Advertising."

47. Quoted in Witt, Paget, and Matthews, *Running as a Woman,* p. 207.

48. Kaid and Tedesco, "Tracking Voter Reaction."

Chapter 9

The author wishes to express her gratitude to Dr. Kim Fridkin Kahn of Arizona State University for her insights and support, Holly Long of Arizona State University for her dedicated research assistance, and Dr. Robert Watson of Florida Atlantic University for his boundless mentoring.

1. *20th Century Presidents,* video documentary, produced by Vision Associates (Atlanta: Jimmy Carter Presidential Library, 1986).

2. On May 10, 1872, in New York City, Victoria Claflin Woodhull became the only woman in U.S. history to be a party's presidential candidate when she accepted the nomination of the Equal Rights Party. Frederick Douglass was her running mate. Gabriel, *Notorious Victoria,* p. 171. Geraldine Ferraro is the only woman nominated to a major party's presidential ticket. She was the Democratic vice presidential running mate of Walter Mondale in 1984. Ferraro and Francke, *Ferraro.* The only woman so far in U.S. history to mount a viable bid on one of the major political party tickets is Elizabeth Dole, who campaigned as a Republican in 1999.

3. Pierce, "Gender Role and Political Culture," p. 22.

4. Conway, Steuernagel, and Ahern, *Women and Political Participation,* p. 21.

5. Cialdini, *Influences,* p. 7.

6. Zimbardo and Leippe, *The Psychology of Attitude,* p. 236.

7. Deaux and Major, "Putting Gender into Context," p. 384.

8. Hoffman and Hurst, "Gender Stereotypes," p. 206.

9. Carroll, *Women as Candidates in American Politics,* p. 95.

10. Ibid, pp. 97–101.

11. Wood, *Gendered Lives,* p. 115.

12. Ibid., p. 120.

13. Ibid, pp. 121–123; R. Edwards, "The Effects of Gender"; Tannen, *You Just Don't Understand,* pp. 43–44.

14. Tannen, *You Just Don't Understand,* pp. 24–25.

15. Jamieson, *Eloquence in an Electronic Age*, p. 82.

16. Dow and Tonn, "Feminine Style," pp. 286–288.

17. Ibid., p. 289.

18. Blankenship and Robson, "A 'Feminine Style,'" p. 353.

19. Jamieson, *Beyond the Double Bind*.

20. Blankenship and Robson, "A 'Feminine Style,'" p. 355.

21. Tolleson-Rinehard and Stanley, *Claytie and the Lady*, p. 3.

22. Jamieson, *Beyond the Double Bind*, p. 3.

23. Ibid, pp. 53–147.

24. Fee and Raposa, "Inside Track," p. 8; LeBlanc, "Some Object to Swift Governing."

25. Goldberg, "2 New Jobs," p. A22.

26. McKinnon, "Fraud Verdict."

27. Bower, "Winning Thread."

28. Jamieson, *Beyond the Double Bind*, p. 190.

29. Ibid., p. 196.

30. Ibid., p. 197.

31. Kinder, "Presidential Character Revisited," p. 253.

32. Tolleson-Rinehard and Stanley, *Claytie and the Lady*, p. 3.

33. Carroll, *Women as Candidates in American Politics*, pp. 97–101.

34. Leeper, "The Impact of Prejudice," p. 254.

35. Huddy and Terkildsen, "The Consequences of Gender Stereotypes," pp. 517–518.

36. White, "Inequality in Symbolism," pp. 61–62; Robson, "Stereotypes and the Female Politician," pp. 210–219.

37. Robson, "Stereotypes and the Female Politician," p. 210.

38. Bower, "Winning Thread," pp. 94–95; Trent and Friedenberg, *Political Campaign Communication*, p. 94.

39. Jamieson, *Eloquence in an Electronic Age*, pp. 82–89.

Chapter 10

1. Schroeder, *24 Years of House Work*, p. 41.

2. Ibid., p. 57.

3. Ibid., p. 110.

4. Ibid., p. 113.

5. Burrell, *A Woman's Place Is in the House*, p. 170.

6. Schroeder, *24 Years of House Work*, pp. 77–78.

7. Ibid., p. 79.

8. Editors' interview with former representative Pat Schroeder, November 16, 2001.

9. Ibid.

10. Schroeder, *24 Years of House Work*, pp. 184–185.

11. See www.publishers.org/home/abouta/president.htm.

Chapter 11

The author would like to thank Danielle Brogan for her able research assistance with the data for this chapter.

1. Iyengar and Kinder, *News That Matters* and *Is Anyone Responsible?;* Kahn, "Senate Elections in the News"; Patterson, *Out of Order;* Bennett, *News;* Wayne, *The Road to the White House 2000*; Hershey, "The Campaign and the Media."

2. Wattenberg, *The Rise of Candidate-Centered Politics.*

3. Heith, "Footwear, Lipstick, and an Orthodox Sabbath."

4. Kahn, "Does Being Male Help?"

5. Abramson, Aldrich, and Rohde, *Change and Continuity,* p. 53.

6. Mayer, "The Presidential Nominations."

7. Stanley, "The Nominations," p. 33.

8. Ibid.

9. Abramson, Aldrich, and Rohde, *Change and Continuity,* p. 53.

10. Stanley, "The Nominations."

11. Heith, "Presidential Polling and the Potential for Leadership," p. 386.

12. Engel, "Feminist Issues," p. A3.

13. Leonard, "Dole's Iowa Showing."

14. Bustillo, "Women's Group Gives Dole Respect."

15. Schemo, "Dole Talks Foreign Policy."

16. Schneider, "The November 6 Vote," p. 227.

17. Bayer, "Dole's Campaign."

18. Auster, "Dole Wasn't Woman Enough," p. 3G.

19. Hua, "Elizabeth Dole May Make Comeback," p. 10.

20. Krum, "Why Can't the President Wear a Dress?"

21. Leonard, "Dole's Iowa Showing."

22. McGrory, "The Muffled."

23. MacPherson, "The Candidate as Symbol."

24. Bayer, "Dole's Campaign."

25. Ibid.

26. Leonard, "Dole's Iowa Showing."

27. Carroll, "Is the 'Steel Magnolia' Now Starting to Wilt?"

28. Overholster, "Why Is Dole Getting Short-Changed?"

29. Krum, "Why Can't the President Wear a Dress?"

30. Ibid.

31. Jones, "Ferraro's Finances," p. A1.

32. Saltman, "On Covering Ferraro," p. D3.

33. Jones, "Ferraro Campaign Delivers Coup de Grace," p. A10.

34. Dole, "Stingy Coverage," p. A24.

35. Overholster, "Why Is Dole Getting Short-Changed?"

36. Ibid.

37. Ibid.

38. Carroll, "Is the 'Steel Magnolia' Now Starting to Wilt?"

39. Woodlief, "Media Eye Women's Style."

40. Ibid.

41. Carroll, "Is the 'Steel Magnolia' Now Starting to Wilt?"

42. Quoted in Woodlief, "Media Eye Women's Style."

43. Patterson, *Out of Order.*

44. Nelson, "The Post-Election Election," p. 170.

45. Polsby, "The Democratic Nomination," p. 57.

46. Gallup survey of October 26–29 (1,520 respondents): 22 percent were more likely to vote for Mondale because of Ferraro, 32 percent were less likely to vote for Mondale because of Ferraro, 3 percent had no opinion, and 43 percent stated there was no difference.

47. Kahn, *The Political Consequences of Being a Woman,* p. 9.

48. Ibid., p. 2.

Chapter 12

An earlier version of this chapter appeared in *White House Studies* 1, no. 3 (Dec. 2001).

1. Cannon, "You Go, Girls"; Saroyan, "Can a Woman Win the White House?"; Rubin, "45,000 Cast Votes."

2. This "dearth" includes Governor Jane Swift of Massachusetts, who succeeded former governor Paul Cellucci in April 2001. See CAWP, "Statewide Elective Executive Women in 2001."

3. For more critical popular perspectives, see Meyer, "Imagining the Impossible"; Dowd, "Why Can't a Woman?"; Erbe, "A Woman Would Be Fine for President, But."

4. Schreiber, "Education and Change"; Ferree, "A Woman for President?"; Cherlin and Walters, "Trends"; Cannon, "You Go, Girls"; Saroyan, "Can a Woman Win the White House?"

5. Pomper, *The Election of 2000.*

6. For a discussion of the methodological challenges, including coverage and sampling error that arise from Internet polling, see Couper, "Web Surveys," pp. 464–494.

7. Rubin, "45,000 Cast Votes."

8. Generally referred to in political communication studies that show that individuals believe that they personally are not affected by media messages while also believing that most others are affected by them. See Thorson, "Ad-Watcher's Toolkit": "The effect, found again and again by researchers, boils down to the fact that most of the people, most of the time, think the media affect others more than themselves." I suggest that there exists a third-person effect with regard to discrimination against a female candidate for the presidency. Most of the people, most of the time, think that they do not discriminate against female candidates but that others do.

9. Crown, *The Approval Motive;* Nunnally, *Psychometric Theory;* Paulhus, "Measurement and Control"; Huddy, "The Political Significance."

10. Lindsay, "Why Two Top Races."

11. For opposing viewpoints, see Henry, "Racial Factors"; Baker and Kleppner, "Race War Chicago Style."

12. Gallup poll, 1987.

13. Lieberman Research poll, 1991.

14. Alexander and Anderson, "Gender as a Factor"; Huddy and Terkildsen, "The Consequences of Gender Stereotypes"; Huddy, "The Political Significance"; Koch, "The Effect of Candidate Gender"; Leeper, "The Impact of Prejudice"; Mandel, "In the Running"; Matland, "Putting Scandinavian Equality to the Test"; Miller et al., "Gender Stereotypes and Decision Context"; Rosenwasser and Seale, "Attitudes Toward a Hypothetical Male or Female Candidate"; Rosenwasser et al. "Attitudes Toward Men and Women in Politics"; Sapiro, "If U.S. Senator Baker Were a Woman."

15. Alexander and Andersen, "Gender as a Factor"; Huddy and Terkildsen, "Gender Stereotypes"; Rosenwasser and Dean, "Gender Roles and Political Office."

16. Matland, "Putting Scandinavian Equality to the Test"; Sapiro, "If U.S. Senator Baker Were a Woman."

17. Erbe, "A Woman Would Be Fine for President, But."

18. Koch, "The Effect of Candidate Gender."

19. Kahn and Goldenberg, "Women Candidates in the News"; Norris, *Women, Media, and Politics.*

20. Trent and Freidenberg, *Political Campaign Communication.*

21. Jane Swift is the successor governor to now Canadian ambassador Paul Cellucci and the mother of twins and an infant daughter.

22. Eagen, "Maternity Leave"; Adamson, "See Jane Play Governor Mom"; Cassidy, "Chuck Hunt."

23. Jamieson, *Beyond the Double Bind,* p. 14.

24. Ibid., p. vii.

25. Ibid.; Kaminer, "Feminism's Identity Crisis"; Sommers, *Who Stole Feminism?*

26. Jamieson, *Beyond the Double Bind,* p. 21.

27. I have formulated this sixth double bind partially in anticipation of critics who may claim that this pessimistic analysis of public opinion and scholarly work regarding the imminent possibility of a women president lands me squarely in the victim camp!

28. N=1,000 U.S. women, margin of error is +/– 5 percent. D'Agostino, "Poll: Women Trending Right on Social Issues," p. 5.

29. Berke, "As Political Spouse, Bob Dole Strays."

30. Baumgardner and Richards, "Why Not Elizabeth Dole?"; see also the Princeton Survey Research Associates Poll in 1995, where 13 percent of women respondents and 10 percent of male respondents considered feminism as the work of the Devil (in Huddy, Neely, and LaFay, "The Polls—Trends," p. 339).

31. Fertik, "Elizabeth Dole."

32. Berke, "As Political Spouse, Bob Dole Strays."

33. Eagen, "Back-Biting Hubby"; McGrory, "The Muffled."

34. Pitney, "That 70s Candidate."

35. Baumgardner and Richards, "Why Not Elizabeth Dole?"

36. Ponnuru, "Gore-Dole 2000!"

37. Nichols, "Will Any Woman Do?"

38. Witt, Paget, and Matthews, *Running as a Woman.*

39. Birnbaum, "Money, Money Everywhere!"

40. MacKenzie, "Cash-Strapped Elizabeth Dole Quits."

41. Bruni, "With Eye on the Vice Presidency."

42. Langton, "International."

43. Fertik, "Elizabeth Dole."

Chapter 13

1. Chisholm, *The Good Fight.*

2. Smith and Fox, "Research Note," pp. 205–221.

3. Leeper, "The Impact of Prejudice," pp. 248–261; Rosenwasser and Seale, "Attitudes Toward a Hypothetical Male or Female Candidate."

4. Hamilton and Sherman, "Stereotypes."

5. Ibid., p. 3.

6. Bem, "The Measurement of Psychological Androgyny," pp. 155–162.

7. Matassa, "The 'Mom' Against All Those Dark Suits," p. A1.

8. Teitell, "Family Affair," p. 63.

9. Mezy, "Does Sex Make a Difference?" pp. 492–501.

10. Huddy and Terkildsen, "Gender Stereotypes," pp. 119–147.

11. Ibid.

12. Roper Starch Worldwide, "Women in Elected Office Survey Identifies Obstacles for Women as Political Leaders," (Deloitte and Touche survey), us.deloitte.com/pub/wilpoll/default.htm, 2001.

13. Ibid.

14. Gordon and Miller, "Does the Oval Office Have a Glass Ceiling?"

15. Kinder, "Presidential Character Revisited."

16. Huddy and Terkildsen, "The Consequences of Gender Stereotypes."

17. Rosenwasser and Seale, "Attitudes Toward a Hypothetical Male or Female Candidate."

18. Koch, "Candidate Gender."

19. Clark and Clark, "The Gender Gap in 1996."

20. Cited in Peffley and Hurwitz, "Whites' Stereotypes of Blacks."

21. Re criminal activity, see Entman, "Blacks in the News"; re affirmative action, see Reeves, *Voting Hopes or Fears?*

22. Sigelman et al., "Black Candidates, White Voters."

23. Peffley and Hurwitz, "Whites' Stereotypes of Blacks."

24. Voss and Lublin, "Black Incumbents, White Districts."

25. Ibid.

26. Huddy and Sears, "Opposition to Bilingual Education," pp. 133–143.

27. Oboler, *Ethnic Labels,* pp. xv–xvi.

28. De la Garza, Falcon, and Garcia, "Will the Real Americans Please Stand Up?"

29. Ferraro, *Ferraro: My Story,* p. 273.

30. Snyder, "Self-Fulfilling Stereotypes."

31. Mendelberg, *The Race Card.*

Chapter 14

1. Ferraro, *Ferraro: My Story,* p. 312.

2. Ibid., p. 322.

3. As quoted in Keen, "Geraldine Ferraro," p. 12A.

4. Editors' interview with Geraldine Ferraro, November 16, 2001.

5. Ibid.

6. Keen, "Geraldine Ferraro," p. 12A.

7. Editors' interview with Geraldine Ferraro.

Chapter 15

1. Duerst-Lahti and Kelly, "On Governance, Leadership, and Gender," p. 12.

2. Northouse, *Leadership,* p. 3.

3. Duerst-Lahti and Kelly, "On Governance, Leadership, and Gender," p. 13.

4. Neustadt, *Presidential Power.*

5. See Skowronek, *The Politics Presidents Make;* Rose, *The Postmodern President.*

6. See, for example, Kessel, *Presidents;* Cronin and Genovese, *The Paradoxes of the American Presidency.*

7. See, for example, Burke, *The Institutional Presidency;* Weko, *The Politicizing Presidency;* Warshaw, *The Keys to Power.*

8. See, for example, Jones, *Separate but Equal Branches;* Lammers and Genovese, *The Presidency and Domestic Policy.*

9. See, for example, Kernell, *Going Public;* Tulis, *The Rhetorical Presidency;* Hart, *The Sound of Leadership;* Stuckey, *The President as Interpreter-in-Chief;* Maltese, *Spin Control;* Han, *Governing from Center Stage.*

10. Wayne, *The Road to the White House 2000*, pp. 209–210.

11. Cronin and Genovese, *The Paradoxes of the American Presidency*, pp. 32–37.

12. Ibid., pp. 118–127.

13. Greenstein, *The Presidential Difference*, pp. 194–200.

14. Wayne, *The Road to the White House 2000*, p. 185.

15. Ibid., pp. 187–189.

16. For a discussion on this trend in the news coverage, see Patterson, *Out of Order;* and Sabato, *Feeding Frenzy*.

17. Cronin and Genovese, *The Paradoxes of the American Presidency*, p. 31.

18. Waterman, Wright, and St. Clair, *The Image-Is-Everything Presidency*, pp. 39–42.

19. "Women in Elected Office, 2001, Fact Sheet Summaries," Center for the American Woman and Politics, Eagleton Institute of Politics, Rutgers University, 2001.

20. For a discussion of potential women candidates, see Han, "The Next Contender."

21. Huddy and Terkildsen, "Gender Stereotypes."

22. Kahn, *The Political Consequences of Being a Woman*.

23. McGlen and O'Connor, *Women, Politics and American Society*.

24. Conway, Steuernagel, and Ahern, *Women and Political Participation*, p. 100.

25. De Conde, *Presidential Machismo*, p. 5.

26. Northouse, *Leadership*, pp. 208–209.

27. Stapleton, "Introduction," p. 33.

28. Genovese, "Women as National Leaders," pp. 214–215.

29. Gergen, *Eyewitness to Power*, p. 349.

30. Jones, *Separate but Equal Branches*, p. 105.

31. Cronin and Genovese, *The Paradoxes of the American Presidency*, p. 179.

32. Whitney et al., *Nine and Counting*, pp. 125–127.

33. Genovese, "Women as National Leaders," p. 215.

34. Cronin and Genovese, *The Paradoxes of the American Presidency*, pp. 207–209.

35. Han, *Governing from Center Stage*, pp. 2–3.

36. See Tulis, *The Rhetorical Presidency;* see also Milkis and Nelson, *The American Presidency*.

37. See Gelderman, *All the President's Words;* Lammers and Genovese, *The Presidency and Domestic Policy*.

38. Tannen, *You Just Don't Understand*, pp. 24–25.

39. Jamieson, *Beyond the Double Bind*, pp. 94–95.

40. Graber, *Mass Media and American Politics*, pp. 272–273.

41. Paletz and Entman, *Media Power Politics*.

42. Rice, "Women Out of the Myths and into Focus," pp. 45–49.

43. See Tuchman, *Hearth and Home*, pp. 7–8; Paletz, *The Media in American Politics*, pp. 135–139.

44. See Braden, *Women Politicians*.

45. Kahn, *The Political Consequences of Being a Woman*, pp. 134–136.

46. Ferraro and Francke, *Ferraro: My Story*.

47. Genovese and Thompson, "Women as Chief Executives," p. 7.

Chapter 16

1. For information on the relationship between the president and Congress in foreign policy, see Crabb and Holt, *Invitation to Struggle*.

2. The executive agreement usually takes one of two forms: an accord negotiated between the president or a representative with an official from another nation, or an agreement negotiated in line with prior congressional approval or consent. The increased use of executive agreements has eroded the congressional oversight capability of the Senate.

3. On this theme, see Mervin, "The Bully Pulpit II."

4. Logan, "Elite Analysis of Democracies' International Policy," p. 5.

5. This indifference was the result of Americans' tendency to become self-absorbed in their own lives and localities, leaving little time to pay attention to world events. See Almond, *The American People and Foreign Policy,* pp. 53, 76. Conversely, Richard Barnet uses a Marxist analysis to contend that the "manipulation" of U.S. public opinion on foreign policy matters is the result of broad efforts by political and economic elites to ensure access to overseas markets. See Barnet, *The Roots of War.*

6. Nacos, "Presidential Leadership," p. 547.

7. Putnam, "Diplomacy and Domestic Politics," p. 434.

8. Papayoanou, "Economic Interdependence," p. 117.

9. Putnam, "Diplomacy and Domestic Politics," p. 426.

10. The reasons for the Senate rejection of the League of Nations were the intransigence and unwillingness to compromise of both Wilson and isolationist members of the Senate (nicknamed the "Irreconcilables"), including William Borah of Idaho and Hiram Johnson of California. For background information, see Knack, *To End All Wars,* pp. 227–270.

11. The GOP wanted assurances that the president would support Republican proposals for a ballistic missile defense system. While the White House was silent, opponents of the CTBT were able to convince many Republican senators that the treaty would seriously harm the ability of the United States to defend itself. Moderate Republicans hoped to postpone the vote on the treaty until after Clinton left office, but Democratic senator Byron L. Dorgan tried to force Senate Majority Leader Trent Lott to open the floor for debate on the CTBT. Dorgan threatened to delay Senate business unless Lott held hearings and a vote on the treaty. Lott released the treaty to the floor for a vote, where it fell well short of the two-thirds needed for ratification and was defeated fifty-one to forty-eight. The *New York Times* later quoted a senior administrative official as saying that Dorgan's action was "a sharp stick in the eye of the Republicans. . . . they called our bluff." Broder, "Quietly and Dexterously."

12. Longworth, "Albright Promises New Push."

13. Wildavsky's thesis was based on research that found that until the Vietnam era, presidents were able to secure approval for their foreign policy programs 70 percent of the time but were only able to secure approval for 40 percent of their domestic policies. See Parsons, "Exploring the 'Two Presidencies' Phenomenon," p. 495.

14. McGlen and Sarkees, "Headline Series," p. 84.

15. This notion forms the core of the bureaucratic politics model of the policy process, which holds that the large bureaucracies in Washington, D.C., primarily determine the policy priorities of the federal government because of their institutional power. For an overview of the various theories on policy formation, see Landy, *The New Politics of Public Policy.*

16. WFPG endeavors to help women enter the foreign service and gain employment in academia or research institutions devoted to foreign and security policy through mentoring and research programs.

17. Tickner, *Gender in International Relations;* Grant and Newland, *Gender and International Relations.*

18. The quote from Washington's Farewell Address served as a constant reminder to successive administrations to shun political or military ties to foreign nations. However, bilateral and multilateral economic treaties were common during the nineteenth century. The Monroe Doctrine, for example, pledged U.S. noninterference in European affairs in exchange for European noninterference in the Western Hemisphere (including no colonization).

19. Although the idea of American exceptionalism is a long-standing component of U.S. foreign policy, the authors conclude that there is a disconnect between the political rhetoric of elites and the actual implementation of foreign policy. In other words, elites use the idea of exceptionalism as a means to justify actions or to garner public support. See Lepgold and McKeown, "Is American Foreign Policy Exceptional?" p. 369.

20. Kerry, *The Star-Spangled Mirror,* p. 3.

21. Ibid., p. 3.

22. For a more thorough examination of the phenomenon of the "favorite son" thesis, see Farrar-Myers, "The Collapse of an Inherited Agenda."

23. Tickner, "Searching for the Princess?" p. 45.

24. Fukuyama, "Women and the Evolution of World Politics."

25. Jaquette, "States Make War," p. 129.

26. Haftendorn and Schissler, *The Reagan Administration.*

27. For an overview of the feminist emphasis placed on these three areas, see Byron and Thorburn, "Gender and International Relations."

28. Gillies, *Between Principle and Practice,* p. 278.

29. Foot, *Rights Beyond Borders.*

30. Byron and Thorburn, "Gender and International Relations," p. 217.

31. Ibid.

32. Albright, "Women and Foreign Policy," p. 6.

33. Enloe, *Bananas, Beaches and Bases.*

34. Peterson, *Gendered States,* p. 32.

35. Byron and Thorburn, "Gender and International Relations," p. 214.

36. Buvinic, "Women in Poverty," p. 43.

37. Ibid., p. 39.

38. Albright, "Women and Foreign Policy."

39. Hunt, "Women's Vital Voice," p. 5.

40. An example of this type of program was the 1996 Bosnian Women's Initiative. Microloans not only have a proven record of success in promoting economic opportunities, but they also have a 98 percent repayment rate.

41. Haass, "Fatal Distraction," p. 114.

Chapter 17

1. Thomas Jefferson to Albert Gallatin, January 13, 1807, in Julian P. Boyd, ed., *Papers of Thomas Jefferson* (Princeton, NJ: Princeton University Press, 1950).

2. In one example, Joint Publication 1-02 (a Department of Defense pamphlet) defines national security as "a collective term encompassing both national defense and foreign relations of the United States. Specifically, the condition provided by: (a) a military or defense advantage over a foreign nation or group of nations, or (b) a favorable foreign relations position, or (c) a defense posture capable of successfully resisting hostile or destructive action from within or without, overt or covert."

3. Sarkesian, *U.S. National Security,* p. 5.

4. Smoke, *National Security,* p. 301.

5. National Security Forum for Women, June 11–12, 1985, had the theme "Challenges to U.S. National Security." In *Proceedings of the National Security Forum for Women* (Washington, DC: Department of Defense, 1985), p. 97.

6. Graham, "Albright."

7. Elizabeth Dole, Transcript of Campaign Address to the College of Charleston, September 27, 1999; for a copy of the speech go to Dole's website at www.elizabethdole.org.

8. Mann, "Who Says?"

9. Schemo, "Dole Talks Foreign Policy."

10. Sorensen, *Decision Making,* pp. 84–85.

11. Ibid.

12. Dole, Transcript of Campaign Address, September 27, 1999.

13. Cited in Jeffreys-Jones, *Changing Differences,* p. 188.

14. Brands, *The Use of Force,* pp. 3–4.

15. Tucker and Hendrickson, *Imperial Temptation,* p. 16.

16. Huddy and Terkildsen, "The Consequences of Gender Stereotypes."

17. In Jeffreys-Jones, *Changing Differences,* pp. 186, 190.

18. Ibid.

19. Lippman, *Madeleine Albright.*

20. Dole, Transcript of Campaign Address, September 27, 1999.

21. Hook and Spanier, *American Foreign Policy,* p. 354.

22. Ibid.

23. Sarkesian, *Presidential Leadership,* p. 257.

24. Sherrill, *Why They Call It Politics,* p. 46.

25. Quoted in Shoemaker, *The NSC Staff,* p. 42.

26. Goulden, *Superlawyers,* pp. 228–229.

27. Sarkesian, *U.S. National Security,* p. 82.

28. Destler, *The National Economic Council.*

29. Transcript, Executive Order Establishing the Homeland Security Council, White House, October 8, 2001. See the White House website for speeches and transcripts, www.whitehouse.gov/news/releases/2001, or www.whitehouse.gov/response.

30. Transcript, First Meeting of the Homeland Security Council, October 29, 2001.

Chapter 18

1. See the Elizabeth Dole official 2000 campaign website and her speech declaring the close of her candidacy in 1999, which can be found at www.2000gop.com/dole.

2. Ibid.

Chapter 19

1. White House Project, "Who's Talking: An Analysis of Sunday Morning Talk Shows," www.thewhitehouseproject.org/research/index.html.

2. Bystrom, Robertson, and Banwart, "Framing the Fight"; Devitt, "Framing Gender"; Kahn, "Does Being Male Help?"; Smith, "When All's Fair."

3. During the press conference announcing the results of this report, several women members of Congress spoke of how they tried to get booked on news shows and the difficulty they experienced.

4. The White House Project report revealed that Senator John McCain was by far the most frequent guest on Sunday morning talk shows.

5. Gertzog, "The Matrimonial Connection"; Kincaid, "Over His Dead Body."

6. Rajakaarunanayake, "Sri Lanka's Bandaranaike Family."

7. American Association of University Women, *Gender Gaps;* Canada and Pringle, "The Role of Gender"; Sadker and Sadker, *Failing at Fairness.*

8. Sadker and Sadker, *Failing at Fairness.*

9. McGlen et al., *Women, Politics, and American Society.*

10. See polls by Gallup and the White House Project, 1996–2002.

11. Hendershot, "The Double Standard."

12. McGlen et al., *Women, Politics, and American Society.*

13. *Duren v. Missouri,* 439 U.S. 357 (1979).

14. Burrell, *A Woman's Place Is in the House;* Costantini, "Political Women."

15. Based on author interviews.

16. Ibid.

17. Kurtz, "The All Boys Network."

18. Ibid.

19. Johnson, "Women Are Almost Never on Sundays."

20. Based on author interviews.

21. Clift and Brazaitis, *Madam President.*

22. Ibid.

23. See the White House Project homepage, www.thewhitehouseproject.org.

Bibliography

Abramson, Paul, John Aldrich, and David Rohde. *Change and Continuity in the 1984 Elections.* Washington, DC: Congressional Quarterly Press, 1986.

Adamson, Rondi. "See Jane Play Governor Mom." *Ottawa Citizen,* April 20, 2001, 14.

Aday, Sean, and James Devitt. *Style over Substance: Newspaper Coverage of Female Candidates: Spotlight on Elizabeth Dole.* Washington, DC: Women's Leadership Fund, 2001.

Albright, Madeleine. "Women and Foreign Policy: A Call to Action." Remarks at the Women's Conference, Los Angeles, October 5, 1999. *U.S. Department of State Dispatch* 10, no. 8 (October 1999).

Alexander, Deborah, and Kristi Andersen. "Gender as a Factor in the Attribution of Leadership Traits." *Political Research Quarterly* 46, no. 3 (1993): 527–546.

Almond, Gabriel. *The American People and Foreign Policy.* New York: Praeger, 1960.

American Association of University Women. *Gender Gaps: Where Schools Still Fail Our Children.* Washington, DC: AAUW, 1998.

Auster, Elizabeth. "Dole Wasn't Woman Enough to Be President." *Cleveland Plain Dealer,* October 24, 1999, 3G.

Ayers, B. Drummond, Jr. "Nothing Wasted, Something Gained." *New York Times,* October 21, 1999, A24.

Baer, D. "The Political Interests of Women." In Lois Duke Whitaker, ed., *Women in Politics: Outsiders or Insiders?* 3rd ed. Upper Saddle River, NJ: Prentice Hall, 1999, pp. 99–118.

Baker, Stephen C., and Paul Kleppner. "Race War Chicago Style: The Election of a Black Mayor." In Terry Clark, ed., *Research in Urban Policy.* Greenwich, CT: JAI Press, 215–238.

Banwart, Mary Christine, and Dianne Bystrom. "Gender Influences on Gathering Political Information: Examining Perceptions of and Sources for Obtaining Political Knowledge in Elections." Paper presented at the annual meeting of the National Communication Association, Atlanta, November 2001.

Banwart, Mary Christine, and Diane B. Carlin. "The Effects of Negative Political Advertising on Gendered Image Perception and Voter Intent: A Longitudinal Study." Paper presented at the annual meeting of the National Communication Association, Atlanta, November 2001.

Barabak, Mark Z. "Dole Drops Bid for Presidency, Leaves a Legacy." *Los Angeles Times,* October 21, 1999, A1.

Barnett, Richard. *The Roots of War.* New York: Atheneum, 1972.

Baumgardner, Jennifer, and Amelia Richards. "Why Not Elizabeth Dole?" *The Nation,* April 5, 1999, 6.

Bayer, Amy. "Dole's Campaign Could Transform GOP 'Gender Gap.'" *San Diego Union Tribune,* August 21, 1999, A1.

Beck, Paul Allen. *The Politics of Congressional Elections.* 5th ed. New York: Longman, 2000.

Bem, Sandra Lipsitz. "The Measurement of Psychological Androgyny." *Journal of Consulting and Clinical Psychology* 42 (1974): 155–162.

Bennett, W. Lance. *News: The Politics of Illusion.* White Plains, NY: Longman, 1996.

Berke, Richard L. "As Political Spouse, Bob Dole Strays from Campaign Script." *New York Times,* May 17, 1999, 1.

———. "Running with (and from) a Famous Name." *New York Times,* March 14, 1999, 4.

Birnbaum, Jeffrey. "Money, Money, Everywhere!" *Fortune,* July 19, 1999, 80.

Blankenship, Jane, and Deborah C. Robson. "A 'Feminine Style' in Women's Political Discourse: An Exploratory Essay." *Communication Quarterly* 43 (1995).

Bower, Carol Lynn. "Winning Thread: The Political Message and Communicative Style in Arizona's 1998 Gubernatorial Election." Master's thesis: Arizona State University, 2001.

Braden, Maria. *Women Politicians and the Media.* Lexington: University of Kentucky Press, 1996.

Brands, H. W. *The Use of Force After the Cold War.* College Station: Texas A&M University, 2000.

Braude, Ann. *Radical Spirits: Spiritualism and Women's Rights in Nineteenth-Century America.* Boston: Beacon Press, 1989.

Broder, John M. "Quietly and Dexterously, Senate Republicans Set a Trap." *New York Times,* October 14, 1999.

Brown, Seyom. *The Faces of Power: United States Foreign Policy from Truman to Clinton.* New York: Columbia University Press, 1994.

Bruni, Frank. "With Eye on the Vice Presidency, Elizabeth Dole Plans to Endorse Bush for President." *New York Times,* January 3, 2000, A14.

Burke, John. *The Institutional Presidency.* Baltimore: Johns Hopkins University Press, 1992.

Burrell, Barbara C. "Campaign Finance: Women's Experience in the Modern Era." In Sue Thomas and Clyde Wilcox, eds., *Women and Elective Office.* Oxford: Oxford University Press, 1998: 30–37.

———. *A Woman's Place Is in the House: Campaigning for Congress in the Feminist Era.* Ann Arbor: University of Michigan Press, 1994.

———. "Women's and Men's Campaigns for the U.S. House of Representatives, 1972–1982." *American Politics Quarterly* 13 (1985): 251–272.

———. "Women's Political Leadership and the State of the Parties." In Daniel Shea and John Green, eds., *The State of the Parties: The Changing Role of Contemporary American Parties.* Lanham, MD: Rowman and Littlefield, 1994.

Busch, Andrew. "New Features of the 2000 Presidential Nominating Process." In William Mayer, ed., *In Pursuit of the White House 2000.* New York: Chatham House, 2000.

Bustillo, Miguel. "Women's Group Gives Dole Respect, Not Passion." *Los Angeles Times,* October 18, 1999, A17.

Buvinic, Mayra. "Women in Poverty: A New Global Underclass." *Foreign Policy* 108 (Fall 1997).

Byron, Jessica, and Diana Thorburn. "Gender and International Relations: A Global

Perspective and Issues for the Caribbean." *Feminist Review* 59 (Summer 1998): 211–233.

Bystrom, Dianne G. "Candidate Gender and the Presentation of Self: The Videostyles of Men and Women in U.S. Senate Campaigns." Ph.D. diss., University of Oklahoma, 1995.

———. "Media Content and Candidate Viability: The Case of Elizabeth Dole." In Mitchell S. McKinney, Dianne G. Bystrom, Lynda Lee Kaid, and Diana B. Carlin, eds., *Communicating Politics: Engaging the Public in Democratic Life.* New York: Peter Lang, 2002.

Bystrom, Dianne G., and Lynda Lee Kaid. "Are Women Candidates Transforming Campaign Communication? A Comparison of Advertising Videostyles in the 1990s." In Cindy Simon Rosenthal, ed., *Women Transforming Congress.* Norman: University of Oklahoma Press, 2002.

Bystrom, Dianne G., Lynda Lee Kaid, and Jerry Miller. "The Evolution of Videostyle for Women Candidates: Advertising as a Form of Debate." Paper presented at the annual meeting of the National Communication Association, Chicago, November 1997.

Bystrom, Dianne G., and Jerry Miller. "Gendered Communication Styles and Strategies in Campaign 1996: The Videostyles of Women and Men Candidates." In Lynda Lee Kaid and Dianne G. Bystrom, eds., *The Electronic Election: Perspectives on the 1996 Campaign Communication.* Mahwah, NJ: Lawrence Erlbaum, 1999.

Bystrom, Dianne G., Terry Robertson, and Mary C. Banwart. "Framing the Fight: An Analysis of Media Coverage of Female and Male Candidates in Primary Races for Governor and U.S. Senate in 2000." *American Behavioral Scientist* 44 (2001): 1999–2013.

Canada, Katherine, and Richard Pringle. "The Role of Gender in College Classroom Interactions: A Social Context." *Sociology of Education* 68 (1995): 161–186.

Cannon, Carl M. "You Go, Girls." *National Journal,* July 24, 1999, 2142–2147.

Carroll, Joe. "Is the 'Steel Magnolia' Now Starting to Wilt?" *The Irish Times,* October 16, 1999.

Carroll, Susan J. *Women as Candidates in American Politics.* Bloomington: Indiana University Press, 1994.

Cassidy, Tina. "Chuck Hunt, First Husband a Former Farmer." *Boston Globe,* April 15, 2001, A1.

CAWP (Center for the American Woman and Politics). "Women in the U.S. Senate, 1922–2002." Eagleton Institute of Politics, Rutgers University, 2001, www.rci.rutgers.edu/~cawp/facts/cawpfs.html.

Cherlin, Andrew, and P. B. Walters. "Trends in United States' Men's and Women's Sex Role Attitudes." *American Sociological Review* 36, no. 4 (1981): 453–460.

Chisholm, Shirley. *The Good Fight.* New York: Harper and Row, 1973.

———. *Unbought and Unbossed.* Boston: Houghton Mifflin, 1970.

Cialdini, Robert B. *Influences: Science and Practice.* Needham Heights, MA: Allyn and Bacon, 2001.

Clark, Cal, and Janet Clark. "The Gender Gap in 1996: More Meaning than a 'Revenge of the Soccer Moms.'" In Lois Duke Whitaker, ed., *Women in Politics: Outsiders or Insiders?* Upper Saddle River, NJ: Prentice-Hall, 1999, 68–86.

Clift, Eleanor, and Tom Brazaitis. *Madam President: Shattering the Last Glass Ceiling.* New York: Scribner, 2000.

Cohen, Marty, David Vard, Hans Noel, and John Zaller. "Party Reform: The Resurgence of Parties in Presidential Nominations, 1980–2000." Paper presented at the annual meeting of the American Political Science Association, San Francisco, 2001.

Common Cause. "The Critical Role of Television in Political Campaigns." In *Chan-*

neling Influence: The Broadcast Lobby and the $70 Billion Free Ride. Washington, DC: Common Cause, 1997. See www.commoncause.org.

Conway, M. Margaret, Gertrude A. Steuernagel, and David W. Ahern. *Women and Political Participation: Cultural Change in the Political Arena.* Washington, DC: Congressional Quarterly Press, 1997.

Cook, Elizabeth A., Sue Thomas, and Clyde Wilcox, eds. *The Year of the Woman: Myths and Realities.* Boulder, CO: Westview Press, 1994.

Cooper, John Milton. *The Warrior and the Priest: Woodrow Wilson and Theodore Roosevelt.* Cambridge: Belknap/Harvard University Press, 1983.

Costain, Anne. "After Reagan: New Party Attitudes Toward Gender." In Janet Boles, ed., *American Feminism: New Issues for a Mature Movement. The Annals* 515, 1991, pp. 114–125.

———. *Inviting Women's Rebellion: A Political Process Interpretation of the Women's Movement.* Baltimore: Johns Hopkins University Press, 1994.

———. "Women's Claims as a Special Interest." In Carol Mueller, ed., *The Politics of the Gender Gap.* Newbury Park, CA: Sage, 1988, 150–172.

Costain, Anne, Richard Braunstein, and Heidi Berggren. "Framing the Women's Movement." In Pippa Norris, ed., *Women, Media, and Politics.* New York: Oxford University Press, 1997.

Costain, Anne, and Heather Fraizer. "Media Portrayal of 'Second Wave' Feminist Groups." In Simone Chambers and Anne Costain, eds., *Deliberation, Democracy, and the Media.* Lanham, MD: Rowman and Littlefield, 2000.

Costantini, Edmund. "Political Women and Political Parties." *American Journal of Political Science* 34 (1990): 741–770.

Costello, Cynthia B., and Anne J. Stone. *The American Woman 2001.* New York: W. W. Norton, 2001.

Cott, Nancy. "Across the Great Divide: Women in Politics Before and After 1920." In Louise Tilly and Patricia Gurin, eds., *Women, Politics, and Change.* New York: Russell Sage, 1992.

Couper, Mick P. "Web Surveys: A Review of Issues and Approaches." *Public Opinion Quarterly* 64 (2000): 464–494.

Crabb, Cecil V., and Pat M. Holt. *Invitation to Struggle: Congress, the President, and Foreign Policy.* Washington, DC: Congressional Quarterly Press, 1980.

Cronin, Thomas E., and Michael A. Genovese. *The Paradoxes of the American Presidency.* New York: Oxford University Press, 1998.

Crown, Marlow. *The Approval Motive.* New York: Wiley and Sons, 1964.

D'Agostino, Joseph A. "Poll: Women Trending Right on Social Issues." *Human Events,* March 26, 1999, 5.

Darcy, R., Susan Welch, and Janet Clark. *Women, Elections and Representation.* Lincoln: University of Nebraska Press, 1994.

Deaux, Kay, and Brenda Major. "Putting Gender into Context: An Interactive Model of Gender-Related Behavior." *Psychological Review* 84 (1987).

DeConde, Alexander. *Presidential Machismo: Executive Authority, Military Intervention, and Foreign Relations.* Boston: Northeastern University Press, 2000.

de la Garza, Rodolfo O., Angelo Falcon, and F. Chris Garcia. "Will the Real Americans Please Stand Up: Anglo and Mexican-American Support of Core American Political Values." *American Journal of Political Science* 40, no. 2 (May 1996): 335–351.

Delli Carpini, Michael X., and Scott Keeter. *What Americans Know About Politics and Why It Matters.* New Haven, CT: Yale University Press, 1996.

Destler, I. M. *The National Economic Council, A Work in Progress: Policy Analyses in International Economics.* Washington, DC: International Economics, 1996.

Devitt, James. *Framing Gender on the Campaign Trail: Women's Executive Leadership and the Press.* Washington, DC: Women's Leadership Fund, 1999.

Dolan, Kathleen. "Gender Differences in Support for Women Candidates: Is There a Glass Ceiling in American Politics?" *Women and Politics* 17, no. 2 (1997): 27–41.

———. "Voting for Women in the 'Year of the Woman.'" *American Journal of Political Science* 42 (Winter 2001): 272–293.

Dole, Bob. "Stingy Coverage." *Washington Post,* September 15, 1999, A24.

Dow, Bonnie J., and Mari Boor Tonn. "Feminine Style and Political Judgment in the Rhetoric of Ann Richards." *Quarterly Journal of Speech* 79 (1993): 286–288.

Dowd, Maureen. "Why Can't a Woman." *New York Times,* October 24, 1999, D15.

Duerst-Lahti, Georgia, and Rita Mae Kelly. "On Governance, Leadership, and Gender." In Georgia Duerst-Lahti and Rita Mae Kelly, eds., *Gender, Power, Leadership, and Governance.* Ann Arbor: University of Michigan Press, 1995.

Eagen, Margery. "Back-biting Hubby Shows Us What Libby's Made Of." *Boston Herald,* May 20, 1999.

———. "Maternity Leave Spoils Governor Jane on Taxpayer Dime." *Boston Herald,* April 15, 2001, 2.

Edwards, Renee. "The Effects of Gender, Gender Role, and Values on the Interpretation of Messages." *Journal of Language and Social Psychology* 17 (1998).

Engel, Margaret. "Feminist Issues Alone Not a Magnet to Women Voters." *New York Times,* September 14, 1984, A3.

Enloe, Cynthia. *Bananas, Beaches and Bases: Making Feminist Sense of International Politics.* Berkeley: University of California Press, 1990.

Entman, Robert. "Blacks in the News: Modern Racism and Cultural Change." *Journalism Quarterly* 69 (1999): 341–361.

Erbe, Bonnie. "A Woman Would Be Fine for President, But." *San Diego Union-Tribune,* January 19, 2000, B7.

Evans, Sara. *Personal Politics: The Roots of Women's Liberation in the Civil Rights Movement and the New Left.* New York: Random House: 1980.

Farrar-Myers, Victoria A. "The Collapse of an Inherited Agenda: George Bush and the Reagan Foreign Policy Legacy." *White House Studies* 1, no. 1 (2001): 33–49.

———. "The Fundraiser-in-Chief: Bill Clinton's Legacy for Presidential Campaign Finance." In Michael A. Genovese and David Adler, eds., *The Presidency and the Law After Clinton.* Lawrence: University Press of Kansas, 2002.

Fee, Gayle, and Laura Raposa. "Inside Track—Maher: Jane Is Incorrect Politically." *Boston Globe,* February 14, 2001, 8.

Ferguson, Thomas. "'Organized Capitalism,' Fiscal Policy, and the 1992 Democratic Campaign." In Lawrence Dodd and Calvin Jillson, eds., *New Perspectives on American Politics.* Washington, DC: Congressional Quarterly Press, 1994, 118–139.

Ferraro, Geraldine, with Linda Bird Francke. *Ferraro: My Story.* New York: Bantam Books, 1985.

Ferree, Myra Marx. "A Woman for President?" *Public Opinion Quarterly* 38, no. 4 (1974): 390–399.

Fertik, Bob. "Elizabeth Dole: America's First Woman President?" *Political Women,* January 8, 1999, www.wlo.org/pw/990108.htm.

Foot, Rosemary. *Rights Beyond Borders: The Global Community and the Struggle for Human Rights in China.* New York: Oxford University Press, 2000.

Forman, S. E. *The Life and Selected Writings of Thomas Jefferson.* Indianapolis: Bobbs-Merrill, 1900.

Fred, Sheryl. "Gender Politics: Women Donors Making a Financial Statement." See http://www.opensecrets.org/newsletter/ce64/01gender.htm, 1999.

Freeman, Jo. *A Room at a Time: How Women Entered Party Politics.* Lanham, MD: Rowman and Littlefield, 2000.

————. "Whom You Know vs. Whom You Represent." In Mary Katzenstein and Carol M. Mueller, eds., *The Women's Movements of the United States and Western Europe*. Philadelphia: Temple University Press, 1987.

Friedan, Betty. *The Feminine Mystique*. New York: W. W. Norton, 2001.

Fuchs, Lawrence H. *The American Kaleidoscope: Race, Ethnicity and Civic Culture*. Middletown, CT: Wesleyan University Press, 1990.

Fukuyama, Francis. "Women and the Evolution of World Politics." *Foreign Affairs* 77, no. 5 (September–October 1998).

Fuller, Margaret. *Woman in the Nineteenth Century*. New York: W. W. Norton, 1971.

Gabriel, Mary. *Notorious Victoria*. Chapel Hill, NC: Algonquin Books, 1998.

Gamson, William. *Talking Politics*. Cambridge: Cambridge University Press, 1992.

Geiger, Stephen F., and Byron Reeves. "The Effects of Visual Structure and Content Emphasis on the Evaluation and Memory of Political Candidates." In Frank Biocca, ed., *Television and Political Advertising: Psychological Processes*. Hillsdale, NJ: Lawrence Erlbaum, 1991.

Gelderman, Carol. *All the President's Words: The Bully Pulpit and the Creation of the Virtual Presidency*. New York: Walker, 1997.

Genovese, Michael A. "Women as National Leaders: What Do We Know?" In Michael A. Genovese, ed., *Women as National Leaders*. Newbury Park, CA: Sage, 1993.

Genovese, Michael A., and Seth Thompson. "Women as Chief Executives: Does Gender Matter?" In Michael A. Genovese, ed., *Women as National Leaders*. Newbury Park, CA: Sage, 1993.

Gergen, David. *Eyewitness to Power: The Essence of Leadership: Nixon to Clinton*. New York: Simon and Schuster, 2000.

Gertzog, Irwin N. "The Matrimonial Connection: The Nomination of Congressmen's Widows for the House of Representatives." *Journal of Politics* 42 (1980): 820–833.

Gillies, David. *Between Principle and Practice: Human Rights in North-South Relations*. Montreal: McGill-Queen's Universities, 1996.

Goldberg, Carey. "2 New Jobs for Massachusetts Official: Acting Governor and Mother of Twins." *New York Times,* February 15, 2001, A22.

Gordon, Ann, and Jerry L. Miller. "Does the Oval Office Have a Glass Ceiling? Gender Stereotypes and Perceptions of Candidate Viability." *White House Studies* 1, no. 3 (2001): 325–333.

Goulden, Joseph. *Superlawyers*. New York: Dell, 1973.

Graber, Doris. *Mass Media and American Politics*. Washington, DC: Congressional Quarterly Press, 1997.

Graham, Victoria. "Albright: Woman President Sooner Rather Than Later." *WomensEnews,* October 19, 2001.

Grant, Rebecca, and K. Newland. *Gender and International Relations*. Bloomington: Indiana University Press, 1991.

Green, John, Paul Herrnson, Lynda Powell, and Clyde Wilcox. "Individual Congressional Campaign Contributors: Wealthy, Conservative and Reform-Minded." See http://www.opensecrets.org/pubs/donors/donors.htm, 1998.

Greenstein, Fred I. *The Presidential Difference: Leadership Style from FDR to Clinton*. Princeton, NJ: Princeton University Press, 2000.

Griffith, Elisabeth. *In Her Own Right: The Life of Elizabeth Cady Stanton*. Washington, DC: Oxford University Press, 1985.

Gurko, Miriam. *The Ladies of Seneca Falls: The Birth of the Women's Rights Movement*. New York: Random House, 1987.

Haass, Richard. "Fatal Distraction: Bill Clinton's Foreign Policy." *Foreign Policy* 108 (Fall 1997).

Haftendorn, Helga, and Jakob Schissler. *The Reagan Administration: A Reconstruction of American Strength?* New York: Walter de Gruyter, 1988.

Hale, Jon. "The Democratic Leadership Council: Institutionalizing Party Faction." In Daniel Shea and John Green, eds., *The State of the Parties: The Changing Role of Contemporary American Parties*. Lanham, MD: Rowman and Littlefield, 1994, 250–262.

Hamilton, David, and Jeffrey Sherman. "Stereotypes." In Robert S. Wyer and Thomas K. Srull, eds., *Handbook of Social Cognition*. Hillsdale, NJ: Lawrence Erlbaum, 1994.

Hammond, Grant T. "Time for a Revolution: The Transition from National Defense to International Security." In Grant T. Hammond, ed., *Plowshares into Swords: Arms Races in International Politics, 1840–1991*. Columbia: University of South Carolina Press, 1993, 148.

Han, Lori Cox. *Governing from Center Stage: White House Communication Strategies During the Television Age of Politics*. Cresskill, NJ: Hampton Press, 2001.

———. "The Next Contender: Assessing the Pool of Women Candidates for President." *White House Studies* 1, no. 3 (2001).

Hart, Roderick P. *The Sound of Leadership: Presidential Communication in the Modern Age*. Chicago: University of Chicago Press, 1987.

Havel, J. T. *U.S. Presidential Candidates and the Elections: A Biographical and Historical Guide*. New York: Simon and Schuster Macmillan, 1996.

Heith, Diane J. "Footwear, Lipstick, and an Orthodox Sabbath: Media Coverage of Non-Traditional Candidates." *White House Studies* 1, no. 3 (2001).

———. "Presidential Polling and the Potential for Leadership." In Lawrence Jacobs, Martha Kumar, and Robert Shapiro, eds., *Presidential Power: Forging the Presidency for the 21st Century*. New York: Columbia University Press, 2000, 380–407.

Heldman, Caroline, Susan J. Carroll, and Stephanie Olson. "Gender Differences in Print Media Coverage of Presidential Candidates: Elizabeth Dole's Bid for the Republican Nomination." Paper presented at the annual meeting of the American Political Science Association, Washington, DC, August 2000.

Hendershot, Thomas R. "The Double Standard on the Stump." *Washington Post*, January 6, 2001, B8.

Henry, Charles P. "Racial Factors in the 1982 California Gubernatorial Campaign." In Michael B. Preston, Lenneal J. Henderson, and Paul L. Puryear, eds., *The New Black Politics*. New York: Longman, 1987.

Herrnson, Paul. *Party Campaigning in the 1980s*. Cambridge, MA: Harvard University Press, 1988.

Herrnson, Paul S., and John C. Green, eds. *Multiparty Politics in America*. Lanham, MD: Rowman and Littlefield, 1997.

Hershey, Marjorie Randon. "The Campaign and the Media." In Gerald M. Pomper, ed., *The Election of 2000*. New York: Chatham House, 2001.

Hinkley, David. "Shirley Chisholm Riding Alone." *Daily News*, March 3, 1999, 19.

Hoffman, Curt, and Nancy Hurst. "Gender Stereotypes: Perception or Rationalization?" *Journal of Personality and Social Psychology* 58 (1990).

Hook, Steven W., and John Spanier. *American Foreign Policy Since World War II*. Washington, DC: Congressional Quarterly Press, 2000.

Hua, Lee Siew. "Elizabeth Dole May Make Comeback as Bush's No. 2." *Straits Times*, November 10, 1999, 10.

Huddy, Leonie. "The Political Significance of Voters' Gender Stereotypes." In Michael Delli Carpini, Leonie Huddy, and Robert Y. Shapiro, eds., *Research in Micropolitics*. Greenwich, CT: JAI Press, 1994.

Huddy, Leonie, Francis Neely, and Marilyn LaFay. "The Polls—Trends: Support for the Women's Movement." *Public Opinion Quarterly* 64 (2000): 309–350.

Huddy, Leonie, and David Sears. "Opposition to Bilingual Education: Prejudice or the Defense of Realistic Interests?" *Social Psychology Quarterly* 58, no. 2 (June 1995): 133–143.

Huddy, Leonie, and Nayda Terkildsen. "The Consequences of Gender Stereotypes for Women Candidates at Different Levels and Types of Office." *Political Science Quarterly* (Fall 1993).

———. "Gender Stereotypes and the Perception of Male and Female Candidates." *American Journal of Political Science* 37, no. 1 (February 1993): 119–147.

Hunt, Swanee. "Women's Vital Voice: The Costs of Exclusion in Eastern Europe." *Foreign Affairs* 76, no. 4 (July–August 1997).

Iyengar, Shanto, and Donald Kinder. *Is Anyone Responsible? How Television Frames Political Issues.* Chicago: University of Chicago Press, 1991.

———. *News That Matters: Television and American Opinion.* Chicago: University of Chicago Press, 1987.

Iyengar, Shanto, Mark D. Peters, and Donald Kinder. "Experimental Demonstrations of the 'Not-So-Minimal' Consequences of Television News Programs." *American Political Science Review* 76 (1982): 848–858.

Iyengar, Shanto, Nicholas A. Valentino, Stephen Ansolabehere, and Adam F. Simon. "Running as a Woman: Gender Stereotyping in Political Campaigns." In Pippa Norris, ed., *Women, Media, and Politics.* New York: Oxford University Press, 1997.

Jacobson, Gary C. *The Politics of Congressional Elections.* 5th ed. New York: Addison Wesley, 2000.

Jamail, J. "The Inquiring Fotographer." *New York Daily News,* January 28, 1972, 45.

———. "The Inquiring Fotographer." *New York Daily News,* January 30, 1964, 35.

———. "The Inquiring Fotographer." *New York Daily News,* December 11, 1963, 53.

Jamieson, Kathleen Hall. *Beyond the Double Bind: Women and Leadership.* New York: Oxford University Press, 1995.

———. *Eloquence in an Electronic Age: The Transformation of Political Speechmaking.* New York: Oxford University Press, 1988.

Jaquette, Jane S. "States Make War." In "Fukuyama's Follies: So What If Women Ruled the World?" *Foreign Affairs* 78, no. 1 (January–February 1999).

Jeffers, H. Paul. *Commissioner Roosevelt: The Story of Theodore Roosevelt and the New York City Police, 1895–1897.* New York: John Wiley, 1994.

Jeffreys-Jones, Rhodri. *Changing Differences: Women and the Shaping of American Diplomacy, 1917–1994.* New Brunswick, NJ: Rutgers University Press, 1997.

Jennings, Kent. "Women in Party Politics." In Louis Tilly and Patricia Gurin, eds., *Women, Politics and Change.* New York: Russell Sage, 1992.

Johnson, Peter. "Women Are Almost Never on Sundays." *USA Today,* December 5, 2001, 4D.

Jones, Alex. "Ferraro Campaign Delivers Coup de Grace to 'Boys on Bus' Era." *New York Times,* November 3, 1984, A10.

———. "Ferraro's Finances: Is the Press Being Fair?" *New York Times,* August 24, 1984, A1.

Jones, Charles O. *Separate but Equal Branches: Congress and the Presidency.* New York: Chatham House, 1999.

Josyln, Richard A. *Mass Media and Elections.* Reading, MA: Addison Wesley, 1984.

Kahn, Kim Fridkin. "The Distorted Mirror: Press Coverage of Women Candidates for Statewide Office." *Journal of Politics* 56 (1994): 154–173.

———. "Does Being Male Help? An Investigation of the Effects of Candidate Gender and Campaign Coverage on Evaluations of U.S. Senate Candidates." *Journal of Politics* 54 (1992): 497–517.

————. "Does Gender Make a Difference? An Experimental Examination of Sex Stereotypes and Press Patterns in Statewide Campaigns." *American Journal of Political Science* 38 (1994): 162–195.

————. *The Political Consequences of Being a Woman.* New York: Columbia University Press, 1996.

————. "Senate Elections in the News: Examining Campaign Coverage." *Legislative Studies Quarterly* 16, no. 3 (1991).

Kahn, Kim Fridkin, and Edie N. Goldenberg. "Women Candidates in the News: An Examination of Gender Differences in the U.S. Senate Campaign Coverage." *Public Opinion Quarterly* 55 (1991): 180–199.

Kaid, Lynda Lee. "Political Advertising: A Summary of Research Findings." In B. Newman, ed., *The Handbook of Political Marketing.* Thousand Oaks, CA: Sage, 1999.

Kaid, Lynda Lee, and Dorothy K. Davidson. "Elements of Videostyle: Candidate Presentations Through Television Advertising." In Lynda Lee Kaid, Dan Nimmo, and Keith R. Sanders, eds., *New Perspectives on Political Advertising.* Carbondale: Southern Illinois University Press, 1986.

Kaid, Lynda Lee, and John C. Tedesco. "Tracking Voter Reaction to the Television Advertising." In Lynda Lee Kaid and Dianne G. Bystrom, eds., *The Electronic Election: Perspectives on the 1996 Campaign Communication.* Mahwah, NJ: Lawrence Erlbaum, 1999.

Kaminer, Wendy. "Feminism's Identity Crisis." *Atlantic,* October 1993, 51–68.

Keen, Judy. "Geraldine Ferraro Says It's About Time for a Female VP." *USA Today,* July 21, 2000, 12.

Kenski, Kate, and Kathleen Hall Jamieson. "The 2000 Presidential Campaign and Differential Growths in Knowledge: Does the 'Knowledge Gap' Hypothesis Apply to Gender as Well as Education?" Paper presented at the annual meeting of the American Political Science Association, San Francisco, CA, August 2001.

Kern, Montague. *30-Second Politics: Political Advertising in the 1980s.* New York: Praeger, 1989.

Kernell, Samuel. *Going Public: New Strategies of Presidential Leadership.* Washington, DC: Congressional Quarterly Press, 1997.

Kerry, Richard J. *The Star-Spangled Mirror: America's Image of Itself and the World.* Savage, MD: Rowman and Littlefield, 1990.

Kessel, John H. *Presidents, the Presidency, and the Political Environment.* Washington, DC: Congressional Quarterly Press, 2001.

Kincaid, Diane. "Over His Dead Body: A Positive Perspective on Widows in the U.S. Congress." *Western Political Quarterly* 31 (1978): 96–104.

Kinder, Donald R. "Presidential Character Revisited." In Richard R. Lau and David O. Sears, eds., *Political Cognition.* Hillsdale, NJ: Lawrence Erlbaum, 1986, 233–255.

Knack, Thomas J. *To End All Wars: Woodrow Wilson and the Quest for a New World Order.* New York: Oxford University Press, 1992.

Koch, Jeffrey. "Candidate Gender and Women's Psychological Engagement in Politics." *American Politics Quarterly* 25, no. 1 (January 1997): 118–133.

————. "The Effect of Candidate Gender on Citizens' Evaluations of Senate Candidates." Paper presented at the American Political Science Association Annual Meeting, New York, 1994.

Krum, Sharon. "Why Can't the President Wear a Dress?" *The Guardian,* October 26, 1999.

Kurtz, Howard. "The All Boys Network." *Washington Post,* December 5, 2001, C1.

Lammers, William W., and Michael A. Genovese. *The Presidency and Domestic Policy: Comparing Leadership Styles, FDR to Clinton.* Washington, DC: Congressional Quarterly Press, 2000.

Landy, Mark K. *The New Politics of Public Policy.* Baltimore: Johns Hopkins University Press, 1995.

Langton, James. "International: Mrs. Dole Aims to Make Bob a First Gentleman." *Sunday Telegraph* (London), February 21, 1999.

LeBlanc, Steve. "Some Object to Swift Governing from Hospital Bed." Associated Press, May 9, 2001, BC.

Lebsock, Suzanne. "Women and American Politics, 1880–1920." In Louise A. Tilly and Patricia Gurin, eds., *Women, Politics, and Change.* New York: Sage, 1990.

Leeper, Mark S. "The Impact of Prejudice on Female Candidates: An Experimental Look at Voter Inference." *American Politics Quarterly* 19 (1991): 248–261.

Leonard, Mary. "Dole's Iowa Showing Quells the Naysayers—For Now; 3rd Place Finish Demonstrates Her Appeal to Women, Aides Say." *Boston Globe,* August 21, 1999, A3.

Lepgold, Joseph, and Timothy McKeown. "Is American Foreign Policy Exceptional? An Empirical Analysis." *Political Science Quarterly* 110, no. 3 (Fall 1995).

Lindsay, Leon. "Why Two Top Races Bucked the Democratic Tide in California Election." *Christian Science Monitor,* November 9, 1982, 14.

Lipman, Thomas W. *Madeleine Albright and the New American Diplomacy.* Boulder, CO: Westview Press, 2000.

Logan, Mark P. "Elite Analysis of Democracies' International Policy." *Perspectives on Political Science* 29, no. 1 (Winter 2000).

Longworth, R. C. "Albright Promises New Push for Test-Ban Treaty." *Chicago Tribune,* November 11, 1999.

MacKenzie, Hilary. "Cash-strapped Elizabeth Dole Quits Presidential Race." *Ottawa Citizen,* October 21, 1999.

MacPherson, Myra. "The Candidate as Symbol, as Pioneer, as Fighter, and Daughter." *The Washington Post,* October 19, 1984.

Maltese, John Anthony. *Spin Control: The White House Office of Communications and the Management of Presidential News.* Chapel Hill: University of North Carolina Press, 1994.

Mandel, Ruth B. *In the Running: The New Woman Candidate.* Boston: Beacon, 1981.

———. "The Political Woman." In S. Matteo, ed., *American Women in the 1990s: Today's Critical Issues.* Boston: Northeastern University, 1996.

———. "Women's Leadership in American Politics: The Legacy and the Promise." In Cynthia B. Costello and Anne J. Stone, eds., *The American Woman, 2001.* New York: W. W. Norton, 2001.

Mann, Judy. "Who Says a Woman Can't Be President? We Do." *New York Times,* January 28, 2000.

Matassa, Mark. "The 'Mom' Against All Those 'Dark Suits'—Murray's Theme Spells Out How She's Different but Doesn't Quell Criticism of Her as 'Less Filling.'" *Seattle Times,* September 4, 1992, A1.

Matland, Richard. "Putting Scandinavian Equality to the Test: An Experimental Evaluation of Gender Stereotyping of Political Candidates in a Sample of Norwegian Voters." *British Journal of Political Science* 24 (1994): 273–292.

Mayer, Henry. *All on Fire: William Lloyd Garrison and the Abolition of Slavery.* New York: St. Martin's Press, 2000.

Mayer, William G. "The Presidential Nominations." In Gerald M. Pomper, ed., *The Election of 2000.* New York: Chatham House, 2001.

McCombs, Maxwell, and Donald Shaw. "The Agenda Setting Function of the Mass Media." *Public Opinion Quarterly* 36 (1972): 176–187.

McGlen, Nancy E., Karen O'Connor, Laura van Assendelft, and Wendy Gunter-Canada. *Women, Politics, and American Society.* Englewood Cliffs, NJ: Prentice Hall, 1998.

McGlen, Nancy E., and Meredith Reid Sarkees. "Headline Series: The Status of Women in Foreign Policy." *Women's International Network News* 21, no. 4 (Autumn 1995).

————. *Women in Foreign Policy: The Insiders.* New York: Routledge, 1993.

McGrory, Mary. "The Muffled vs. the Sycophant." *Washington Post,* October 14, 1984.

McKinnon, S. "Fraud Verdict Leaves Career in Disarray." *Arizona Daily Star,* September 4, 1997.

Melich, Tanya. *The Republican War Against Women.* New York: Bantam, 1998.

Melucci, Alberto. *Challenging Codes: Collective Action in the Information Age.* Cambridge: Cambridge University Press, 1996.

Mendelberg, Tali. *The Race Card.* Princeton, NJ: Princeton University Press, 2001.

Mervin, David. "The Bully Pulpit II." *Presidential Studies Quarterly* 25, no. 1 (Winter 1995): 19–23.

Meyer, Carol H. "Imagining the Impossible." *Journal of Women and Social Work* 11, no. 1 (Spring 1996): 8–10.

Mezy, Susan Gluck. "Does Sex Make a Difference? A Case Study of Women in Politics." *Western Political Quarterly* 31 (1978): 492–501.

Milkis, Sidney M., and Michael Nelson. *The American Presidency: Origins and Development.* Washington, DC: Congressional Quarterly Press, 1999.

Miller, Nathan. *Theodore Roosevelt: A Life.* New York: William Morrow, 1992.

Miller, P., Todd Shields, Ellen Riggle, and Mitzi Johnson. "Gender Stereotypes and Decision Context in the Evaluation of Political Candidates." Paper presented at the annual meeting of the Midwest Political Science Association, Chicago, 1995.

Mitchell, Susan. *American Attitudes: Who Thinks What About the Issues That Shape Our Lives.* Ithaca, NY: New Strategist Publications, 1998.

"Mothers Replacing the Career Woman." *New York Times,* January 18, 1956, p. 13.

Mueller, M. "The Empowerment of Women." In M. Mueller, ed., *The Politics of the Gender Gap.* Newbury Park, CA: Sage, 1988.

Nacos, Brigitte Lebens. "Presidential Leadership During the Persian Gulf Conflict." *Presidential Studies Quarterly* 24, no. 3 (Summer 1994).

Nelson, Candice J. "Women's PACs in the Year of the Woman." In Elizabeth A. Cook, Sue Thomas, and Clyde Wilcox, eds., *The Year of the Woman: Myths and Realities.* Boulder, CO: Westview, 1994, 185–197.

Nelson, Michael. "The Post-Election Election: Politics by Other Means." In Michael Nelson, ed., *The Elections of 2000.* Washington, DC: Congressional Quarterly Press, 2001.

Neustadt, Richard. *Presidential Power.* New York: Wiley, 1960.

Newman, J. *Perception and Reality: A Study Comparing the Success of Men and Women Candidates.* Washington, DC: National Women's Political Caucus, 1994.

Newport, Frank, David W. Moore, and Lydia Saad. "Long-term Gallup Poll Trends: A Portrait of American Public Opinion Through the Century." See http://www.gallup.com/poll/release/pr991220.asp, 1999.

Nichols, John. "Will Any Woman Do?" *Progressive* 63, no. 7 (July 1999): 31.

Noble, Iris. *Emmeline and Her Daughters: Pankhurst Suffragettes.* New York: Messner, 1971.

Norris, Pippa. *Women, Media and Politics.* New York: Oxford University, 1997.

Northouse, Peter G. *Leadership: Theory and Practice.* Thousand Oaks, CA: Sage Publications, 1997.

Nunnally, Jum. *Psychometric Theory.* New York: McGraw-Hill, 1978.

Oboler, Suzanne. *Ethnic Labels, Latino Lives: Identity and the Politics of (Re)Presentation in the United States.* Minneapolis: University of Minnesota Press, 1995.

Olson, Lynne. *Freedom's Daughters: The Unsung Heroines of the Civil Rights Movement from 1830 to 1970.* New York: Scribner, 2001.

Overholster, Geneva. "Why Is Dole Getting Short Changed?" *Washington Post,* September 13, 1999.

Page, Benjamin, and Robert Shapiro. "Educating and Manipulating the Public." In Michael Margolis and Gary Mauser, eds., *Manipulating Public Opinion: Essays on Public Opinion as a Dependent Variable.* Pacific Grove, CA: Brooks/Cole, 1989.

Paletz, David L. *The Media in American Politics: Contents and Consequences.* New York: Longman, 2002.

Paletz, David L., and Robert M. Entman. *Media Power Politics.* New York: Macmillan, 1981.

Palmer, Beverly Wilson, Holly Byers Ochoa, and Carol Faulkner. *Selected Letters of Lucretia Mott.* Champaign: University of Illinois Press, 2001.

Pankhurst, Emmeline. *My Own Story.* New York: Greenwood, 1985.

Papayoanou, Paul A. "Economic Interdependence and the Balance of Power." *International Studies Quarterly* 41, no. 1 (March 1997).

Parsons, Karen Toombs. "Exploring the 'Two Presidencies' Phenomenon:' New Evidence from the Truman Administration." *Presidential Studies Quarterly* 24, no. 3 (Summer 1994).

Patterson, Thomas E. *Out of Order.* New York: Vintage Books, 1994.

Patterson, Thomas E., and Robert D. McClure. *The Unseeing Eye: The Myth of Television Power in National Politics.* New York: G. P. Putnam, 1976.

Paulhus, P. "Measurement and Control of Response Bias." In John P. Robinson, Phillip R. Shavert, and Lawrence Wrightsman, eds., *Measures of Social Psychological Attitudes.* New York: Academic Press, 1991.

Peffley, Mark, and Jon Hurwitz. "Whites' Stereotypes of Blacks: Sources and Political Consequences." In Jon Hurwitz and Mark Peffley, eds., *Perception and Prejudice.* New Haven, CT: Yale University Press, 1998, 58–99.

Penley, Nellie, and Marie Sullivan. "Ladies at Odds over Woman as President." *Bangor Daily News,* January 28, 1964, 1.

Peterson, V. Spike. *Gendered States: Feminist Revisions of International Relations Theory.* Boulder: Lynne Rienner Publishers, 1992.

Pierce, P. A. "Gender Role and Political Culture: The Electoral Connection." *Women and Politics* 9 (1989).

Pitney, John J. "That 70s Candidate: Jimmy Carter with Helmet Hair." *Reason* 31, no. 2 (June 1999): 48.

Polman, Dick. "A Woman in the White House: Did Dole Help or Hurt Cause?" *Philadelphia Inquirer,* October 24, 1999, D1.

Polsby, Nelson. "The Democratic Nomination and the Evolution of the Party System." In Austin Ranney, ed., *The American Elections of 1984.* Durham: Duke University Press, 1985.

Polsby, Nelson, and Aaron Wildavsky. *Presidential Elections: Strategies and Structures of American Politics.* New York: Chatham House, 2000.

Pomper, Gerald. *The Election of 2000.* New York: Chatham House, 2001.

Ponnuru, Ramesh. "Gore-Dole 2000! A Place for Mrs. D." *National Review,* July 12, 1999, 22.

Price, David. *Bringing Back the Parties.* Washington, DC: Congressional Quarterly Press, 1984.

Purvis, June. *Emmeline Pankhurst: A Biography.* New York: Routledge, 2002.

Putnam, Robert. "Diplomacy and Domestic Politics: The Logic of Two-Level Games." *International Organization* 42 (Summer 1998).

Rajakaarunanayake, Hilary. "Sri Lanka's Bandaranaike Family Sets Parliamentary Record." *Japan Economic Newsletter,* October 19, 2000.

Reeves, Keith. *Voting Hopes or Fears? White Voters, Black Candidates, and Racial Politics in America.* New York: Oxford University Press, 1997.

Rice, Patricia. "Women Out of the Myths and into Focus." In *Women and the News*. New York: Hastings House, 1978.

Robson, Deborah Carol. "Stereotypes and the Female Politician: A Case Study of Senator Barbara Mikulski." *Communication Quarterly* 48 (2000): 210–219.

Rochon, Thomas R. *Culture Moves: Ideas, Activism, and Changing Values*. Princeton, NJ: Princeton University Press, 1998.

Roper Starch Worldwide. "Women in Elected Office Survey Identifies Obstacles for Women as Political Leaders." Deloitte and Touche, http://us.deloitte.com/pub/wilpoll/default.htm, 2001.

Rose, Richard. *The Postmodern President*. Chatham, NJ: Chatham House, 1991.

Rosenberg, Emily S. *Spreading the American Dream: American Economic and Cultural Expansion, 1890–1945*. New York: Hill and Wang, 1982.

Rosenwasser, Shirley M., and Norma Dean. "Gender Roles and Political Office." *Psychology of Women Quarterly* 13 (1989): 77–85.

Rosenwasser, Shirley M., Robyn R. Rogers, Sheila Fling, Kayla Silvers-Pickens, and John Butemeyer. "Attitudes Toward Women and Men in Politics." *Political Psychology* 8, no. 2 (1987): 191–200.

Rosenwasser, Shirley M., and Jana Seale. "Attitudes Toward a Hypothetical Male or Female Candidate—a Research Note." *Political Psychology* 9, no. 4 (1988): 591–598.

Rowe, E. "What Counts Is Content of Vote." *Bangor Daily News* (February 7, 1964): 10.

Rubin, Lisa. "45,000 Cast Their Votes for a Woman President in New Survey." White House Project, www.thewhitehouseproject.org/press_frame.html (February 23, 2001).

Rule, Wilma. "Why Women Don't Run: The Critical Contextual Factors in Women's Legislative Recruitment." *Western Political Quarterly* 34 (1981): 60–77.

Sabato, Larry J. *Feeding Frenzy: Attack Journalism and American Politics*. Baltimore: Lanahan Publishers, 2000.

Sadker, Myra, and David Sadker. *Failing at Fairness: How America's Schools Cheat Girls*. New York: Scribner's, 1995.

Saltman, David. "On Covering Ferraro." *Washington Post*, November 10, 1984, D3.

Sapiro, Virginia. "If U.S. Senator Baker Were a Woman." *Political Psychology* 9 (1982): 591–598.

Sarkesian, Sam C. *Presidential Leadership and National Security. Styles, Institutions, and Politics*. Boulder, CO: Westview Press, 1988.

———. *U.S. National Security: Policymakers, Processes, and Politics*. Boulder, CO: Lynne Rienner Publishers, 1995.

Saroyan, Strawberry. "Can a Woman Win the White House?" *George* 4, no. 2 (February 1999): 94.

Schemo, Diana Jean. "Curiosity in Dole Exceeds Support." *New York Times*, October 7, 1999, A28.

———. "Dole Talks Foreign Policy, but Women Want Something Else." *New York Times*, September 28, 1999, A23.

Schneider, William. "The November 6 Vote for President: What Did It Mean?" In Austin Ranney, ed., *The American Elections of 1984*. Durham: Duke University Press, 1985.

Schreiber, E. M. "Education and Change in American Opinions on a Woman for President." *Public Opinion Quarterly* 42, no. 2 (Summer 1978): 171–182.

Schroeder, Pat. *24 Years of House Work . . . and the Place Is Still a Mess*. Kansas City: Andrews McMeel, 1998.

Seebach, L. "How Not to Elect Women to Office." *Rocky Mountain News*, November 29, 1998, B1.

Seltzer, R. A., J. Newman, and M. V. Leighton. *Sex as a Political Variable: Women as Candidates and Voters in U.S. Elections.* Boulder, CO: Lynne Rienner Publishers, 1997.

Shapiro, Virginia. *The Political Integration of Women: Role, Socialization, and Politics.* Urbana: University of Illinois Press, 1983.

Shelby, Joyce. "Chisholm Hits Old Trail in Library Fete." *Daily News,* November 13, 1998, Suburban, p. 1.

Sherrill, Robert. *Why They Call It Politics: A Guide to American Government.* New York: Harcourt Brace Jovanovich, 1979.

Shoemaker, Christopher C. *The NSC Staff: Counseling the Council.* Boulder, CO: Westview Press, 1991.

Sigelman, Carol, Lee Sigelman, Barbara J. Walkosz, and Micheal Nitz. "Black Candidates, White Voters: Understanding Racial Bias in Political Perceptions." *American Journal of Political Science* 39, no. 1 (1995): 243–266.

Skidmore, Max J. *Legacy to the World: A Study of America's Political Ideas.* New York: Peter Lang, 1998.

———. "Theodore Roosevelt on Race and Gender." *Journal of American Culture* 21, no. 2 (Summer 1998).

Skowronek, Stephen. *The Politics Presidents Make: Leadership from John Adams to George Bush.* Cambridge: Belknap/Harvard University Press, 1993.

Smith, Eric R. A. N., and Richard L. Fox. "Research Note: The Electoral Fortunes of Women Candidates for Congress." *Political Research Quarterly* 54, no. 1 (2001): 205–221.

Smith, Kevin B. "When All's Fair: Signs of Parity in Media Coverage of Female Candidates." *Political Communication* 14 (1997): 71–81.

Smoke, Richard. *National Security and the Nuclear Dilemma.* New York: Random House, 1987.

Snyder, Mark. "Self-Fulfilling Stereotypes." In P. S. Rothenberg, ed., *Race, Class, and Gender in the United States: An Integrated Study.* New York: Worth, 2001, 511–516.

Sommers, Christina Hoff. *Who Stole Feminism?* New York: Touchstone, 1994.

Sorensen, Theodore. *Decision Making in the White House: The Olive Branch or the Arrows.* New York: Columbia University, 1963.

Stalcup, Brenda. *Women's Rights Movements: Opposing Viewpoints.* San Diego: Greenhaven Press, 1996.

Stambough, Stephen J., and Valerie R. O'Regan. "Female Candidates for Executive Office: The Road to the Governor's Mansion." In Robert P. Watson and Colton C. Campbell, eds., *Campaigns and Elections: Issues, Concepts, and Cases.* Boulder, CO: Lynne Rienner Publishers, 2003.

Stanley, Harold. "The Nominations: The Return of the Party Leaders." In Michael Nelson, ed., *The Elections of 2000.* Washington, DC: Congressional Quarterly Press, 2001.

Stanton, Elizabeth Cady. *The Woman's Bible.* New York: Prometheus, 1999.

Stapleton, Jean. "Introduction." In Cynthia B. Costello and Anne J. Stone, eds., *The American Woman 2001–2002: Getting to the Top.* New York: W. W. Norton, 2001.

Stuart, Douglas. *Organizing for National Security.* Carlisle, PA: Strategic Studies Institute, U.S. Army War College, 2000.

Stuckey, Mary E. *The President as Interpreter-in-Chief.* Chatham, NJ: Chatham House, 1991.

Sullivan, David B. "Images of a Breakthrough Woman Candidate: Dianne Feinstein's 1990, 1992, and 1994 Campaign Television Advertisements." *Women's Studies in Communication* 21 (1998): 7–26.

Tager, James. *The Women's Chronology.* New York: Henry Holt, 1994.

Tannen, Deborah. *You Just Don't Understand: Women and Men in Conversation.* New York: Ballantine, 1990.

Teitell, Beth. "Family Affair: New Lieut. Gov.—and New Mother—Jane Swift Works Out the Details of Being the State's Highest-Profile Working Mom." *Boston Herald,* November 13, 1998, 063.

Theilmann, John M., and Al Wilhite. *Discrimination and Congressional Campaign Contributions.* New York: Praeger, 1991.

"Thomas Jefferson to Albert Gallatin." In Julian P. Boyd, ed., *Papers of Thomas Jefferson.* Princeton, NJ: Princeton University Press, 1950.

Thomas, Sue, and Clyde Wilcox. *Women and Elective Office: Past, Present, and Future.* New York: Oxford University Press, 1998.

Thorson, Esther. "Ad-Watcher's Toolkit: How to Read Campaign Ads, 1998." See www.pbs.org/pol/ad/ads/toolkit_text.htm.

Tickner, J. Ann. *Gender in International Relations: Feminist Perspectives of Achieving Global Security.* New York: Columbia University Press, 1992.

———. "Searching for the Princess?" *Harvard International Review* 21, no. 4 (Fall 1999).

Tolleson-Rinehart, Sue, and Jeanie R. Stanley. *Claytie and the Lady: Ann Richards, Gender, and Politics in Texas.* Austin: University of Texas Press, 1994.

Trent, Judith S., and Robert V. Friedenberg. *Political Campaign Communication: Principles and Practices.* Westport, CT: Praeger, 1995.

Tuchman, Gaye. *Hearth and Home: Images of Women in the News.* New York: Oxford University Press, 1978.

Tucker, Robert W., and David C. Hendrickson. *Imperial Temptation: The New World Order and America's Purpose.* New York: Council on Foreign Relations, 1992.

Tulis, Jeffrey K. *The Rhetorical Presidency.* Princeton, NJ: Princeton University Press, 1987.

Tyler, Alice Felt. *Freedom's Ferment: Phases of American Social History from the Colonial Period to the Outbreak of the Civil War.* Minneapolis: University of Minnesota Press, 1944.

Uhlaner, Carole Jean, and Kay Lehman Schlozman. "Candidate Gender and Congressional Campaign Receipts." *Journal of Politics* 48 (1986): 30–50.

Vaccaro, E. B. "Sen. Smith in Race to the Finish." *Bangor Daily News,* July 7, 1987, 1.

Voss, Stephen D., and David Lublin. "Black Incumbents, White Districts: An Appraisal of the 1996 Congressional Elections." *American Politics Research* 29, no. 2 (March 2001): 141–182.

Ward, Geoffrey C., Martha Saxton, and Ann D. Gordon. *Not for Ourselves Alone: The Story of Elizabeth Cady Stanton and Susan B. Anthony.* New York: Alfred A. Knopf, 1999.

Warshaw, Shirley Anne. *The Keys to Power: Managing the Presidency.* New York: Longman, 2000.

Washington, Shirley. *Outstanding Women Members of Congress.* Washington, DC: U.S. Capitol Historical Society, 1995.

Waterman, Richard W., Robert Wright, and Gilbert St. Clair. *The Image-Is-Everything Presidency: Dilemmas in American Leadership.* Boulder, CO: Westview Press, 1999.

Watson, Robert P. *The Presidents' Wives: Reassessing the Office of First Lady.* Boulder, CO: Lynne Rienner Publishers, 2000.

Wattenberg, Martin. *The Rise of Candidate-Centered Politics: Presidential Elections of the 1980s.* Cambridge, MA: Harvard University Press, 1991.

Wayne, Stephen J. *The Road to the White House 2000: The Politics of Presidential Elections.* New York: Bedford St. Martin's, 2001.

Weber, Douglas. "Sex, Money and Politics: The Gender Gap in Campaign Contributions." See http://www.opensecrets.org/pubs/gender/index/htm, 1999.

Weir, Sara J. "The Feminist Face of State Executive Leadership." In Lois Duke Whitaker, ed., *Women in Politics: Outsiders or Insiders?* Upper Saddle River, NJ: Prentice Hall, 1999.

Weko, Thomas J. *The Politicizing Presidency: The White House Personnel Office, 1948–1994.* Lawrence: Kansas University Press, 1995.

West, Darrell M. *Air Wars: Television Advertising in Election Campaigns, 1952–1992.* Washington, DC: Congressional Quarterly Press, 1994.

White, Anne Barton. "Inequality in Symbolism: Cultural Barriers to Female Candidates in Political Advertising." *New Political Science* 28 (1994): 61–62.

Whitehouse, Beth. "Twin Billing: She's a Working Mother Who Is Pregnant with Twins. Can Jane Swift Govern Both Massachusetts and Her Growing Family?" *Newsday,* April 20, 2001, B6.

Withey, Lynne. *Dearest Friend: A Life of Abigail Adams.* New York: Free Press, 1981.

Whitney, Catherine, Barbara Mikulski, Susan Collins, Barbara Boxer, Dianne Feinstein, and Kay Bailey Hutchinson, eds. *Nine and Counting: The Women of the Senate.* New York: William Morrow, 2000.

Witt, Linda, Karen M. Paget, and Glenna Matthews. *Running as a Woman: Gender and Power in American Politics.* New York: Free Press, 1994.

Wolffe, Richard. "Dole Blames Cash Woes as She Quits Republican Contest." *Financial Times,* October 21, 1999, 10.

Wood, Julie T. *Gendered Lives: Communication, Gender, and Culture.* Belmont, CA: Wadsworth, 1999.

Woodlief, Wayne. "Media Eye Women's Style, Not Substance." *Boston Globe,* November 21, 1999.

Yeomans, Jeannine. "Women Candidates Run Harder for Campaign Cash." See http://www.womensnews.org/article.cfm/dyn/aid/235/context/archive, 2000.

Yepsen, David. "Beat the Press: 10 Rules for Surviving the Media." Paper presented at the Candidates and Campaigns Workshop, Des Moines, IA, October 2001.

"YWCA Study Finds That Women Are Usually Contented with Roles." *New York Times,* April 24, 1957, p. 37.

Zaller, John R. "The Myth of Massive Media Impact Revived: New Support for a Discredited Idea." In D. Muntz, ed., *Political Persuasion and Attitude Change.* Ann Arbor: University of Michigan Press, 1996.

Zimbardo, Philip G., and M. R. Leippe. *The Psychology of Attitude Change and Social Influence.* New York: McGraw-Hill, 1991.

The Contributors

Carol Lynn Bower returned to college as a mature student, after a career in the media, to complete two Ph.D.'s at the Hugh Downs School of Human Communication and the Department of Political Science at Arizona State University. She investigates the intersection of politics and rhetoric with an emphasis on gendered political discourse. Her work includes examinations of female candidacies, the historic 1998 Arizona election, first ladies' communication construction, and the White House press corps.

Dianne Bystrom is director of the Carrie Chapman Catt Center for Women and Politics and a professor at Iowa State University. She is the author of numerous publications on women and politics.

Anne N. Costain is professor of political science at the University of Colorado at Boulder and Associate Vice President of the University of Colorado system. She is the author of *Inviting Women's Rebellion: A Political Process Interpretation of the Women's Movement* (1992) and coeditor of *Social Movements and American Political Institutions* (1998) and *Deliberation, Democracy, and the Media* (2000).

John Davis is a Washington, D.C.–based research consultant in national security and foreign affairs and adjunct professor at Howard University. He was formerly with the National Defense University.

Erika Falk is senior researcher at the Annenberg Public Policy Center (APPC) in Washington, D.C. She has just completed her dissertation at the University of Pennsylvania on press coverage of women who have run for U.S. president. She has also written reports for APPC on issue advertising, civility in the House of Representatives, and free time for candidates on network newscasts. Falk has published articles on women and politics, civility in Congress, and the history of rhetoric. Prior to coming to the Annenberg School, she was a reporter and producer for public radio.

Victoria A. Farrar-Myers is associate professor of political science at the University of Texas at Arlington. She specializes in presidential-congressional relations and the policymaking process. Farrar-Myers is the coauthor of *Legislative Labyrinth: Congress and Campaign Finance Reform* and has contributed to *The Presidency and the Law After Clinton*, *American Political Parties: Decline or Resurgence?* and *Campaigns and Elections: Issues, Concepts, and Cases* (Lynne Rienner Publishers). Her research has been published in such journals as *Congress and the Presidency, White House Studies*, and *American Review of Politics*. During 1997–1998, she served as an American Political Science Association Congressional Fellow.

Ann Gordon is assistant professor of political science at Ohio University. She was honored with the Carrie Chapman Catt Center Prize for research on women and politics and is the recipient of a Goldsmith Research Award from the Shorenstein Center on the Press, Politics, and Public Policy at Harvard University. Gordon served as guest editor for a special issue of *White House Studies* entitled "A Woman President: Is America Ready?" and is coauthor of the forthcoming book *When Stereotypes Collide: Race, Gender, and Videostyle in Congressional Campaigns*.

Lori Cox Han is assistant professor of political science at Austin College in Sherman, Texas. She received her Ph.D. from the University of Southern California in 1997. Her first book, *Governing from Center Stage: White House Communication Strategies During the Television Age of Politics,* was published in 2001 as part of the Political Communication Series with Hampton Press. Her work has also appeared in journals such as *White House Studies.* A former journalist, her research interests focus on the U.S. presidency and the media and politics. She is currently working on a book assessing the public presidency of George H. W. Bush, 1989–1993.

Melissa Haussman received her doctorate from Duke University in 1994 and teaches government at Suffolk University in Boston. Her primary research and teaching interests are in the areas of U.S. and Canadian gender politics and law. She is a member of the Research Network on Gender and the State, which includes feminist researchers from numerous countries. For this project, she has written on federal and provincial abortion law reform in Canada and is working on a study of the gendered effects of health insurance cuts in Canada. Haussman is also a member of the Washington Center College Liaison Advisory Board and an elected town meeting member in Arlington, Massachusetts.

Diane J. Heith is assistant professor of government and politics at St. John's University. She has written articles on polling and the presidency for *Public Opinion Quarterly*, *Presidential Studies Quarterly,* and *White House Studies* and has coauthored an article on the Clinton health care debate and political advertising for the *Journal of Health Politics, Policy, and Law.* She is currently working on a book examining the use of public opinion polls in six administrations.

Kathleen Hall Jamieson is professor of communication and the Walter H. Annenberg Dean of the Annenberg School for Communication at the University of Pennsylvania. She is also director of the Annenberg Public Policy Center. She is the author or coauthor of ten books, including *Everything You Think You Know About Politics . . . and Why You're Wrong* (2000) and *Beyond the Double Bind: Women and Leadership* (1995). Jamieson is an expert on political campaigns and has received numerous teaching and service awards and many fellowships and grants. In 2001, she was elected a Fellow of the American Academy of Arts and Sciences.

Carole Kennedy is assistant professor of political science at San Diego State University. Her research interests include campaigns and elections and women in politics, and her work has been published in *Political Research Quarterly, American Journal of Political Science,* and *White House Studies.*

Tom Lansford is assistant professor of political science at the University of Southern Mississippi at Gulf Coast and a research fellow at the Frank Maria Center for International Politics and Ethics. Lansford is the author of *Evolution and Devolution: The Dynamics of Sovereignty and Security in Post–Cold War Europe* (2000), and *Lords of Foggy Bottom* (2002); coauthor of *Untying the Gordian Knot: Great Power Interests in the Persian Gulf* (1999); and coeditor of *Teaching Old Dogs New Tricks: International Organizations in the Twenty-First Century* (2000) and *Theodore Roosevelt* (2002); and has published many scholarly articles and essays.

Jerry Miller is associate professor in the School of Interpersonal Communication and the John Casses Director of Forensics at Ohio University. Miller was awarded the 2002 Carrie Chapman Catt Center Prize for Research on Women and Politics and has been the recipient of several teaching and forensic coaching awards. He is coauthor of the forthcoming book, *When Stereotypes Collide: Race, Gender and Videostyle in Congressional Campaigns*. His research and publications focus on political communication, campaign communication, and the mass media.

Karen O'Connor is director of the Women and Politics Institute and a professor in the Department of Government at American University. O'Connor is the editor of the journal *Women and Politics* and the author or coauthor of several books, including *American Government: Continuity and Change* (7th ed., 2002); *Women, Politics, and American Society* (3rd ed., 2002); and *No Neutral Ground: Abortion Politics in an Age of Absolutes,* in addition to several articles on women and politics, women and the law, and judicial politics.

Max J. Skidmore is University of Missouri Curators' Professor of Political Science at the University of Missouri at Kansas City. He is the author of numerous books and scores of articles and chapters on politics, political thought, popular culture, American studies, and the presidency. His most recent books are *Social Security and Its Enemies* (1999) and *Legacy to the World: A Study of America's Political Ideas* (1998). He currently is working on a book for St. Martin's Press: *Former Presidents as Private Citizens*.

Robert P. Watson has written, edited, or coedited thirteen books, including *The Presidents' Wives: Reassessing the Office of First Lady* (Lynne Rienner Publishers, 2000); has published over 100 scholarly articles, chapters, and reviews; and is the founder and editor of the journal *White House Studies*. He directed the first-ever *Report to the First Lady 2001,* which was presented to Laura Bush and Lynne Cheney; appeared on C-SPAN's *Book TV* program; was a guest for CNN.com's coverage of the 2001 presidential inaugural; and has been quoted or interviewed by CNN, MSNBC, *USA Today,* the *Los Angeles Times,* and dozens of media outlets. He taught formerly at the University of Hawaii at Hilo and now teaches at Florida Atlantic University.

Index

263

About the Book

Madam President? The question is not *if,* but rather *when* the United States will elect a female president—but timing is not the only uncertainty involved in shattering this most visible glass ceiling in U.S. society.

Who will be included in the field of candidates for Madam President, and why? How will she have to position herself for a viable run at the Oval Office? Once in office, will she encounter gender-based biases in her handling of military and foreign affairs? Will Madam President blend seamlessly with the long line of Mr. Presidents—or will the very nature of the presidency be irrevocably changed?

Anticipating Madam President's insightful blend of analysis, profiles, and interviews with prominent political women illustrates the realities of women in the upper echelons of public life, as well as the challenges likely to face a woman in one of the world's most powerful political positions.

Robert P. Watson is visiting associate professor of political science at Florida Atlantic University. He is editor of the journal *White House Studies* and author of numerous books on gender, the presidency, and U.S. politics, including *The Presidents' Wives: Reassessing the Office of First Lady* and *First Ladies of the United States: A Biographical Dictionary.* **Ann Gordon** is assistant professor of political science at Ohio University. She is coauthor of *When Stereotypes Collide: Race, Gender, and Videostyle in Congressional Campaigns* (forthcoming).